CAMBRIDGE LIBRARY COLLECTION

Books of enduring scholarly value

Classics

From the Renaissance to the nineteenth century, Latin and Greek were compulsory subjects in almost all European universities, and most early modern scholars published their research and conducted international correspondence in Latin. Latin had continued in use in Western Europe long after the fall of the Roman empire as the lingua franca of the educated classes and of law, diplomacy, religion and university teaching. The flight of Greek scholars to the West after the fall of Constantinople in 1453 gave impetus to the study of ancient Greek literature and the Greek New Testament. Eventually, just as nineteenth-century reforms of university curricula were beginning to erode this ascendancy, developments in textual criticism and linguistic analysis, and new ways of studying ancient societies, especially archaeology, led to renewed enthusiasm for the Classics. This collection offers works of criticism, interpretation and synthesis by the outstanding scholars of the nineteenth century.

A Treatise on Hannibal's Passage of the Alps

The controversy over the route taken by Hannibal, the Carthaginian army and his famous elephants in their crossing of the Alps to attack Rome in 218 BCE began within fifty years of the event and has continued for many centuries. A particular scholarly dispute emerged in the 1850s between Robert Ellis (1819/20–85) and William John Law (1786–1869), and was fought in the pages of the *Journal of Classical and Sacred Philology* and in books. Ellis, a classical scholar, had surveyed the Alpine passes in 1852 and again in 1853, when he published this work, claiming that the Little Mount Cenis route was the one used. Law responded immediately in the *Journal*, and later published his own theory, to which Ellis riposted in 1867 with *An Enquiry into the Ancient Routes between Italy and Gaul*, also reissued in this series. Modern scholarship doubts, however, that either man was right.

T0371078

Cambridge University Press has long been a pioneer in the reissuing of out-of-print titles from its own backlist, producing digital reprints of books that are still sought after by scholars and students but could not be reprinted economically using traditional technology. The Cambridge Library Collection extends this activity to a wider range of books which are still of importance to researchers and professionals, either for the source material they contain, or as landmarks in the history of their academic discipline.

Drawing from the world-renowned collections in the Cambridge University Library and other partner libraries, and guided by the advice of experts in each subject area, Cambridge University Press is using state-of-the-art scanning machines in its own Printing House to capture the content of each book selected for inclusion. The files are processed to give a consistently clear, crisp image, and the books finished to the high quality standard for which the Press is recognised around the world. The latest print-on-demand technology ensures that the books will remain available indefinitely, and that orders for single or multiple copies can quickly be supplied.

The Cambridge Library Collection brings back to life books of enduring scholarly value (including out-of-copyright works originally issued by other publishers) across a wide range of disciplines in the humanities and social sciences and in science and technology.

A Treatise on Hannibal's Passage of the Alps

In which his Route Is Traced over the Little Mont Cenis

Robert Ellis

CAMBRIDGE
UNIVERSITY PRESS

CAMBRIDGE
UNIVERSITY PRESS

University Printing House, Cambridge, CB2 8BS, United Kingdom

Cambridge University Press is part of the University of Cambridge.
It furthers the University's mission by disseminating knowledge in the pursuit of
education, learning and research at the highest international levels of excellence.

www.cambridge.org
Information on this title: www.cambridge.org/9781108075770

This edition first published 1853
This digitally printed version 2014

ISBN 978-1-108-07577-0 Paperback

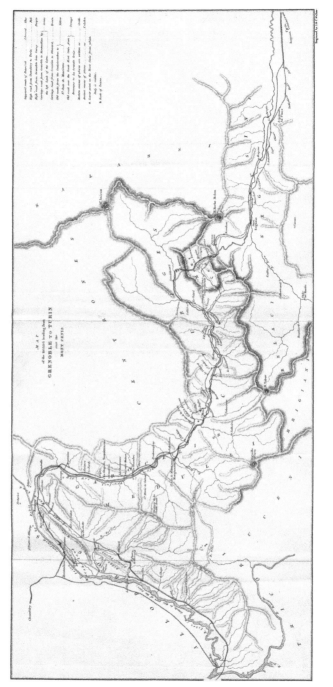

The material originally positioned here is too large for reproduction in this reissue. A PDF can be downloaded from the web address given on page iv of this book, by clicking on 'Resources Available'.

A

TREATISE

ON

HANNIBAL'S PASSAGE OF THE ALPS

IN WHICH HIS ROUTE IS TRACED OVER THE

LITTLE MONT CENIS,

BY

ROBERT ELLIS, B.D.,

FELLOW OF ST JOHN'S COLLEGE, CAMBRIDGE.

———

CAMBRIDGE: J. DEIGHTON.
LONDON: JOHN W. PARKER AND SON.
———
1853.

PREFACE.

IN the course of a series of excursions in the Alps, the attention of the Author had naturally been drawn to the subject of Hannibal's passage of those mountains. On a subsequent examination of Polybius' account of that expedition, it appeared almost certain that the prominent and distinguishing characteristics of the pass which Hannibal crossed could only be found on the pass of the Mont Cenis. A general acquaintance with the passes, by which it had been conjectured that Hannibal entered Italy, led at first to this conclusion. The close proximity to the plains of Piedmont of the summit of the pass which Hannibal crossed, the precipitous nature of the descent into Italy, and the immense losses which the Carthaginians incurred in consequence, all tended to identify this pass with that of the Mont Cenis. It was also beyond a doubt, that from neither the Great nor the Little St Bernard, nor from the Mont Genevre, was it possible to see the Italian plain. None of the roads over these passes, nor any accessible point in their neighbourhood, could command the view which the Carthaginian army saw from the crest of the Alps. The situation of the Mont Cenis, as might be judged from the map, rendered it, however, not improbable, that such a view might be obtained from the immediate neighbourhood of the road over its summit. As this route, then, had a considerable amount of *a priori* probability in its favour, a probability shared by no other pass, it seemed likely that an examination of it in detail might lead to its complete identification with the line of Hannibal's march into Italy. Accordingly, in the month of July, 1852, and in the months of April and May, 1853, the requisite examination was made. A period of nearly six weeks was, altogether, spent upon the investigation, some days being lost in consequence of unfavourable weather. A great quantity of snow was found upon the ground during the spring months, and rendered the character of the pass more in accordance with what it would have been at the time of Hannibal's passage of the Alps.

It is now, it may be said, universally admitted, that the great test, by which the claims of every pass must be tried, is the narrative of Polybius. The following investigation has, accordingly, been conducted on this principle. In the translation of Polybius, which accompanies it, the exact meaning of the historian, and his peculiarities of narration, have been preserved as far as possible. To gain this end, of the utmost importance in the present case, nothing beyond a merely literal version of the Greek has been attempted.

Less attention has been paid to Livy's narrative ; but his evidence has not been neglected. An examination of the objections brought against the Mont Cenis, and an enquiry into the antiquity of that pass, conclude the investigation. The testimony of Polybius, and that of Livy, have been kept, almost entirely, distinct from one another; and the question of the old roads across the Alps has also been considered by itself, and a third and independent body of evidence deduced from its discussion.

The thanks of the Author are due to the Syndics of the Pitt Press for the liberality with which they have undertaken the printing of the present work.

St John's College,
Dec. 23, 1853.

CONTENTS.

CHAPTER V.

CHAPTER VI.

CHAPTER VII.

CHAPTER VIII.

Directions for the insertion of the Maps and Plans.

A TREATISE

ON

HANNIBAL'S PASSAGE OF THE ALPS.

CHAPTER I.

Introduction.—Brief notice of Hannibal's march from New Carthage.—
Polybius' estimation of the lengths of the different parts of the
whole march from New Carthage to the plains of Italy.—A peculiarity in Polybius' mode of narration observed.—Division of the
march from the passage of the Rhone to the country of the Insubrian
Gauls into seven stages.

A PERIOD of more than twenty years of peace succeeded the close of the first Punic war. It was not
however a peace which could be expected to endure.
The mutual exhaustion of the contending parties had
obliged them for a time to desist from the further prose-
cution of hostilities : but the power of neither the Romans
nor the Carthaginians was inwardly shattered; and the
rivalry and hatred with which they had long regarded each
other were necessarily increased rather than diminished
by the losses which both had suffered. These losses,
severe as they had been, were gradually repaired; each
nation recovered its former vigour, and looked forward to
the renewal of a strife, which the deeply-rooted animosity,
the clashing interests, and the ambitious spirit of both
parties, plainly forewarned them could have no end but in
the complete subjection of Rome or Carthage. The first
Punic war had established an inveterate rivalry between
the two cities : the event of the second war was to determine which should fall.

1

The struggle which was to decide this question at
length approached.   In the year 219 B. c. the peace between the Romans and Carthaginians was formally broken;
hostile declarations were exchanged at Carthage, and preparations for the contest were made on both sides.   The
news of the rupture reached Hannibal at New Carthage in
Spain, a country which he had in a great measure reduced
under the Carthaginian yoke; and where the continual
growth and consolidation of the power of their enemy had
given much umbrage and disquiet to the Romans.   It was
there he meditated the invasion of Italy and the fall of
Rome, and resolved upon that march which has associated
his name for ever with the Alps.   His preparations for the
invasion had commenced before he was aware of the
rupture of the peace, and by the spring of the year 218
they were finally completed.

A fortunate conjuncture of circumstances had enabled
him to secure allies in Italy.   The Romans were at this
time, and had been for some years previously, making gradual encroachments upon the territories of the Cisalpine
Gauls: and the Gauls, feeling that they were of themselves
incapable of resisting the growing might of Rome, readily
embraced the opportunity of forming an alliance with the
great enemy of the Roman name.   In anticipation of such
an event, and before he had received the news that the
Romans had declared war against the Carthaginians, Hannibal had despatched an embassy from Spain into Cisalpine
Gaul, to ascertain and confirm the disposition of the inhabitants towards the Carthaginian alliance, and to discover also,
whether the passage of the Alps was practicable or not.

The return of his envoys he was now awaiting.   At
length they arrived at New Carthage, and brought back
the intelligence, that the Cisalpine Gauls were very favourably disposed towards the Carthaginians.   The passage
of the Alps they also reported to be practicable, although
exceedingly difficult and unavoidably attended with great
labour[1].   Impossible, however, they were assured that it
was not.   For the Gauls themselves had frequently, not

[1] Polyb. III. 34.

only in remote, but also in recent times, crossed the mountains with large armies[1]: and although the march of the Carthaginian host, encumbered with its elephants and baggage, would be much less easily performed than that of an army of barbarians; still the difference was not so great as to lead them to conclude the passage impracticable. The receipt of this intelligence determined the course of Hannibal. His resolution of penetrating across the Alps into Cisalpine Gaul was finally taken, and at the end of May the army began its march from New Carthage.

It consisted at first of 90,000 foot and 12,000 horse, besides elephants and baggage-animals. All, however, did not quit the Spanish territory. Some were lost in subduing the nations between the Ebro and the Pyrenees: and when the march was resumed after the reduction of these tribes, a detachment of 11,000 was left behind under Hanno, and an equal number of men were dismissed to their own homes. 50,000 foot and 9000 horse were all that crossed the Pyrenees and entered Gaul. After the passage of the Rhone this number was diminished to 38,000 foot and 8000 horse[2]. Of these, 20,000 foot and 6000 horse alone survived the passage of the Alps, and succeeded in reaching the plains of the Po.

Hannibal's route from New Carthage lay, as just intimated, northward; and was directed along the coast of Spain. The river Ebro was crossed, the nations between it and the Eastern Pyrenees were subdued, the extremity of those mountains was passed, and Transalpine Gaul entered. After the passage of the Pyrenees, Hannibal still kept for a time near the sea, but at length turned inland, and crossed the Rhone at a distance of nearly four days' march from the sea. Proceeding subsequently along the left or eastern bank of the Rhone for four days more, he

---

[1] Polyb. III. 48.

[2] It is difficult to account for the loss of 13,000 men between the Pyrenees and the Rhone. The ordinary casualties seem insufficient to explain it. Perhaps a number of the Iberians had deserted on entering Gaul, and returned to their own country, having been disappointed at not being included in the number of those whom Hannibal had allowed to do so.

reached, at the end of that period, a district called the Island, of which Polybius gives a particular description. Having left the Island, Hannibal struck off towards the Alps, effected his passage across them, and descended into the plains of the Po. The whole of this march, from New Carthage to the Italian plains, has been divided by Polybius (iii. 39) into five stages, which terminate, respectively, at the passage of the Ebro, at Ampurias (Emporium), at the passage of the Rhone, at the foot of the first Alpine ascent, and at the commencement of the plains of Italy. The last two of these stages, in which the passage of the Alps is included, are all with which this book is immediately concerned.

Before, however, proceeding to the examination of this part of Polybius' narrative, it will be necessary to give the distances comprised in each stage of the march, from New Carthage to the commencement of the plains of Italy. They are laid down by Polybius as follows (iii. 39):

" From this city (New Carthage) to the river Ebro the distance is 2600 stadia : again from this river to Emporium 1600 stadia; and from thence also to the passage of the Rhone about 1600 stadia: for these distances have been now measured in paces and marked carefully by the Romans at intervals of eight stadia. From the passage of the Rhone, as they (the Carthaginians) marched along the bank of the river, in the direction of its sources, as far as the ascent of the Alps on the way to Italy, there was a further distance of 1400 stadia. *There still remains to be estimated the passage of the Alps, a march of about* 1200 *stadia;* and, after crossing these mountains Hannibal would immediately arrive at the plains of Italy lying around the Po. The whole length of his march from New Carthage would consequently amount to about 9000 stadia[1]."

The first thing requisite to be observed here is Polybius' scale of measurement. He computes, it will be perceived, by lengths of 200 stadia, or 25 Roman miles. Doubtless, with his deficient means of estimating distances,

---

[1] The sum of the distances given by Polybius only amounts really to 8400 stadia.

he found himself unable to determine the lengths of the several marches more closely, at least in such parts of the route
as the Romans had not measured. Yet for these parts also
he employs the same rule of computation, it not being apparently his object to aim at greater accuracy. This fact
must always be borne in mind in the investigation of Hannibal's route, in order that too much stress may not be
laid upon discrepancies of distance, when not great: while,
at the same time, due attention should still be paid to the
statements of distances, given by so careful an authority as
Polybius, and a too great laxity avoided in accommo-
dating them to actual routes. It must therefore be remembered that Polybius' measure of distance is 25 Roman
miles, in computing the length of a march of several days'
duration.

The passage marked in italics, in the quotation given
above from Polybius, is more particularly connected with
the following investigation. It supplies at once one of the
conditions, which the pass to be identified with that which
Hannibal crossed must satisfy. This condition may be
thus stated:

" The length of the route over the Alps, beginning at
the commencement of the ascent of the mountains, and
terminating at the commencement of the plains of Italy,
must be about 150 Roman miles[1]."

That the termination of this part of the march was at
the commencement of the plains of Italy, is clearly stated by
Polybius. That "the ascent of the Alps on the way to Italy"
means the place where the route first became mountainous,
the point where the army was first obliged to ascend the
mountains,—this seems also sufficiently plain·; for it appears scarcely probable that any other meaning can be
attached to the expression of Polybius, τὴν ἀναβολὴν
τῶν Ἄλπεων τὴν εἰς Ἰταλίαν. There is however a certain
amount of vagueness in it, and a different interpretation
might be possible.

The narrative of Polybius, from the time when the
march was resumed after the passage of the Rhone, up to

---

[1] Condition II.

the time of Hannibal's arrival in the plains of Italy, will now be given in full, with the exception of three chapters and part of a fourth. The passages omitted include the end of the fifty-sixth chapter, and all the fifty-seventh, fifty-eighth, and fifty-ninth chapters. These parts of the narrative are passed over, as not bearing upon the question of Hannibal's passage of the Alps, but as relating either to the operations of the Roman armies, or else containing general reflections upon the subject of history.

There is, however, one peculiarity in Polybius' style of narration, especially in this part of his history, upon which it will previously be necessary to make some observations. The peculiarity alluded to is this: that the historian, before entering into the details of a particular march, event, or military transaction, gives, in a few lines, what may be regarded as a short statement or summary of the occurrences which took place at that particular period. Having done this, he proceeds to make such observations, and give such explanations, as appear necessary, or to narrate at length the various circumstances that attended the facts in question, whenever they were of such importance as to deserve minute consideration. The short summary serves frequently, in point of fact, as an argument to the succeeding and more detailed account. The whole of that portion of Polybius' narrative now about to be given, may be considered with much probability as written in this manner, and will divide itself into seven parts. Four of these relate to the actual passage of the Alps; two to the march from the place where the Rhone was crossed, to the commencement of the mountains; and one to the march from the foot of the Alps, on the Italian side, to the territories of the Insubrian Gauls, the allies of Hannibal. The first division will consist of the march from the passage of the Rhone to the district called the Island; the second, the march from the Island to a certain defile and town at the commencement of the Alps; the third, the march from the town just mentioned to the neighbourhood of a certain λευκόπετρον ὀχυρόν, or ' strong [1]

---

[1] ' Strong,' of course, in a military point of view.

white rock,' where the army encountered great danger from an attack of the Alpine Gauls; the fourth, the march from this rock to the summit of the pass; the fifth, the circumstances which took place while the army remained on the summit of the pass; the sixth, the descent from the summit of the Alps to the commencement of the plains of Italy; and the seventh, (all of which will not be given) the march from the foot of the Alps to the country of the Insubrians.

These form the seven parts, into which the narrative seems to be divided. The correctness of the supposition, that this mode of narration was adopted by Polybius, will be best seen by an inspection of the historian's own words. Accordingly, those parts of his account, which are supposed to be the summaries in question, will, in the extract from Polybius which now follows, be distinguished by being printed in capital letters. Those passages also of the narrative, which bear more particularly on the present question, and afford a clue to the determination of the features of the country through which Hannibal passed, will be brought prominently forward by being printed in italics. Polybius' account of the march, thus arranged, will form the substance of the next chapter.

CHAPTER II.

Polybius' Narrative of Hannibal's March, from the passage of the Rhone to the capture of Turin.

Polybius. Book III. Part of Chap. 49.

HANNIBAL, HAVING CONTINUED HIS MARCH FOR FOUR SUCCESSIVE DAYS FROM THE PASSAGE (OF THE RHONE) CAME TO THE DISTRICT CALLED THE ISLAND, A POPULOUS AND CORN-PRODUCING TRACT OF COUNTRY, WHICH DERIVES ITS NAME FROM THE VERY CIRCUMSTANCE (OF ITS FORMATION). For the Rhone flowing on one side of this district, and a river called the Scaras[1] on the other, sharpen it into a point at their confluence. It is similar in size and form to the so-called Delta in Egypt; excepting that, in the case of the Delta, the sea forms one side (i. e. the third side) by joining the mouths of the rivers (which form the other two sides); whereas the third side of the Island is formed by *mountains difficult of approach and entrance, and, it may be said, almost inaccessible.* When Hannibal arrived at the Island, he found two brothers contending for the royal power, and encamped with their armies opposite each other; and when the elder brother tried to induce him to second his efforts in acquiring the sovereignty, he listened to the overtures which were made to him: for it was sufficiently evident what advantages he would derive from the assistance of the Gaul at the present juncture. By their combined forces, the second claimant of the sovereignty was attacked and expelled; and Hannibal afterwards received great assistance from the victor. For he not only abundantly supplied the army with corn and all other necessaries, but also exchanged such of their arms and accoutrements as were old and worn out, and equipped afresh all the forces at a time when such aid was very opportune. He also furnished the mass of the soldiers with clothing and shoes, a provision which was of great service for the passage of the mountains. The most signal benefit however which he conferred upon them was, that as they were apprehensive of danger while they marched through the territory of the Gauls who are called Allobroges, he covered their rear with his own troops, and secured for them a safe advance until they approached the passage of the Alps.

---

[1] The manuscripts have Σκάρας or Σκώρας. 'Ισάρας is only conjectural. It has been thought better to adhere to the MS. reading.

Chap. 50.

HANNIBAL, IN THE COURSE OF TEN DAYS, HAVING ADVANCED ALONG THE RIVER-SIDE FOR A DISTANCE OF 800 STADIA, COMMENCED THE ASCENT OF THE ALPS, AND FOUND HIMSELF IN A SITUATION OF THE GREATEST DANGER. For as long as the army continued *in the plain*, all the petty chieftains of the Allobroges refrained from attacking them, *partly from the fear of their cavalry*, and partly from fear of the Barbarians who formed their escort. But when these last had returned to their own country, and Hannibal, with his army, was advancing towards *the places which were difficult of passage*, the chieftains of the Allobroges collected a sufficient body of forces, and took possession of *the advantageous posts* along the road by which Hannibal was obliged to make his ascent. Had they concealed their plans, they must have altogether destroyed the Carthaginian army; and, even after their purpose was detected, they inflicted great injury upon the troops of Hannibal, although the loss which they themselves incurred was equally great. For, when the Carthaginian general discovered that they had occupied the advantageous posts, he halted his troops, and encamped *near the heights*: he then sent forward a party of the Gauls, who acted as his guides, to discover the plan of the enemy, and the whole scheme of their operations. The Gauls executed his commission; and the Carthaginian general found, from the intelligence they brought, that the enemy guarded very vigilantly their posts during the daytime, but withdrew at night *to a town in the neighbourhood.* To counteract therefore their designs, he determined upon operations of the following nature. He set his army in motion *and advanced in open view; and, when he drew near to the difficult places, he encamped at a short distance from the enemy.* When night came on, *he ordered the watch-fires to be lighted,* and left in the camp the mass of his forces; while he himself, *with the most active of his troops, purposely equipped for such a service, penetrated in the night through the defile, and seized the posts which had been before occupied by the enemy, who had now retired to the town, according to their usual practice.*

Chap. 51.

WHEN this had been accomplished, and day appeared, the Barbarians, observing what had taken place, desisted for a time from their original design; but when they subsequently saw the numbers of the baggage-animals and the cavalry *laboriously, and, in an extended line, defiling through the difficult places*, they were induced, by this circumstance, to attack the line of march. When this was done, and the Barbarians had fallen upon them on many points, a great loss ensued to the Carthaginians, especially in horses and baggage-animals: and this was caused, *not so much by the attacking enemy, as by the nature of the ground.* For the way by which the Carthaginians had to advance *was not only narrow and rugged, but also precipitous, so that at every shock or commotion, numbers of the animals with their burdens were carried down the precipices.* This confusion was mainly caused by the horses which were wounded. Some of these, rendered unruly by their wounds, fell back upon the baggage-animals; and others, in their impetuous advance, drove before them all that fell in their way upon this difficult ground. Very great confusion was thus created. When Hannibal saw this, and reflected that even those who escaped such dangers would have no chance of preservation ultimately, if the baggage-animals were lost, he set in motion the soldiers who, during the night, had taken possession of the heights, and rushed down to the succour of the foremost column in the line of march[1]. By this movement many of the enemy were destroyed, *in consequence of Hannibal attacking them from the heights above them; but the loss which he caused to his own army was equally great.* For the tumult on the line of march was increased on both sides (Allobroges and Carthaginians) in consequence of the shouts of the newly-arrived troops, and their intermingling in the conflict. But when Hannibal had destroyed the greater number of the Allobroges, and forced the remnant of them to fly homewards, then all the baggage-animals and horses which were left, with much labour and trouble effected their passage through the difficult places. Meanwhile, Hannibal collected as many of his soldiers as he could after this perilous service, and fell upon the town from which the enemy had made their attack: and finding it almost deserted, in consequence of all its inhabitants having gone out in hope of plunder, he became master of it. This capture ensured him many present and subsequent advantages. *He recovered immediate possession of a number of his horses and beasts of burden, and the men who had been made prisoners with them,* and gained a supply of corn and cattle sufficient for two or three days' consumption. But the chief advantage which resulted was, that he inspired such great alarm among the people adjacent to the ascent[2], that none of them for the future ventured lightly to attack him.

---

[1] Read here with Casaubon, Gronovius, and Bekker, προλαβοῦσι.

[2] (i. e.) adjacent to the district where he then was, which was that where the ascent to the mountains first began.

Chap. 52.

HAVING then encamped there and remained one day, he proceeded onwards. DURING THE DAYS IMMEDIATELY FOLLOWING HE LED ON THE ARMY SAFELY FOR SOME DISTANCE : BUT ON THE FOURTH DAY HE AGAIN HAD TO ENCOUNTER GREAT DANGERS. For the people who lived along his route, having formed a treacherous design against him, went out to meet him with crowns and branches of trees,—now these among Barbarians are considered almost universally as tokens of amicable intentions, as is the case with the herald's wand among the Greeks. But Hannibal, cautious of giving too easy credence to them, made careful enquiry into their aims and intentions. They alleged their perfect knowledge of the capture of the town, and the destruction of the people who had attempted to injure Hannibal; and affirmed that those events had induced them to seek that interview, as they were anxious to prevent the occurrence of mutual hostilities. They also promised to give some of their own people as hostages to the Carthaginians. Hannibal continued for a long time on his guard against them, and distrusted their representations: but when he considered, that if he were to accept their overtures, he would, in all probability, render them more cautious[1] and well disposed; whereas, if he rejected them, he would certainly incur their open hostility;—(for these reasons) he assented to their proposals, and affected to engage in alliance with them. The Barbarians gave the hostages they had promised, supplied the troops with cattle in great abundance, and so unreservedly placed themselves in the hands of the Carthaginians, that the latter trusted to them as guides through the difficult places they next encountered. *When these Barbarians had led the way in the van for two days*, the tribes before mentioned having collected their forces and followed on the rear of the Carthaginians, attacked them as they were passing through *a difficult and precipitous ravine.*

Chap. 53.

ALL would again have been lost, had it not been that Hannibal, still to a certain extent distrusting the Barbarians, and providing against the issue, *had placed his baggage-animals and cavalry in the van, and his heavy infantry in the rear.* The protection which these afforded mitigated the calamity, *for the heavy infantry succeeded in withstanding the attacks of the Barbarians.* Not-

---

[1] This word probably relates to the safety of the hostages, which would be compromised by the bad faith of the Barbarians.

withstanding this circumstance however, *a considerable number of men, baggage-animals, and horses were destroyed. For the Barbarians, being in possession of the heights, and marching along the mountain-sides in a parallel line to the Carthaginian columns, kept rolling down rocks from above upon part of the army, and wounded others from a nearer distance by hurling stones at them.* So utter was the consternation, and so great the danger occasioned by this attack, *that Hannibal was obliged to pass the night with half his army near a certain strong white rock, away from the cavalry and baggage-animals, thereby affording protection to the latter,* until they had with difficulty defiled through the ravine, an operation which occupied the whole night. HANNIBAL HAV-ING ON THE FOLLOWING DAY, WHEN THE ENEMY HAD RETIRED, RE-JOINED HIS CAVALRY AND BAGGAGE-ANIMALS, LED ON HIS ARMY TO THE HIGHEST SUMMITS OF THE ALPS, WITHOUT MEETING AGAIN WITH ANY CONSIDERABLE BODY OF THE BARBARIANS, ALTHOUGH PARTS OF HIS ARMY WERE HARASSED BY THEM AT VARIOUS PLACES ON THE ROAD. For they, watching their opportunity, assaulted and carried off the baggage-animals, sometimes from the rear, and sometimes from the van, of the line of march. Upon these occasions, the elephants were of very great service; for the Barbarians were so much alarmed at the extraordinary appearance of these animals, that they were deterred from attacking any part of the line of march where the elephants were to be found. ON THE NINTH DAY HANNIBAL ARRIVED AT THE SUMMIT OF THE MOUNTAINS; AND, EN-CAMPING THERE, REMAINED TWO DAYS, AS HE WISHED TO GIVE SOME REPOSE TO THOSE TROOPS WHO HAD ALREADY ARRIVED SAFELY, AND TO WAIT FOR THOSE WHO HAD FALLEN BEHIND. During this period many of the horses which had broken loose in their fright, and many of the baggage-animals which had got rid of their burdens, unexpectedly joined them in the camp, having followed apparently the tracks of the army.

Chap. 54.

THE snow was now gathering around the summits of the mountains (for it was near the time of the setting of the Pleiades[1]); and Hannibal, observing that the soldiers were much dispirited by the sufferings they had already undergone, and the anticipation of those which yet awaited them, called them together and endeavoured to raise their spirits. *The prospect of Italy offered itself as the only means by which this result could be attained.* For Italy lies extended beneath these mountains in such a manner, that, when both are seen together, the Alps seem to occupy the

---

[1] The last week in October.

position of a citadel to the whole of Italy. Accordingly Hannibal, *pointing out to his men the plains circumjacent to the Po,* and
reminding them of the goodwill which the Gauls who dwelt there
entertained towards them, and at the same time *indicating to
them the quarter in which Rome itself lay,* succeeded to a certain
degree in raising their drooping spirits. THE FOLLOWING DAY HE
BROKE UP HIS CAMP, AND COMMENCED HIS DESCENT, DURING WHICH HE
ONLY SUFFERED FROM FURTIVE ATTACKS ON THE PART OF THE ENEMY;
YET IN CONSEQUENCE OF THE SNOW AND THE NATURE OF THE GROUND,
HIS LOSS WAS NEARLY AS GREAT AS IT HAD BEEN DURING THE AS-
CENT. *For as the way down was narrow and steep,* and the snow
made every one uncertain of his path ; *all, both men and animals,
that fell out of the track or missed their footing, were carried down
the precipices.* Still, however, they bore these hardships with
the patience of men already habituated to similar calamities.
*But when they arrived at a place where it was impossible for the
elephants or baggage-animals to pass on account of the narrowness
of the way (the broken ground which previously occurred here for
a length of a stadium and a half having recently suffered additional
disruption), the army was again greatly dispirited and perplexed.*
The Carthaginian general at first proposed to make a circuit
round the difficult ground, but as the fresh snow that had fallen
rendered this impracticable, he desisted from his attempt.

Chap. 55.

FOR the circumstances were peculiar and extraordinary.
Upon the snow previously existing, and which had remained
from the preceding winter, the snow of the present year had
lately fallen. Now they found this latter snow easy to penetrate
and soft, because it was fresh, and not as yet of any depth. But
as soon as they had trodden through this, and reached the com-
pacted snow beneath, they were unable to penetrate it; but
both their feet slipped away along its surface, as is sometimes the
case with people walking over ground of which the surface is
covered with mud. But what ensued was still more calamitous.
As the men were unable to penetrate the lower snow, whenever
upon falling they tried to support themselves upon their hands and
knees and to get up again, they only found that they made themselves slip still more, and carried with them whatever they laid
hold upon for support—for the declivity was one of excessive
steepness. The baggage-animals, on the contrary, when they fell,
broke through the surface of the lower snow in their attempt to
rise, and there remained firmly fixed with their burdens, in consequence of the weight they bore, and the compact nature of
the old snow. Accordingly Hannibal, giving up all hope of car-

rying out his first plan, *encamped about the crest of the ridge,* having first cleared away the snow upon it.   He then employed large numbers of his soldiers *in building up the precipice,* a task of great labour and difficulty.   *In one day a way was completed sufficient for the passage of the horses and baggage-animals.* Hannibal, therefore, made them pass at once; and then encamping in a position where snow was found no longer, he let them loose to seek pasturage.   He then employed parties of the Numidians in turn upon the construction (of the path along the broken precipice); and, *after three days of hardship,* he managed with difficulty to make the elephants pass.   They were indeed reduced by famine to a miserable condition.   For the summits of the Alps, and the acclivities of the passes, are entirely without trees and quite barren, in consequence of the snow which remains there both winter and summer, while the lower half of the mountains, on both sides, abounds in underwood and trees, and is altogether habitable.

Chap. 56.

HANNIBAL, having reassembled his whole force, continued his descent, and *on the third day after leaving the precipices which have been described, reached the plain,* having lost, during his whole march, many of his soldiers from hostile attacks, and by crossing rivers, and many also in the Alps, on account of the precipices and other difficulties of the route; while the loss of horses and baggage-animals from the last causes was still greater than that of men.   THUS AT LENGTH, HAVING COMPLETED HIS MARCH FROM NEW CARTHAGE IN FIVE MONTHS, AND HIS PASSAGE OF THE ALPS IN FIFTEEN DAYS, HE BOLDLY DESCENDED INTO THE PLAINS OF THE PO, AND THE COUNTRY OF THE INSUBRIANS.   Of his Libyan forces, 12,000 infantry were all that survived; and of his Iberian forces, 8000; the cavalry that were left not amounting to more than 6000 ; and this statement of numbers is given by Hannibal himself in the inscription upon the column at Lacinium.

*   *   *   *   *   *

Chap. 60.

WE have already mentioned the amount of the forces with which Hannibal invaded Italy.   *Upon his entry, having encamped at the very foot of the Alps,* he spent some time in restoring the strength of his troops.   For the whole army had not only suffered very severely during the ascent and descent, and in the rugged country about the summit of the pass; but they were also in a wretched condition from the want of provisions they had experienced, and the unavoidable neglect of their bodily health. Many indeed were depressed to the lowest state by the privations and incessant hardships they had undergone. For it was impossible to convey food in quantities sufficient for so many thousand men, through a country which presented such difficulties : and even of the provisions which they did convey with them, the greater part was lost when the beasts which carried them perished. And thus, having begun his march, after the passage of the Rhone, with 38,000 infantry, and more than 8000 cavalry, he lost, as I have before mentioned, nearly half his whole force in the passage of the Alps; and even those who did survive, had become from incessant hardship quite savage in appearance and condition. Hannibal, therefore, used his utmost efforts to revive the spirits of his army, and to restore the strength of both men and horses. When the army had now completely recovered, Hannibal tried to effect an alliance with the Taurini, *a nation dwelling at the foot of the mountains,* who were at war with the Insubrians, and distrusted the Carthaginians. Upon their rejection of the offers of Hannibal, he invested their principal city; and, having taken it after three days' siege, he put to the sword all that had opposed him, and inspired such terror in the minds of the neighbouring barbarians, that they all came immediately and threw themselves upon his protection. The remaining tribes also of the Celtæ, who dwelt in the plains, were very anxious to co-operate with the Carthaginians according to their original intention; but the Roman legions having already passed through the country where the greater part of them dwelt, and so cut them off (from the Carthaginians), they either remained neutral, or were even obliged in some cases to join the Roman army. When Hannibal considered these things, he determined to lose no time, but to advance forward and achieve some success, which might serve to encourage all those who were willing to share the fortunes of the Carthaginians.

CHAPTER III.

THE course of Hannibal's march from New Carthage has been already traced. After crossing the Pyrenees and the Rhone, he proceeded upwards along the eastern bank of that river until he came to a district called the Island, which Polybius compares in form and size to the Egyptian Delta. One side of this triangular district was formed by the Rhone, another by the confluent stream of a river called the Scaras, and the third by a range of almost inaccessible mountains extending across from the Scaras to the Rhone. The first division of the march from the passage of the Rhone to the plains of Italy terminates at this district, and must of course be supposed to end at the point where Hannibal first came upon its borders: for that would be the place where he would naturally be said to arrive at it, besides being the only definite point where the march could be broken off. Now, as Hannibal marched along the bank of the Rhone, which formed one side of the Island; and as the Scaras, a river falling into the Rhone, formed its second side; it must have been at the junction of these two rivers that the account of Hannibal's march is broken off by Polybius; and it must be from the same place that he afterwards resumes it, when he has completed the narration of the events which took place at the Island. The first point therefore to determine is, what was this river which Polybius calls the Scaras.

Now the name *Scaras* is unknown in Roman geography, but may be shewn to be virtually identical with Isaras; and the river *Scaras* must consequently be the Roman Isara, the modern Isère. The word Isara or Isaras is plainly a compound word, the elements of which are Is-aras. Of the derivation of its latter element *aras* there can be little doubt. It is of the same origin as the Roman Arar, (the Saône) which is a reduplication of the syllable *ar*, one of those syllables consisting either of the vowel *a* alone, or of the same vowel combined with various consonants, which form, either singly or reduplicated, the appellations of water and rivers in many languages, both of the East and the West. There might be cited, as examples, the Persian *ab*, the Latin *aqua*, the *Ach* or *Ache* of the Austrian Alps, the Swiss or French *Aa*, the Swiss *Aar*, the *Anas* of Bœtica, and many other words of similar formation. The *Is* of the word *Isaras* has however another origin, and is identical with the Celtic *uisg* or *uisge* "water," a term which is still applied to some of the streams of the Scotch Highlands, and from which, by corruption, such names of rivers as Ouse, Usk, Esk, Exe, &c., are derived. Of the Celtic *uisg*, the Romans, as in the case of the Usk, formed the word *Isca*, which may thus be taken as the classic form of the Celtic word. The two elements therefore, which enter into the name *Is-aras* are *Isca* and *Aras*; which, when blended into one word, would give *Iscaras* as the primitive form of *Isaras*. By the omission of the initial vowel, the Greek word *Scaras* at once results; while the Latin *Isara* is clearly but a more euphonious form of *Iscaras*. We may thus conclude that *Scaras* and *Isara* are both merely different forms of one word, *Iscaras*, and that the river Scaras of Polybius is the modern Isère. The Isca and the Aras would, in all probability, be the names of the two principal rivers which united to form the Iscaras; the Isca being upon this supposition identified with the Upper Isère, the river of the Tarantaise; and the Aras with the Arc, the river of the Maurienne[1].

The distances given by Polybius are in perfect accord-

---

[1] Similar derivations of the names of rivers are given by Dr Donaldson in his *Varronianus*, p. 45, (2nd Edit.)

ance with the conclusion that the Scaras and the Isère are identical. From the point where Hannibal passed the Rhone to the "ascent of the Alps," the length of the march was 1400 stadia. From the Island also, that is to say, from the junction of the Rhone and the Scaras, there was à march of 800 stadia to the same point. There was therefore a distance of 600 stadia or 75 Roman miles from the point where the Rhone was crossed, to the junction of the Scaras and the Rhone. The place where the Carthaginians passed the Rhone was also at a distance of about 1600 stadia or 200 Roman miles from Emporium, and nearly four days' march from the sea.

These distances are in themselves almost, if not quite, sufficient to prove, that Hannibal crossed the Rhone at or near Roquemaure, and that the Scaras of Polybius was the Isère. The question has been argued satisfactorily by M. Deluc upon these grounds[1]. Following the Roman itineraries as far as possible, he gives the distance between the ancient Emporium and Roquemaure at 206.2 Roman miles; the distance between the eastern embouchure of the Rhone and a point on that river opposite Roquemaure at $64\frac{1}{2}$ Roman miles; and the distance from this latter point to the junction of the Rhone and Isère at 75 Roman miles. The last of these distances is accurately the same as the distance of 600 stadia, deduced from Polybius as the length of the march from the passage of the Rhone to the confluence of the Scaras. The actual 206.2 Roman miles between Emporium and Roquemaure make also a distance nearly in accordance with that given by Polybius, who states it as being about 1600 stadia or 200 Roman miles. Finally, the distance of $64\frac{1}{2}$ Roman miles, from the point on the Rhone opposite Roquemaure to the eastern embouchure of the Rhone, would be a distance that might be well described as rather under four days' march, as Han-

[1] *Histoire du passage des Alpes par Annibal.* Ukert conjectures that Hannibal crossed the river lower down, in the neighbourhood of Beaucaire; a supposition which is also adopted in a very able article in the *Philological Museum*, on Hannibal's passage of the Alps. On many material points, however, as will be afterwards found, the views advocated in this treatise receive the sanction of the learned writer of the article alluded to.

nibal, after having passed the Rhone, marched to the con-fluence of the Scaras, a distance of 75 Roman miles, in four complete days.

The description which Polybius gives of the district called the Island, though not minutely accurate, is yet sufficiently so for its recognition. Two sides of it, he says, were bounded by the Rhone and the Scaras : its third side was formed by a chain of almost impracticable mountains. These mountains spoken of by Polybius form what is called the Chartreuse range, the celebrated monastery of the Grande Chartreuse being inclosed among them. They extend northward from Grenoble to the outlet of the lake of Bourget, and form the connecting link between the Alps and the Jura, though not strictly belonging to either mountain-system. On the east, they are separated from the Alps by the Vale of Graisivaudan, (the French part of the valley of the Isère) by the valley of Chambéry, and by the lake of Bourget. On the south-west, they are also separated from the Alps by a portion of the Vale of Graisi-vaudan. On the north-west, the Rhone divides them from the Jura : and on the west, the river Guiers, which marks the frontier between France and Savoy, and a line drawn from Les Echelles to Moirans, may be assigned as the limits between them and the hilly part of the district between the Rhone and the Isère. The character which Polybius gives these mountains is perfectly accurate. Their extreme western face rises suddenly and precipi-tously from the country they overlook, and presents a long barrier of rock so apparently impracticable, as fully to bear out Polybius' strong expressions, that these mountains were difficult of approach and entrance, and almost inac-cessible.

Yet, though the Island of Polybius may thus be iden-tified by the nature of the boundaries he has assigned to it, his acquaintance with it does not seem to have been per-fect. The comparison of it to the Egyptian Delta is not very fortunate. It is considerably less in size than the Egyptian district, and does not entirely resemble a Delta in form. For, in order that this comparison might hold, the course of the Rhone, from the confluence of the

Isère to the foot of the Chartreuse mountains near St Genix, ought to be straight. Yet the course of this river (reckoning upwards) is only straight as far as Lyons. It there changes its direction from north to east, assumes subsequently, for a short distance, a north-easterly course, and finally makes a sudden flexure towards the south-east, retaining the same direction as far as St Genix. The only way of accounting for this defective description of the Island seems to be, by supposing Polybius not to have been personally acquainted with the northern parts of that district. It is true that he would have no maps to assist him in forming a conception of the country, but could only judge of its figure and nature by the eye. Yet, even with these disadvantages, it hardly appears probable that he could have been ignorant of the flexures of the Rhone above Lyons, or could have looked upon it as running a straight course. The length also of the base of the Chartreuse mountains, extending from Moirans to St Genix, is much too short to allow them to be cited as standing in the same relation to the Island that the sea does to the Egyptian Delta. If, however, we suppose Polybius only to have visited the southern parts of the Island, the resemblance which he finds between it and the Egyptian Delta is readily understood. The Isère does actually run nearly a straight course from the edge of the base of the Chartreuse mountains near Moirans down to its confluence with the Rhone, and therefore corresponds perfectly to the eastern arm of the Nile. The course of the Rhone also from Lyons downward may be considered straight, and will thus represent the western branch of the Nile, if its course above Lyons be supposed unknown, and the river be imagined, as was probably the case with Polybius, to preserve the same direction above that city which it does below. Upon this supposition, the Rhone above Lyons would be conceived by Polybius, not as penetrating from the lake of Geneva between the Jura and the Chartreuse mountains, but as lying on the west, instead of the east, of the Jura range. The mountains therefore which Polybius speaks of as forming the third side of the Island, would not now be merely the Chartreuse range, but would include, besides, the extremity of the Jura, extending as a continuation of the Chartreuse mountains from the Rhone to the Ain, and thus nearly reaching the imaginary prolongation of the Rhone above Lyons. Both these systems of mountains would appear from the country of the Island as a connected group, and would naturally be considered to form as such one of the boundaries of the district.

Upon the supposition therefore that Polybius had not visited the northern parts of the country between the Rhone and the Isère, the discrepancies in the imagined resemblance between the Island and the Egyptian Delta may be accounted for; for the similarity holds good to the eye, if the course of the Rhone above Lyons be supposed unknown, and the Jura and Chartreuse mountains be taken together as one mountain boundary. That Polybius also exaggerates the size of the Island is another argument that he was not fully acquainted with it. Yet, if he was ignorant of any district in it, that district must have been the ·northern or more remote portion of the Island: for, if he was acquainted with those parts of it, he could not have been ignorant of the southern parts. That the Island was the country between the Rhone and the Isère, appears clearly, as has been previously shewn, from the distances given by Polybius, and from the identity of the names Scaras and Isaras. The defective resemblance between this tract of country and the Egyptian Delta does not invalidate this fact, but only leads us to conclude that Polybius had not visited the northern parts of the country; a conclusion which will be found of some importance in the investigation of the route by which Hannibal reached the first ascent of the Alps[1].

---

[1] It may be here observed, that this country, though not conforming accurately to the shape of a Delta, but only taking that form in the mind of one not thoroughly acquainted with it, is yet exceedingly well described by the native name of 'the Island.' With the exception of the line drawn from the Isère near Moirans to the Rhone near St Genix, a line hardly exceeding 20 miles in length, those two rivers form its entire boundary Consequently, out of a circumference of nearly 180 miles, it is surrounded for about 160 miles, or eight-ninths of the whole circuit,

This route is the subject which has now immediately to be considered. After having established the elder of the two contending brothers in the sovereignty of the Island, Hannibal resumed his march under the escort of a band of the men of that district[1]. This march must be supposed to be resumed from the point where Polybius breaks off his narrative of the previous march; from the confluence, that is to say, of the Rhone and the Isère. And here a difficulty at once arises to be resolved: for the resumed march is said to have lain *by the river side* for a distance of 800 stadia or 100 Roman miles. Which then of the two rivers, the Rhone and the Isère, from whose junction he started, was the river which Hannibal followed up?

The previous narrative of Polybius would at first lead us to imagine that it was the Rhone. For in the 39th chapter it is stated, that, after the passage of the Rhone, Hannibal went along the very river bank towards its source, until he arrived at the ascent of the Alps on the way to Italy. Now from this account it is certainly most natural to conclude, that it was the same river which was followed up all the way to the beginning of the Alpine ascent; and not in the first part of the march the Rhone, and in the second the Isère. Another apparent argument in favour of the Rhone is, that Hannibal's operations in the Island must have obliged him to cross the Isère, and led him away from the banks of that river. This last argument is however of no weight. The transactions in the Island are quite episodical to the rest of the march, and seem to be kept perfectly distinct by Polybius, who breaks off his narrative of the progress of the army, for the purpose of relating them, at the junction of the Rhone and the Isère,

---

by the waters of two large and navigable rivers. Under these circumstances, and considering that it is an inland district, the name of 'Island,' as applied to it, is a very expressive and appropriate designation.

[1] The Island afterwards formed part of the country of the Allobroges. This does not, however, appear to have been the case in the time of Hannibal, for Polybius speaks of 'the Gauls called Allobroges,' as if they were entirely a different people. See *Philological Museum*, 'Hannibal's Passage of the Alps.'

as if to intimate that the bulk of the army went no further
northward at that time along the Rhone. The transactions
at the Island stand indeed, in their relation to this part of
the march, quite in the same position as the subjection of
the Spanish nations between the Ebro and the Pyrenees
does to the march along the coast in that part of Spain. To
subdue these nations, Hannibal must have left the coast,
and penetrated into the interior of the country; and yet,
in spite of these inevitable deviations, Polybius makes
Hannibal's march to lie throughout along the coast of
Spain from New Carthage to Emporium. Indeed, had he
adopted any other system, great confusion must have been
the result, and all estimation of distances nearly impracticable. All the marchings and countermarchings therefore, which Hannibal performed in the course of his operations against these Spanish tribes, from the time he left
the coast-road until the time that he returned to it, are
entirely omitted by Polybius in his relation of the progress
of the great march. The transactions at the Island seem
to be treated by him in the same manner. Before proceeding to relate them, he arrests the march of the army
at the confluence of the Isère with the Rhone, measuring
the distance up to that point. No distances whatsoever
are mentioned while the operations in the Island are
related. After concluding his account of those events, the
estimation of distances again begins; and this estimation
of distances must clearly be commenced, as has already
been often repeated, at the place where the last measurement of distances terminated, or at the junction of the
Rhone and the Isère.

The first argument against the supposition that Hannibal followed up the Rhone from the junction of the two
rivers is derived from the fact, that the whole Carthaginian
army must in that case have passed the Isère, and that the
passage of that river is not mentioned by Polybius. It is
true that, in order to carry on his operations in the Island,
Hannibal must have crossed the Isère with part of his
army; but there is no sufficient reason for concluding that
the baggage and the elephants were then brought across.
Had they been so, the silence of Polybius on the subject

would be difficult to account for. There were indeed several rivers crossed by Hannibal in Gaul, of which Polybius takes no notice; but these rivers would all be small streams, which the army would pass by wading. The Isère cannot be ranked in this class. It is, at its junction with the Rhone, a navigable river with a deep and rapid current, and presents an obstacle to the passage of an army too important to be omitted in silence in a narrative such as that of Polybius. With the exception of hostile opposition on the part of the inhabitants, all the difficulties and dangers, which attended the passage of the incumbrances of the army across the Rhone, must have been repeated in the case of the Isère, the lesser width of the latter river being the only circumstance that would make any difference. And yet no word about difficulty or danger is spoken by Polybius with respect to the Isère, nor does he take notice of any preparations having been made to effect the passage of the river.

Suppose, however, Hannibal to have brought all his army across the Isère, and to have directed his march upon the Alps along the side of the Rhone. In this case, the first mountains that he would encounter upon his way would be the Chartreuse group, the foot of which he would reach when he arrived in the neighbourhood of St Genix, at the junction of the Guiers with the Rhone. St Genix would thus be the earliest place, where the first ascent of the Alps could be fixed.

But the first ascent of the Alps lay at a distance of 100 Roman miles from the junction of the Rhone and the Isère, reckoned along the river side. St Genix should therefore lie at about that distance from the confluence of these two rivers. Now from Valence to Lyons the Itinerary of Antoninus reckons 71 Roman miles. Allowing 6 Roman miles for the distance from the confluence of the Rhone and the Isère to Valence, there remain 65 for the distance to Lyons. Above Lyons there are no ancient or modern roads along the Rhone to assist us in determining the distance to St Genix: but the length of the river between St Genix and Lyons is about the same as its length between Lyons and the confluence of the Isère, and we may therefore take the probable length of a march along the river as being the same in both cases.   The distance from the junction of the Rhone and Isère to St Genix, reckoned along the Rhone, would thus be about 130 Roman miles, instead of the 100 given by Polybius, a discrepancy which seems greater than ought to occur, though perhaps not so great, considering the manner in which Polybius measures, as to be decidedly conclusive against the supposition of Hannibal's having followed up the Rhone[1].

It has already been conjectured, in discussing Polybius' account of the Island, and in endeavouring to account for his imperfect conception of the nature of that district, that he had not visited its northern parts.   If such were the case, it would be a strong argument that Hannibal never followed up the Rhone to the foot of the mountains ; for otherwise Polybius, who had examined the whole of Hannibal's route, must have visited the northern parts of the Island, and have thus been enabled to form a more accurate idea of its nature and figure.

It may also be mentioned, that the very cursory manner in which Polybius speaks of the Chartreuse mountains in his description of the Island, and his not applying to them the name of Alps, would hardly lead us to expect that he considered them as forming the very portion of that great mountain system which Hannibal first encountered.   We should rather imagine that he looked upon them as mountains independent of the Alps, and with which he had no further concern, than in as far as they formed one of the boundaries of the district called the Island.

---

[1] M. Deluc, who supposes that Hannibal brought his whole army into the Island, and subsequently crossed the Chartreuse mountains, makes him leave the Rhone at Vienne, and strike straight across the country to St Genix. It seems however impossible, that, if Hannibal had adopted this route, Polybius could have spoken of him as keeping along the very bank of the river to the foot of the mountains; or that the sharers in the expedition, from whom the accounts of it must have been derived, should have failed to observe, that they had turned their backs upon the Rhone at Vienne.

Another objection to the supposition of Hannibal's having followed up the Rhone arises from the fact of the extremely circuitous nature of the route, from the junction of the Rhone and the Isère to St Genix, which the bank of the Rhone affords. It seems indeed nearly twice as long as is requisite. This objection might possibly appear, at first sight, somewhat obviated by the consideration, that the country was not then accurately mapped out, as it is now, and therefore the distances between various points, and their respective bearings, were not sufficiently well known. But it must be remembered, that Hannibal would then be under the escort of the inhabitants of the country he was traversing, whose local knowledge would compensate their want of geographical information: and it is almost impossible to conceive that they, wishing to guide the Carthaginians from the junction of the Rhone and Isère to St Genix, should have conducted him there all the way along the very bank of the Rhone. Yet this, according to Polybius' account, they must have done, if the Rhone were indeed the river which Hannibal followed to the foot of the Alps.

Again, if Hannibal followed up the Rhone to St Genix, he would either subsequently continue to pursue its banks to the lake of Geneva, and enter Italy by the Simplon or the Great St Bernard, or else cross the Chartreuse mountains, and make for the Little St Bernard or the Mont Cenis. Now that Hannibal entered Italy by the Simplon or the Great St Bernard are suppositions so beset with improbabilities that it is hardly necessary to consider them: so that the only point which it is requisite to examine here will be, whether any additional improbability arises from supposing that Hannibal selected the banks of the Rhone as his line of approach to the pass of the Little St Bernard or of the Mont Cenis.

Now, if he chose this line of approach, he must cross the Chartreuse mountains, and subsequently pass through Montmélian on the Isère. Yet, if a general wished to reach Montmélian from the junction of the Rhone and Isère, it would be very much shorter for him to follow up the Isère, rather than to take the line of the Rhone, and cross the Chartreuse mountains. Montmélian is, in fact, by the high road along the north bank of the Isère, only about 100 Roman miles from the confluence of the Rhone and Isère, while the distance along the banks of the Rhone and across the Chartreuse mountains exceeds 160. If then the longer line was adopted, it would naturally be chosen because it was a much easier route. But the line of the Isère is not only the shorter, but at the same time the easier route; for in the other case the Chartreuse mountains have to be crossed, a range of mountains which Polybius mentions as almost impracticable. It is very difficult to imagine that Hannibal would lengthen this part of his journey by more than one half, not in order that he might avoid, but in order that he might cross without necessity, mountains described by Polybius himself, as δυσπρόσοδα, καὶ δυσέμβολα, καὶ σχεδόν, ὡς εἰπεῖν, ἀπροσίτα[1].

From all these considerations the natural conclusion seems to be, that, although the most obvious interpretation of the words 'παρὰ τὸν ποταμόν,' in chap. 39, would lead us to think that Hannibal followed up the Rhone, from the place where he crossed that river up to the first ascent of the Alps ; yet the Isère must nevertheless be taken as the river which led Hannibal to the Alps after the transactions in the Island, and we must suppose that he followed up the Rhone no further than to the point where the Isère joins it. The passage of the Isère not being mentioned by Polybius in his account of the march of the army to the Alps, we shall infer that one part of the army, with the elephants and baggage, remained on the left bank of the Isère, while Hannibal crossed the river with the rest to take part in the affairs of the Island. After the conclusion of these transactions, Hannibal would recross the Isère, and the whole army would be again collected together on the south of the river, and at the place were it flows into the Rhone. From this point the march to the Alps was resumed. It lay, as Polybius informs us, in the beginning of his 50th chapter, for 800 stadia along the river side.

---

[1] See Ukert's *Geographie*, and *Philol. Mus.* Vol. II.

The ascent of the Alps (or to the Alps, as Polybius here expresses it) then commenced; that is to say, the route, previously upon the plain, (ἐν τοῖς ἐπιπέδοις) now first began to ascend the mountains. Here then, having previously concluded that the Carthaginian army never crossed the Isère on their way to the Alps, we have another condition for the determination of Hannibal's route:

‘The commencement of the ascent of the Alps must be situated at a distance of about 100 Roman miles from the junction of the Rhone and the Isère, reckoned along the left bank of the latter river[1].’

---

[1] Condition I.

CHAPTER IV.

Discussion of the narrative of Polybius, from the commencement of the ascent of the Alps to the arrival at the summit of the pass.—The defile at the commencement of the ascent.—Conclusions drawn as to its nature and the character of the neighbouring country.—The 'strong white rock.'—Features of the country in its vicinity.—The 'rock' at a distance of many miles from the summit of the pass.

WHEN the Carthaginians had approached the commencement of the mountain route, the men of the Island returned to their own country, and left them to penetrate alone into the Alps. They encountered almost immediately the greatest dangers. A difficult pass, through which they were obliged to march, was commanded by the Allobroges, who had taken possession of the heights above the road. This pass was situated, it is clear, at or very near the commencement of the ascent. Its nature, and the features of the surrounding country, will now have to be investigated.

The first features presented to our notice are certain 'advantageous posts,' which Polybius afterwards mentions as 'heights.' The elevation of these heights was evidently considerable, and their access difficult, at least from the side where Hannibal lay with his army : for the Allobroges would hardly have ventured to abandon them during the night, had they not then thought them perfectly secure from occupation on the part of the Carthaginians. It is also mentioned, that when Hannibal set forward to seize them in the night, the soldiers whom he selected for this service were active and lightly equipped, in order that they might be better enabled to contend with the difficulties of the mountains. It appears, besides, from the account of the battle of the next day, that Hannibal's posts on the heights were at some distance from the road through the pass, along which his army was defiling when it was attacked by the Allobroges. For as the Carthaginians were skirting the edge of the precipices which lay below the road, and Hannibal was in position on the heights, the Allobroges attacked the army on its march, from the ground above the road, and placed themselves between Hannibal and the rest of the Carthaginians. This is clear from what subsequently followed, when Hannibal at length charged down from the heights and routed the Allobroges, destroying an equal number both of his own army and of the enemy: for the Carthaginians, being below the Allobroges, were forced over the precipices by the success of the attack upon the enemy above them, who were driven down in confusion towards the precipices. Now, had there not been a considerable interval between Hannibal and the rest of his army, the Allobroges would scarcely have dared to occupy the intervening space, and expose themselves immediately to attack from Hannibal, and this before they had any time to inflict much loss upon the Carthaginian army. With respect then to these heights, the inference seems to be, that they were of considerable elevation, and not readily accessible from the side where the Carthaginians lay, though probably more easily gained from the side of the Allobroges, a circumstance which would induce them to abandon their posts during the night with less apprehension.

When Hannibal seized in the night the posts which had been abandoned by the Allobroges, he first passed through τὰ στενά 'the defile.' There was then, as might have been otherwise concluded, a defile in this part of the route, and Hannibal was obliged to pass through it on his march to seize the heights.

Polybius describes the way by which the Carthaginians had to advance, as being narrow and rugged, and also precipitous. A great number of horses and baggage-animals are said besides to have been lost down the precipices, when the Allobroges attacked the Carthaginians. In some part, therefore, of the line of advance, a narrow and rugged way along the edge of a precipice must be found for the Carthaginians.

Two other points which demand attention are suggested by the history of the events which preceded and followed the battle at the defile. On the evening of the day before the battle, Hannibal advanced into the immediate neighbourhood of the defile, and encamped not far from the enemy, their position being on the heights or advantageous posts. Previously also to his setting out in the night to seize these posts, he commanded the camp fires to be lighted; no doubt with the intention that the Allobroges might see them, and, concluding that the Carthaginians were permanently encamped till the morning, and meditated no further movement for the present, might, according to their custom, leave their posts for the night, and retire to the neighbouring town. The truth of this supposition is confirmed by its being said, that Hannibal advanced to the place where he encamped, in open view of the enemy. There must consequently be found, immediately below the defile, a place of encampment for Hannibal's army visible from the heights commanding the defile.

The town to which the Allobroges retired for the night presents a second subject for consideration. This town would be situated above the defile, and not far from it: for it is not likely that the Allobroges would have retired to any considerable distance from their strong posts. Indeed, Polybius expressly describes it as a town in the neighbourhood of the heights. Above the defile therefore, and near it, must be found a place where a town either stands or might have stood. But more than this is even requisite: for Hannibal, having taken the town, encamped there for a whole day. The place sought must thus be sufficiently large, not merely for the site of a town, but also for the encampment of an army as numerous as Hannibal's, which at this time probably amounted to more than 40,000 men, besides elephants, cavalry-horses, and beasts of burden. An open district or valley among the mountains seems to be required in this place.

Such then are the characteristics of the defile and the adjacent country, which the narrative of Polybius suggests to us. The existence of such a defile supplies another important clue by which Hannibal may be traced in his

Alpine route; the character of the pass and the nature of the vicinity presenting several particular features by which it may be identified. We thus derive, from the section of Polybius under consideration, one principal condition, as well as several minor ones, which any route, supposed to be that of Hannibal, must satisfy. The principal condition may be stated as follows[1]:

'At the commencement of the ascent of the Alps, a defile must be found, the character of which, and of the surrounding country, is in accordance with the events related by Polybius to have occurred in that place.'

The minor conditions which this includes may be thus given:

(1) The defile must be commanded by certain heights, of considerable elevation.

(2) These heights must not be easily accessible from below the defile.

(3) The way through the defile must skirt in some place the edge of a precipice.

(4) Immediately below the defile, must be found a place where an army as numerous as that of Hannibal could encamp.

(5) This place of encampment should be visible from the heights commanding the defile.

(6) Above the defile, and near it, must be found an open district, where a town either stands or might have stood, and where an army such as Hannibal's, could have encamped.

The ten days' march from the junction of the Rhone and Isère must be taken as terminating, not at the point where Hannibal left the Isère, but at the town of the Allobroges, which he captured after passing through the defile at the commencement of the Alpine ascent. For from this town the subsequent march of fifteen days through the Alps is clearly reckoned: and the march of ten days ought to terminate where the march of fifteen days be-

---

[1] Condition III.

gins. The distance also of 100 Roman miles along the
river side is hardly of sufficient length to have occupied
the Carthaginians ten days in marching; for even in the
Alps their rate of advance was greater than this. It
would be on the evening of the eighth day after leaving
the confluence of the Rhone and Isère, that Hannibal encamped before the heights occupied by the Allobroges :
on the same night he seized the abandoned heights : on
the ninth day the defile was passed, and the town captured : and on the tenth day the Carthaginians remained
encamped in the neighbourhood of the town. Polybius,
indeed, estimates the length, in distance, of the passage
of the Alps, from the point where Hannibal left the Isère ;
so that it might be natural to expect that the fifteen days
occupied in that passage would be reckoned from the
same point. But, from the rest of the narrative, it seems
plain, that the fifteen days' march is reckoned from the
town, the capture of which makes a natural break in the
history. This town was also, no doubt, very near the
Isère, and thus only a short distance removed from the
point where the march along the river terminated.

The fifteen days' march through the Alps terminated
at the commencement of the great plains of Northern
Italy. (Chap. 39). On the ninth day after leaving the
town, the summit of the pass was gained; and the army
remained encamped there for two days. The descent
then began; but was soon arrested in consequence of
the destruction of the road, by which the army had to
descend. It was only after three days of hardship that
this obstacle was surmounted, and the way made practicable. In one day the path was sufficiently repaired for
the passage of the horses and baggage-animals; but it
was not till the third day that the elephants were able
to pass. On the third day after leaving the place where
the path was broken up, the commencement of the plains
of Italy was reached.

Since the whole march through the Alps occupied
fifteen days, and the march terminated on the third day
after Hannibal passed the place where the path was broken up, it must have been on the thirteenth day that this

3

latter event took place.   But the Carthaginians were detained for three days by the broken path, and consequently could not have arrived at it before the eleventh
day.   The descent therefore from the summit of the
pass could not have commenced later than on the eleventh day.   But Hannibal arrived on the summit of the
pass on the ninth day, and encamped there for two days.
Now the eleventh day cannot be included as one of these
two days, for that day is the latest that can be assigned
to the commencement of the descent.   The ninth and
tenth days were thus the two days spent on the summit of
the pass : and the summit must therefore be supposed to
have been gained on the morning of the ninth day; for
that day could not be included as one of the two during
which the army remained encamped, unless the greater
part of it was spent by the army in its encampment.   A
similar conclusion must be drawn with respect to the three
days lost on the descent.   The army arrived at the broken
path on the eleventh day, the first day of the descent,
and left it on the thirteenth.   The eleventh, the twelfth,
and the thirteenth days are thus the days alluded to by
Polybius in the words, ἐν ἡμέραις τρισὶ κακοπαθήσας, (Chap.
55), which clearly refer to the hardships endured while the
army was obliged to halt in consequence of the path
being broken up.   Now, in order that these three days
may be referred to as passed while the army halted, the
whole or the greater part of each day must have been
consumed at the broken path.   The army must, in consequence, have had its progress arrested on the morning of
the eleventh day.   The greater part of that day, the whole
of the twelfth day, and the greater part of the thirteenth,
were spent at the broken path.   On the evening of the
thirteenth day the elephants were brought down by the
road which Hannibal had restored, and rejoined that part
of the army which had previously passed.   On the fifteenth
day the whole army arrived at the commencement of the
plains of Italy.

As Hannibal is stated to have encamped for two days
at the summit of the pass, the following condition at once
results :

'A place suitable for the encampment of Hannibal's army must be found at the summit of the pass[1].'

Also, since the descent began on the eleventh day, and terminated on the fifteenth, no more than five days were spent on the descent. But of these, more than two were lost at the broken path: (viz.) all the twelfth, and the greater part of the eleventh and thirteenth days. There were therefore less than three days of actual marching between the summit of the pass and the commencement of the plains of Italy. This circumstance supplies another condition[2].

'The commencement of the plains of Italy must be less than three days march from the summit of the pass.'

For several days, after leaving the town of the Allobroges, the march of Hannibal was undisturbed by hostilities: but on the fourth day he again had to encounter great dangers. These dangers resulted from a treacherous attack made upon the Carthaginians by the Alpine Gauls, with whom Hannibal had previously entered into a treaty. The attack took place near a certain strong white rock, περί τι λευκόπετρον ὀχυρόν, and was made on the fourth day's march from the town. A different date is, however, generally assigned to this event. It is usually supposed, not that the attack took place, but that Hannibal met and entered into a treaty with the Gauls who afterwards made the attack, on the fourth day. This view of the case would defer the attack till the seventh day, as the Carthaginians had marched for two days previously under the guidance of the Gauls; or, at any rate, till the sixth day, if the fourth day be included as one of the two which preceded the attack, and during which Hannibal was guided by the Gauls. It will consequently be necessary to consider here, somewhat at length, what is the right interpretation of Polybius' account of these occurrences.

The difference of the two views arises from this cause;

[1] Condition V.   [2] Condition VII.

that, while we have taken Polybius' narrative in this place
to consist, first of a summary statement of the events of
four days, and then of an explanation and a detailed
account of those events: yet it has, on the other hand,
been generally supposed, that the whole is one continuous
narrative; or, at all events, that no part of the details of
the transactions with the Alpine Gauls refers to the three
days preceding the fourth day indicated by the word
τεταρταῖος.

Now the few lines, printed in the translation of Polybius as the summary, comprise two facts: (1) An undisturbed march for some time, i. e. three days: and (2) a
great danger encountered on the fourth day. The two
questions thus suggested for consideration are: (1) How
did it happen that Hannibal's march was undisturbed for
three days? and (2) What were the particulars of the
danger encountered on the fourth day? These two questions, according to our view, Polybius proceeds at once to
resolve; and his explanation either implies or states the
following facts. Hannibal's march was undisturbed for
three days, because the Gauls thought their chance of
destroying the Carthaginian army would be greater, if
they refrained from attacking it until it arrived at a certain difficult pass; and if they were enabled, by previously
gaining the confidence of Hannibal, and becoming his
escort, to assail him when he was off his guard, and open
to great danger from a treacherous attack. They would
besides, by these means, secure a great part of their country from being ravaged by an hostile army, and would also
have time to collect their forces together, and hang upon
the rear of the Carthaginians, the most vulnerable extremity of an army upon its march. Acting in accordance
with this design, they met Hannibal, either on the evening
of the first day, or on the morning of the second day, of
his march from the town; and bore with them boughs and
crowns in token of their amicable intentions. Hannibal
however doubted the sincerity of their professions, but
thought it at last expedient to seem to confide in them.
For two days he pursued his march under their guidance.
These two days were the second and third. On the next

day he was attacked by the Gauls. This day was the fourth : and the treacherous attack was the great danger, which Polybius particularly mentions as having occurred on that day.

Now from this view of the case it may certainly be said, that the history comes out with clearness and precision. Whether what has been regarded as the explanation of a previous summary, were intended as such or not, yet it undoubtedly does explain it perfectly, both with respect to time and circumstances. Such a coincidence, it may be objected, is accidental. This is possible, though not highly probable; for the coincidence is almost too exact to be the effect of chance. There are, besides, other reasons which lead us to conclude, that Polybius' history may in this place be divided into a summary, and a subsequent explanation and detailed narrative. The justice of this conclusion may be perceived, by comparing what is given in this place as a summary, with the two passages given in the translation of Polybius as the previous summaries. These then are the three passages in question :

(1) Hannibal, having continued his march for four successive days from the passage (of the Rhone), came to the district called the Island, a populous and corn-producing tract of country, which derives its name from the very circumstance (of its formation).

For the Rhone &c.

(2) Hannibal, in the course of ten days, having advanced along the river side for a distance of 800 stadia, commenced the ascent of the Alps, and found himself in a situation of the greatest danger.

For as long as &c.

(3) During the days immediately following, he led on the army safely for some distance : but, on the fourth day, he again had to encounter great dangers.

For the people &c.

There are here presented, in one view, what are regarded as being three brief statements of marches, all broken off at points, where observations, explanations, or details, are requisite ; the unfinished sentences, which

follow in each case, being considered as the beginnings
of such particular remarks.   Now, let the events which
occurred, between the passage of the Rhone and the encampment at the town, be considered.   They will be found
to comprise these things; a march of four days along the
Rhone to the frontier of the Island, a number of episodical
transactions at the Island itself, a march of ten days to a
certain town, not far from the commencement of the ascent
of the Alps, and of a battle near the town and its subsequent capture.   In the first two supposed summaries, these
two marches are given, the Island noticed, and the dangers
mentioned which befel the army at the commencement of
the ascent of the Alps.   All the leading events therefore,
which happened between the passage of the Rhone and the
encampment in the neighbourhood of the town, are set
briefly before the reader.   This being the case, these sentences may reasonably be looked upon as summaries of
these important occurrences.   It remains to be considered,
how far, in these two instances, the remainder of the narrative is explanatory of these short statements.

Now the first summary presents to our notice the
march to the Island, and the Island itself.   Of the march
itself, nothing is subsequently said.   It offered, we may
suppose, no circumstances, which called for any particular
observation.   All the latter part of the forty-ninth Chapter
is devoted to a description of the Island; to an account of
the events which took place there, and which formed a
kind of episode to the great expedition; and to a pro-
spective glance at the assistance, which the men of the
Island rendered to Hannibal during the next part of his
march.   All these circumstances may be considered as
incidental to what is stated in the summary.

In the second summary are introduced, the march to
the commencement of the ascent of the Alps, and the
dangers which the Carthaginians encountered in that
neighbourhood.   The long account that follows explains
why, during that march, the army was unassailed by the
Allobroges, gives full particulars of the dangers it afterwards passed through, and brings it to its encampment at

the town of the Allobroges. These events also are all subordinate to those in the previous summary, and carry the history no further onward than where the dangers it alludes to terminated.

Let now the three passages given in page 37, be compared together. The third will, without much difficulty, be seen to have a considerable similarity to the other two; especially to the second, which it resembles with respect to the events it records. In both instances, there is an undisturbed march, succeeded by a dangerous contest. As such is the case, it is not unreasonable to suppose, that the historian would treat the last of these sections of his history in the same manner as the previous section : that having (as he unquestionably does in the previous instance) brought plainly forward in a short statement, the march itself and the dangers at its close, he would then proceed to enter into the requisite details, as he had done just before in that parallel case. This, it will be seen, from reference to page 37 is exactly the mode of narration which it has been concluded that he adopted : and it has already been noticed, how clearly his narrative developes itself on such a supposition. The views, therefore, which have here been taken, with respect to the events which occurred on the fourth day after Hannibal left the town, seem to be perfectly in accordance with Polybius' mode of narration, besides bringing out the history with great clearness, and explaining everything simply and without confusion.

The generally received interpretation of Polybius' narrative is much less satisfactory. According to this interpretation, Hannibal met the deputation of the Gauls on the fourth day after he left the town, and must consequently have been attacked on the sixth or seventh day. Yet Polybius states, (fixing the date with careful precision, ἤδη δὴ τεταρταῖος ὤν), that Hannibal fell again, *when now on his fourth day's march*, into some great danger. What then was this great danger? According to the view we have taken, it was the treacherous attack in the neighbourhood of the rock : according to the general view, it was the meeting with the deputation of Gauls bearing boughs and crowns. But this last supposition is scarcely well founded :

for no great danger could be said to result to Hannibal
from such an encounter, or from such weapons. Neither
is this difficulty by any means explained away by the fact,
that the intentions of these Gauls were treacherous, and
that, two or three days afterwards, they brought Hannibal
into great danger. It was the danger itself, and not the
Gauls from whom he afterwards incurred that danger, that
Hannibal encountered on the fourth day. Nor is it allow-
able thus to compress the events of three or four days
into one; as must be done, if the dangers of the attack
at the Rock, on the sixth or seventh day, are supposed to
be comprised in the pacific interview of the fourth day.
The evident intention of the historian to fix his dates with
accuracy must be completely defeated by such a lax interpretation. Far preferable to a strained explanation of this
nature must be the one, which takes the great danger
spoken of to be nothing else than the treacherous attack
of which Polybius afterwards gives the details, a time
of peril when the whole army was on the very brink
of destruction. This was, in absolute reality, a great
danger: the meeting with the Gallic deputation could
only, at the most, be considered as such in prospect;
being, in fact, only partially conducive to the great dangers, which befel the Carthaginians several days subsequently.

Yet Polybius does not merely say, that Hannibal had,
on the fourth day, to encounter great dangers; but that he
had *again*, on the fourth day, to encounter great dangers.
To what previous event then does this '*again*' refer?
Clearly to the similar part of what has been given above
as the second summary, where, in page 37, it is stated,
that Hannibal found himself in a situation of the greatest
danger. This danger, we know, befel him in consequence
of the attack made upon him at the commencement of the
ascent of the Alps: and the almost complete identity of
the two statements of danger would lead us to expect
something similar on the second occasion. The attack
near the Rock satisfies these expectations completely: but
no resemblance can be found between the battle with the
Allobroges, and the peaceful conference with the Gauls,

who bore boughs and crowns in token of amity. Yet this is the only event which took place on the fourth day, if the general interpretation of Polybius be adopted.

Lastly, it may be urged, that when Polybius says, 'but, on the fourth day he again had to encounter great dangers,' the historian plainly wishes to mark the precise date of some important occurrence; in like manner as he afterwards fixes the great event of the arrival at the summit of the pass, as taking place on the ninth day. But which of the two events was pre-eminent in point of importance: the attack by which the whole Carthaginian army was nearly brought to destruction, or the meeting with a deputation of Gauls bearing boughs and crowns? There can evidently be no question as to the relative importance of these two events: nor, as has been before observed, can the connexion of the first with the second make it be considered as identical with it in respect of date.

From all these arguments it appears, that the interpretation of Polybius, generally accepted, is found, on close examination, to be without foundation; the only satisfactory view that can be taken of the Greek narrative being, that Hannibal was attacked, near 'the strong white rock,' on the fourth day of his march from the town of the Allobroges. In the investigation of Hannibal's route, it is exceedingly important to determine the date of this attack with accuracy: for the 'strong white rock' seems noticed by Polybius, expressly with the view of pointing out the locality where the contest occurred, by mentioning a striking and permanent landmark, which offered itself in that place as a natural monument of the battle fought around it. The place where this remarkable rock, distinguished by its strength and whiteness, is to be sought, must be found by fixing the date of the events which occurred in its neighbourhood; and these events, we have now concluded, occurred on the fourth day after Hannibal left the town. As, therefore, Hannibal remained encamped near the Rock during the fourth night, and as he arrived at the summit of the pass on the ninth morning, the Rock must be situated nearly half-way between the town and the summit of the pass; nearly half-way, that is to say, in point of time, for, in point of distance, the respective difficulties of the way, above and below the rock, must be taken into account. Another condition for the determination of Hannibal's route is thus obtained[1]:

'At a place nearly half-way, in point of time, between the town of the Allobroges and the summit of the pass, a certain 'strong white rock' must be found; and the adjacent country must be in accordance with the events, which are recorded by Polybius to have taken place in the neighbourhood of the rock.'

We have now to consider Polybius' account of the battle which was fought near the rock he so particularly mentions. The Carthaginian army was attacked, he says, while it was passing through a difficult and precipitous ravine, φάραγγά τινα δύσβατον καὶ κρημνώδη. By this expression he probably means a narrow passage bounded by precipitous acclivities, where the way presented considerable difficulty. Polybius afterwards calls this ravine χαράδρα, and says that the army ἐξεμηρύσατο, defiled through it; an operation which occupied a whole night. From this also we should be led to conclude, that there was a narrow passage, where not many could pass at a time, through which the Carthaginians were obliged to make their way. This φάραγξ or χαράδρα will form one of the features of the country, which must be sought for in the neighbourhood of the 'strong white rock.'

As Hannibal proceeded through the country of these Alpine Gauls, the band, which had first met him on his march from the Town, led the way in the van. But as the Carthaginians advanced, other bodies of the Gauls collected on the rear. Each village or district that was passed through, would send out its men to swell the numbers of those who were following up the army; so that, in the two days, during which they allowed Hannibal to march peaceably through their country, they would be

---

[1] Condition IV.

enabled to draw together a considerable force. These movements increased the suspicions of the Carthaginian general, which had never entirely been laid asleep. Aware of the danger to which his rear was exposed, he placed his heavy infantry there, to make head against the Gauls, if they should venture to assail him. The cavalry and baggage were at the same time placed in the van, so as to be beyond the reach of the Gauls hanging upon the rear. What position in the line of march the light infantry occupied is not mentioned: they were probably in the centre, ready to move upon any point where their assistance might be required. That they should have been in a position where they could be easily brought into action, was almost indispensable; for they alone were serviceable in mountain fighting, or capable of driving back an enemy upon difficult ground.

This then was the arrangement of the Carthaginian line of march previous to the attack. The cavalry and baggage were in the van, the light infantry probably in the centre, and the heavy infantry in the rear. One body of the Gauls, now about to put their treacherous design into execution, was leading the way at the head of the Carthaginian columns: another body was hanging on the rear. The army of Hannibal was thus threatened at both extremities of its line of march.

The numbers of the Carthaginians amounted at this time to about 40,000 [1]. The line of march of an army so numerous as this, especially when confined in a mountain valley, must have extended to a length of some miles. The foremost columns and the rear-guard would consequently be several miles apart.

The Gauls at length made their attack: but the prudent arrangements of Hannibal saved the Carthaginian army. The attack upon the rear failed; for the heavy

---

[1] After the passage of the Rhone they amounted to 46,000, of whom 26,000 reached the plains of Italy. Nearly as many were lost upon the descent from the Alps, as there were during the ascent. About 35,000 would thus reach the summit of the Alps. Their numbers at the battle of the Rock may therefore be taken to have been about 40,000.

infantry succeeded in withstanding the efforts of the enemy. The contest here probably took place in a part of the valley where the ground was not difficult: for the heavy infantry would hardly have repelled the mountaineers, if they had had at the same time to contend with the ruggedness of the mountains. Yet, though the Carthaginians were successful upon this quarter, they suffered severe loss, both in men, horses, and baggage-animals. The van therefore was also attacked, for it was there that the cavalry and baggage had been placed by Hannibal. This attack must have been made by the Gauls who were previously mentioned by Polybius as leading the way in the van. They were, however, probably not alone, but had been joined by other parties of Gauls, who were awaiting them there; yet of whose presence Hannibal does not seem to have been aware, as it was his rear which he appears to have thought especially in danger. It is not likely that any of the Gauls who attacked the rear had any share in the destruction of the cavalry and baggage-animals in the van: for they could hardly have managed to make their way along the mountain sides, unopposed by Hannibal, for so long a distance. Neither could the heavy infantry be spoken of by Polybius as rendering the service they did to the army, had the Gauls who had hung upon the rear succeeded in passing all along the mountains so as to fall on the van. When the historian says, τούτων δὲ ἐφεδρευόντων ἔλαττον συνέβη γενέσθαι τὸ πάθος· οὗτοι γὰρ ἔστεξαν τὴν ἐπιφορὰν τῶν βαρβάρων, it seems necessarily to be implied, that the heavy infantry, repelling the enemy in the rear, succeeded in preventing them from inflicting any injury upon the Carthaginians.

The Gauls who attacked the van had the advantage of the ground. As they marched in advance of the Carthaginians, they were enabled to occupy the slopes above the road, along which the army which followed them had to proceed. From this position, (joined perhaps, as has been conjectured, by others of their own countrymen) they assailed the Carthaginian van with rocks and stones. Down the steeper declivities they probably rolled rocks from some distance above: and, where the slope was not sufficiently steep to give the requisite impulse to the rocks, they advanced almost close to the Carthaginians, and hurled heavy stones at them as they passed beneath.   By these attacks a heavy loss in men, horses, and baggage-animals, was sustained.   The foremost column was, in all probability, entirely destroyed, before Hannibal could take any measures for the defence of this division of his army. Seeing the destruction that awaited them, the rest of the cavalry, with the baggage, would halt or fall back, until a safer progress could be ensured for them.

No danger was now to be apprehended on the rear : the heavy infantry there held the Gauls in check, and Hannibal was enabled to devote his personal efforts to the safety of the van.   For this purpose it must have been necessary to gain possession of the heights above the slopes, where the Carthaginians had suffered so severely from rocks and stones.   The light infantry would be the arm to which this service would naturally be entrusted ; but it cannot be said whether they composed all the forces on the occasion.   One half of the Carthaginian army, that is to say, about 20,000 men, were led on by Hannibal in person against the Gauls on the mountains, and succeeded either in driving them back, or in manœuvring so as to make them abandon their posts.   However his purpose may have been effected, he at length took up a position where he was able to guard the rest of his army as it resumed the interrupted march through the ravine. This march was performed during the night, which may have been about to fall when Hannibal took up his position on the heights.   He probably thought that during the night he could draw his army off better from the Gauls in the rear, who perhaps would not suspect that such a movement was contemplated, even if the fatigue and ill success of the conflict of the day had not rendered them indisposed for an immediate renewal of hostilities.   During all the night Hannibal remained in position, separated from the rest of his army as it defiled through the ravine. On the morrow, the Gauls having withdrawn, Hannibal rejoined his cavalry and baggage, and resumed his journey towards the summit of the Alps.

Such, as far as can be collected from the narrative of Polybius, were the progress and termination of the battle of the Rock. The most remarkable circumstance it contains,—a circumstance which gives an important clue by which the scene of this contest may be found,—is the fact of Hannibal's having posted 20,000 men on the heights, away from the rest of his army, and for the sake of ensuring its safety. This circumstance at once suggests the existence of an extent of practicable ground above the slopes on one side of the road, by no means usually to be found in the Alps. It is also worthy of notice, that Hannibal is said to have passed the night χωρὶς τῶν ἵππων καὶ τῶν ὑποζυγίων, an expression which seems to imply that his position was at some considerable distance from the place where he had left his cavalry and baggage; for a slight distance, such as some fifty or a hundred yards, between two divisions of an army, would hardly be considered as amounting to a separation of positions, or have been a sufficiently important movement to have been recorded.

But the extent of the practicable ground on one side of the Carthaginian army seems to have been more than was merely sufficient for the posts of Hannibal's 20,000 men. For these men were placed on the heights in order that they might protect the rest of the army, from which they had separated. They had consequently,—at least such a conclusion appears necessary,—interposed between the Gauls on the heights and their own cavalry. These Gauls would thus be stationed, in all probability, on a more remote part of the same tract of ground where Hannibal had posted his 20,000 men.

The difficult and precipitous ravine, mentioned by Polybius, has been already noticed, and its character conjectured. The slopes where the Gauls attacked the flank of the Carthaginian van, by rolling down rocks and casting stones; and the great extent of practicable ground above these slopes, are the chief features (besides the 'strong white rock') by which the scene of the battle is to be recognized. We have therefore to find in the immediate neighbourhood of the Rock:

(1) A difficult and precipitous ravine, through which the road must pass.

(2) A range of slopes overlooking the road, and liable to be swept, in one or more places, by rocks set in motion from above.

(3) A large extent of practicable ground above these slopes.

(4) A position on this ground, at some distance from the road, where 20,000 men could be stationed, so as to protect completely an army marching along the road beneath, and such as would not expose themselves to be attacked at any serious disadvantage, by an enemy lying beyond them relatively to the road[1].

The portion of Polybius' narrative, relating to the march from the neighbourhood of the Rock to the summit of the pass, is very short, and presents nothing of much consequence. It comprises a short statement of the march; and mentions how the Carthaginians were harassed on their way by occasional predatory attacks on the part of the barbarians, but had not to encounter any formidable opposition to their progress. The only particular observation, which Polybius makes upon this part of the march, refers to the effect which the sight of the elephants produced upon the barbarians; who were so overawed by the appearance of these unknown and gigantic animals, that they were deterred from making any assault upon those parts of the line of march where they were to be found. It does not appear, that these barbarians formed any part of those who had attacked Hannibal in the neighbourhood of the Rock, and who would naturally have been left behind by the Carthaginians. Indeed, had the barbarians, who made the predatory attacks, had any share in the battle of the Rock, the appearance of the elephants could

---

[1] As no attack is said to have been made, either on the army during its night march, or on the protecting troops of Hannibal, we may conclude that neither division was much exposed to molestation on the part of the enemy.

hardly have been so unfamiliar to them, or have overawed
them in the manner it is said to have done. Most probably, they were merely the inhabitants of the several
districts through which the army successively passed, who
seized any favourable opportunity of plundering that occurred, without offering any organized resistance to the
Carthaginians.

It is, however, necessary to notice in this place an
erroneous interpretation of a passage in Polybius, from
which it has been concluded, that the battle of the Rock
took place on the day before Hannibal reached the summit
of the Alps. The Greek narrative runs thus : τῇ δ᾽ ἐπαύριον τῶν πολεμίων χωρισθέντων, συνάψας τοῖς ἱππεῦσι καὶ
τοῖς ὑποζυγίοις προῆγε πρὸς τὰς ὑπερβολὰς τὰς ἀνωτάτω
τῶν Ἄλπεων, κ. τ. λ.

In this passage, it has been supposed that the words
τῇ δ᾽ ἐπαύριον are connected with προῆγε, and that Hannibal consequently gained the summit of the pass on the
day after he fought the battle. Yet this supposition is
unfounded, for all that the Greek implies as having occurred ' on the morrow,' is the junction of the two divisions of the army after the enemy had withdrawn. It is,
besides, by no means natural to suppose, that the day
mentioned as the ἐπαύριον is the same day as that indicated subsequently in the word ἐνναταῖος ; for the latter day
seems clearly to be spoken of by Polybius as later than
the former. Neither would any sufficient time be left, if
this view were adopted, for the series of repeated attacks,
on various parts of the army, and in different localities,
which are recorded to have been made between the neighbourhood of the Rock and the summit of the pass. For
Hannibal reached the summit of the pass on the morning
of the ninth day ; so that scarcely any time could inter-
vene between his arrival there, and his departure from his
position near the Rock, if it were only on the same ninth
morning that he left this position. Indeed, it seems plain
that the Rock must have been at a distance of many miles
from the summit of the pass, for the predatory attacks,
which the Carthaginians suffered during this part of the
march, were, in all probability, made by the inhabitants

of the several districts through which they passed[1]; and
the immediate neighbourhood of the summits of the
Alpine passes was not inhabited in the time of Polybius,
as indeed is generally the case at present, although the
uninhabited regions are now, no doubt, less extensive.   If
the words also of Polybius—ὁλοσχερεῖ μὲν οὐδενὶ περιπίπ-
των ἔτι συστήματι τῶν βαρβάρων, κατὰ μέρη δὲ καὶ κατὰ
τόπους παρενοχλούμενος ὑπ᾽ αὐτῶν· ὧν οἱ μὲν ἀπὸ τῆς οὐρα-
γίας οἱ δὲ ἀπὸ τῆς πρωτοπορείας ἀπέσπων τῶν σκευοφόρων
ἔνια, προσπίπτοντες εὐκαίρως. κ.τ.λ.—if these words be
duly considered, it will be seen, that the events to which
they refer require for their occurrence a considerable
space of time and length of march, and that they are not
such as would have happened in the course of two or three
hours, or on a march of a very few miles, especially
through a district where there were scarcely any, or no
inhabitants.   That the 'strong white rock' of Polybius
should thus have been situated (as is the case with the
'Roche Blanche' on the road of the Little St Bernard,
and the gypsum rock near Termignon on the road of the
Mont Cenis) at a distance of no more than about six
miles below the summit of the pass, appears, from this
passage alone of Polybius, to be a supposition deficient in
probability, even if no account be taken of the previous
part of the narrative, which relates to Hannibal's transactions with the barbarians who afterwards betrayed him,
and from which the natural conclusion is, that it was on
the fourth day that the Carthaginians were attacked near
the 'strong white rock.'   Upon this latter supposition, on
the other hand, ample space and time are allowed for the
events which took place between the Rock and the summit
of the pass; Hannibal being supposed to have left his
position near the Rock on the morning of the fifth day,
and to have arrived at the summit of the pass four days
afterwards.

---

[1] As the van of Hannibal's army was plundered, as well as the rear, it
seems almost certain that these attacks could not have been made by bands
following up the Carthaginians.

4

CHAPTER V.

ON the morning of the ninth day after he had left the town of the Allobroges, Hannibal at length gained the summit of the pass. Here he encamped, and remained during the greater part of the ninth and all the tenth day, waiting for stragglers who had been left behind, and giving some repose to his men after the toils and dangers of the ascent. A respite from toil and a freedom from hostile attacks they indeed obtained, but were exposed in return to new and equally depressing hardships. It was now the end of October. Winter had already reigned for a month upon the higher parts of the Alpine passes; the snow was beginning to collect; and the temperature, during a full half of the twenty-four hours, would be below the freezing point. The rest they had obtained only made them feel the cold still more acutely, by depriving them of all opportunity of exercise; the excitement of enterprise and of overcoming danger and difficulty no longer sustained them; and in the languor of inaction their thoughts naturally reverted to the perils, from which they had only escaped with difficulty and heavy loss, and a renewal of which they expected to await their enfeebled and reduced numbers upon the descent. Their provisions also were probably by this time approaching to exhaustion, and they found themselves encamped on the snowy crest of the Alps, with a barren solitude extending for miles around them. Here, for the first time, we read of the spirits of the army sinking. A feeling of despondency spread through the ranks of the Carthaginians : and on the tenth day[1], after they had been exposed to the severities of a winter's night upon the Alps, their profound dejection aroused the anxiety of their leader, who imme-diately took measures to counteract a state of feeling, which might have proved fatal to the success of the expedition.

From this circumstance we are made aware of one of the most important characteristics of the pass which Hannibal crossed. He had, Polybius says, one only re-source by which he could encourage his desponding army: and that one resource consisted in setting before them the prospect of Italy. Italy was thus visible from the summit of the pass. No modified interpretation[2] of this assertion can be admitted : it cannot be supposed that Polybius would have spoken of Hannibal, either as shewing or as pointing to, that which was at the time out of sight. Nor is it easy to conceive, unless Italy itself lay before their eyes, how the soldiers would have derived much en-couragement from all Hannibal's words. For this it was essential that Italy should be visibly present, and their extrication from the fatal region of the Alps evidently at hand, the utmost limits of the mountains, and the country beyond, being plainly descried. Otherwise Hannibal would have had no foundation on which to ground his encourag-ing exhortations; but all his words would have fallen dead, had the Carthaginians seen, as they would have done on most passes, that the mountains still shut them in on every side, and that ' Alps on Alps' still lay piled before them upon their future course, all the unknown and intricate vallies and ravines among them having still to be threaded, before they could hope to arrive at the invisible plains of Italy.

Yet, though Italy was visible from the summit of the pass, it was not from the place where the Carthaginians were actually encamped, that Italy could be seen. On

---

[1] It was on the tenth day; for on the morrow they began to descend, and their descent commenced on the eleventh day.

[2] See Deluc, *Histoire du passage des Alpes*, pp. 156—159; and *Disser-tation on the passage of Hannibal, by a member of the University of Oxford*, pp. 62— 67.

the tenth morning, after they had remained encamped for a whole day, the ἐνάργεια τῆς Ἰταλίας, or 'manifestation of Italy,' had not taken place. From their encampment then, at that time, Italy was invisible; and Hannibal must have brought them to some other point, from whence the prospect could be obtained. As to the position of this point of view, Polybius says nothing; but we are led to infer that it lay not far distant from the road over the summit of the pass. For, had it lain at any great distance, it is rather difficult to imagine how Hannibal had become aware that there was any point commanding such a view; a circumstance, of which he was probably apprised by his Gallic guides, who would only have been acquainted, from previous knowledge, with what lay in the immediate neighbourhood of the road; as it was not likely that any one, crossing these desolate regions, would have diverged unnecessarily from the track. Besides, had Hannibal made an excursion of any length for the purpose of obtaining a view of Italy, Polybius would naturally have taken some notice of it, and not have passed it over in complete silence. We are therefore led to conclude, that the point from which Italy was seen lay not far from the road over the summit of the pass, but yet was not included in the ground where the Carthaginians encamped, when they first gained the summit.

When Hannibal shewed Italy to his troops, he pointed out to them the plains of the Po, and indicated to them the quarter in which Rome itself lay, τὸν τῆς Ῥώμης αὐτῆς τόπον. The district described as the plains of the Po is well known. It is the vast tract of country, almost entirely level, which lies between the Alps on the North and the Apennines on the south, and which stretches eastward from the roots of the Cottian Alps as far as the Adriatic sea. A part of this country Hannibal pointed out to his soldiers. He also indicated to them the quarter in which Rome itself lay. Here the word is much vaguer than when the plains are spoken of. In the first case it is ἐνδεικνύμενος, in the latter ὑποδεικνύων. Neither is it actually Rome that is spoken of, but only the quarter in which Rome lay. Hannibal gave his army, in fact, a vague no-tion where Rome was situated. He saw, we may imagine, as he would naturally do from the Alps, the range of the Apennines rising beyond the plains of the Po; and gave his men some idea of the situation of Rome, by saying that it lay beyond the range of mountains, which they then descried upon the distant horizon. How far it lay beyond them, he probably did not think it necessary to state, even if he well knew himself; for his object was not to convey information, but encouragement: and he would not have been unwilling to let his army infer, that Rome was situated at a short distance beyond the Apennines. With respect to the plains of the Po, no deception was possible: they could not have supposed that they saw them, unless they actually did so. With respect, however, to the position of Rome, they had no means of determining whether what Hannibal said was strictly true or not; but must have taken it for granted, without question, that Rome lay where he told them that it did, unless such an assertion was palpably extravagant.

It is unnecessary to offer any remarks upon the sagacity which Hannibal evinced in introducing the name of Rome, and in connecting that city with the prospect the Carthaginians then had beneath them. But a short time before, seeing themselves enclosed on all sides by the snows and crags of the Alps, they had abandoned hope, and given way to despair. Now, not only did the fertile plains of Italy greet their sight; but it even seemed, as their eyes possessed themselves of the country upon which they looked down, and rested upon the distant Apennines, which alone, as they believed, separated them from Rome, that the great city itself, the prize for which they had dared so much, was then almost within their grasp.

It was then the sight of the Apennines, which had, in all probability, suggested to Hannibal the idea of Rome, and by means of which he indicated its situation. The condition, therefore, which results from the fact of Italy having been seen from the summit of the pass, will be of the following nature[1]:

---

[1] Condition VI.

'From a point, probably not far from the road over
the summit of the pass, but yet not upon the ground where
the Carthaginians would encamp when they first reached
the summit, the plains of the Po, and, in all probability,
the Apennines also, ought to be visible.'

On the eleventh day after leaving the Town, the Carthaginians began their descent into Italy. The commencement of the march was attended with great disasters.
The declivity of the mountain, down which their route lay,
was excessively steep, and their path was wholly or partially concealed by the snow. Many, in consequence, uncertain where to tread, missed their footing, and great numbers, both of men and beasts, were carried down the precipices. Of the multitudes lost upon the whole descent,
and amounting to nearly 10,000 men, a large proportion
probably perished here. This circumstance presents to us
another characteristic of the pass which the Carthaginians
crossed[1].

'The first part of the descent from the summit of the
pass on the Italian side must be of a precipitous character.'

Heavy, however, as these disasters were, the army bore
them with constancy, having already experienced similar
calamities. On the other side of the pass they had probably been exposed to something of the same nature,
although Polybius, who is very concise with respect to the
latter part of the ascent, does not mention anything of the
kind. Yet a still severer trial soon befel the Carthaginians. They arrived at a place where their line of route
ran along the face of a crumbling precipice, and where the
path had been carried away, together with the face of the
precipice, by a recent landslip. There seems no doubt
that it was an accident of this nature, (of very common
occurrence in the Alps, especially after rainy weather,)
which arrested the further progress of the army of Hannibal. That there was a precipice in this place is evident,

_____

[1] Condition VIII.

both from the events which took place, and from the fact of the Carthaginians being obliged to halt for three days, in consequence of the accident; besides, Polybius, afterwards speaking of this spot, (and perhaps exclusively of it,) uses the words τῶν προειρημένων κρημνῶν. Hannibal also when he remedied the misfortune, 'built up the precipice,' τὸν κρημνὸν ἐξῳκοδόμει; so that it is quite certain there was a precipice here. But this same place is also called ἀπορρώξ, and the ἀπορρὼξ is further described as recently μᾶλλον ἔτι ἀπερρωγυῖα; in which description a slip of the side of the precipice is evidently alluded to. The destruction also, whole or partial, of the path, could hardly be explained on any other supposition[1].

The method by which Hannibal repaired the path, his ' building up the precipice,' may be explained without difficulty; for the words describe graphically the means now resorted to in the Alps to construct or repair a path in similar places. The precipice which had fallen away would not have been one of solid rock, but a very steep declivity of earth, or, what is perhaps more likely, one of earth and loose rocks mingled together. These precipices are necessarily, from the nature of their formation, loosely coherent and very subject to disintegration: the water, in times of rain, easily penetrates them; the cohesion of their parts is thus destroyed or weakened; and, owing to the steepness of the declivity, the outer surface of the precipice breaks up, and a landslip is the result[2]. Such precipices as these always deviate considerably from the vertical: a sheer precipice must be composed of solid rock. Any exception to

---

[1] Livy is quite plain here: he says that the cause of the accident was a 'lapsus terræ,' or landslip.

[2] A part of the road over the Stelvio pass is mentioned as suffering in this manner. 'The steep sides of the mountains along which the road is carried, are of a light crumbling soil, in which are embedded rocks and stones. Heavy rains produce great injury to this part of the road, by washing away the soil and bringing down the rocks. Near Trafoi, the road, for a length of about two English miles, was nearly destroyed by such accidents, and a new one on the opposite bank of the stream was in consequence opened in 1846.'—Murray's *Handbook for Southern Germany*.

this rule is very rare indeed.   Consequently, when Hannibal set his men to work to construct a new path, footing
for the workmen to stand might be found without much
difficulty upon the face of the precipice.   In their case also
it would be more easily penetrable by the feet, in consequence of its having been recently broken up; so that
none of the surface near the line of the destroyed path
could have been hard, but the men might have buried
their feet in the loose ground, and thus secured a tolerably
firm position.

The way in which the precipice was 'built up,' and the
path made or repaired, would be such as is now employed.
Men would be stationed on the declivity, a few yards
below the line of the broken path ; and from thence, with
the aid of materials readily found, such as small rocks,
stones, and earth, they would build up a kind of terrace to
the level of the old path, and so restore to it the width it
had lost[1].   As the path is only said to have been made
impracticable by the landslip for elephants and beasts of
burden, but not for men, we may suppose that some
assistance might be rendered from it to those working

---

[1] The annexed figures, representing profiles or sections of the declivity, may assist in rendering the mode of operation clearer.   Fig. 1 re-
presents a place where the path was partially carried away, *AB* being the
width of the remnant of the path.   In fig. 2, the damage is seen remedied
by means of a terrace (represented by the dark part *BCD*), *ABC* being
the width of the restored path.   In fig. 3, the path is supposed to have
been wholly carried away, the point *A* marking its former position.
In fig. 4, a new path, whose width is *AC*, is seen formed by means of a
terrace.

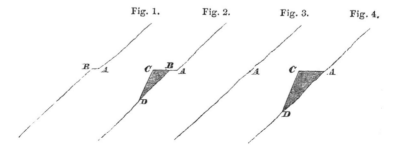

Fig. 1.   Fig. 2.   Fig. 3.   Fig. 4.

below, that materials might have been furnished to them from above, and some help given to them in their arrangement. Such a work must, nevertheless, have been long and tedious : and when it is considered, that these terraces had to be raised along the mountain-side for a length of nearly three hundred yards at least[1], (for the path was probably either destroyed, or more or less damaged, for the whole of the length mentioned by Polybius,) and also to be made sufficiently wide and strong to support the ponderous bulk of the elephants, it will readily be understood how the greater part of three days was occupied in their construction.

No vestiges of Hannibal's work can now be expected to remain. It is only the general features of the place which could have continued unaltered to the present day. What its nature was has been now sufficiently explained. Its position also with respect to the summit of the pass may be easily deduced within certain limits. For Hannibal arrived at the broken path before the first half of the eleventh day had elapsed; and it was on the same day that he began his descent. A condition of the following nature will consequently result[2] :

'At a place, within half a day's march of the summit of the pass, on the Italian side, the path must lie along a precipitous mountain-side liable to be broken up for a length of nearly 300 yards; and the country in the vicinity should be of a nature adapted to Polybius' account of the events which took place in the neighbourhood of the broken path.'

What these occurrences were will now be considered. When Hannibal first perceived that his path was destroyed, and that it was no longer possible for him to descend by the regular way, he attempted to proceed by taking a circuit, and so avoiding the broken ground. An attempt of this nature, among precipices, seems to have bordered upon temerity. Yet Hannibal probably did not intend to

---

[1] If the path was in zigzag, its length would have exceeded the 300 yards, the extent of the broken ground.

[2] Condition IX.

strike out a new line of route for any length of distance, but merely to deviate so far from the ordinary way, as was sufficient to enable him to go round the broken ground, and then to fall again into the regular path. Besides, unless he adopted this expedient, he must have been obliged to remain (as he ultimately was obliged) for a long time upon the snowy ground, until the broken path could be reconstructed. This alternative was in itself almost a desperate one: for the condition of the army must have been now seriously impaired, and their provisions nearly gone, while their courage had again left them when they saw their course arrested.

Hannibal preferred the alternative of immediate peril to that of lengthened hardship. His attempt to effect a circuit was, however, frustrated. The course he had selected brought him upon a very steep declivity of snow, where a mass that was hard and compact, and which Polybius says had remained there since the previous winter, was thinly covered with snow that had freshly fallen. The existence of this mass of old snow gives some clue as to one probable feature of the ground where the circuit was attempted. It seems clearly an isolated patch of snow that Polybius speaks of. We have no reason for imagining that the line of perpetual snow extended, even in those times, when the climate of the Alps was severer than it is at present, as far down as this place would probably be. Fresh snow indeed then covered the ground from the summit of the pass to this neighbourhood, and concealed perhaps in the higher parts of the pass several patches of old snow like the one of which Polybius speaks, but which, as the fresh snow lay more thickly upon them in consequence of the greater elevation, may have escaped notice.

Now the places where patches of permanent snow lie, below the line of perpetual snow, (above which, all the mountains, sheer precipices excepted, are buried beneath it) are principally gullies in the mountain-sides, into the hollows of which the snow naturally drifts, and which occasionally form the channels of avalanches. In consequence of the fall of one of these, old snow may sometimes be found, even at the end of summer, at a very low level[1]. This circumstance gives us some reason to suspect that it was by a gully that Hannibal attempted to make his circuit; a suspicion strengthened by the fact that such a course would be the most natural one to adopt. Whenever a man, descending a mountain where there is no track, finds his progress arrested by arriving at the edge of a range of precipices, he naturally keeps along their summit, till he finds a gully breaking through them from above, and affording him a tolerably safe passage down to their feet. A course of this nature would not improbably be that adopted by Hannibal: although it must, in his case, have been of an easier kind than is usual, as he would never have attempted to bring his whole army, men, animals, and baggage, down by such a line as might be taken by an unencumbered traveller.

When Hannibal's attempt to make a circuit was frustrated, and he found himself obliged to halt, and repair the broken path, he is said to have encamped, περὶ τὴν ῥάχιν, having cleared away the snow upon it. This implies that he not only encamped near it, but also upon it; and the word περί has therefore been translated 'about.' Hannibal encamped on and around this ῥάχις. Now ῥάχις signifies the back or crest of a ridge, 'dorsum montis.' Yet Polybius has previously mentioned no ῥάχις whatever. We first read of it, in connexion with the encampment, as τὴν ῥάχιν; neither has anything gone before, that necessarily implies such a feature in the country; for the precipice, along which the path lay, could not well be described by the word ῥάχις, nor was it possible to encamp upon it. This ridge-back had possibly, owing to Polybius' being personally acquainted with the country, been present in his mind from the time he first brought Hannibal down to the broken path; and this may have led him inadvertently

---

[1] The lowest situation in which I ever observed old snow, was when crossing, in the middle of August, 1850, a gully in the gorge of the Inn, between Martinsbruck in the Engadine, and Finstermünz in the Tyrol. It lay at an elevation of less than 3500 feet above the sea, and about 5000 below the line of perpetual snow.

to make use of the article in connexion with the ῥάχις, when the subsequent course of his narrative required its mention.   However this may be, the account naturally leads us to look, immediately above the broken path, for an encampment for the Carthaginians, partly extending over a ridge-back.

As soon as the path was in a sufficiently advanced stage of completion to allow the horses and baggage-animals to pass, they were immediately brought down, accompanied, no doubt, by a large portion of the army.   Another encampment was then made below the place where the path had been destroyed, and the animals were let loose to find pasturage, this lower district being quite free from snow. This account suggests to us the presence here of a large tract of open pasturage.   How far it lay from the broken path is not stated, but it probably was at no great distance from it.   This open tract of country is the last characteristic of the neighbourhood of the place where the path was broken up, which may be conjectured, from the narrative of Polybius, to have existed.   What is intimated, in addition, by the account of the attempt at a circuit and its frustration, and of the encampment about the ῥάχις, has been already considered above.

Only one condition now remains to be deduced.   It is supplied by the fact, that the part of the plains into which Hannibal entered, after his passage of the Alps had been effected, was occupied by the Taurini.   There is, however, one sentence in Polybius, which seems, at first sight, to imply something different.   In Chap. 56 it is stated, that, after Hannibal had passed the Alps, 'he descended boldly into the plains of the Po, and the territory of the Insubrians.'   From this it might be imagined that he emerged at once from the Alps into the country of the Insubrians, the modern Milanese.   This supposition would make him pass the Alps as far eastward as the St Gothard, or at least as the Simplon, both which suppositions are utterly improbable[1].   But there is little doubt, that the passage

---

[1] According to Ptolemy, Novara was a town of the Insubrians. The river Sesia may thus have been their western boundary. To the west of

above cited, concerning the Insubrians, is one of Polybius' succinct accounts, or summaries before mentioned, and that it merely states the direction and end of a march, the details of which are afterwards to be given[1]. The nature of Hannibal's dealings with the Taurini, which Polybius afterwards relates, perfectly explains what is meant by the word 'boldly,' as applied to his march into the country of the Insubrians. Though no doubt still anxious not to provoke hostilities, he yet did not avoid them so sedulously as he had done during the passage of the Alps, where he only seems to have fought when driven to extremity. From the foot of the Alps a new and bolder system of action was at once adopted.

It is not, however, necessary to take for granted that the passage relating to the Insubrians is a mere summary. It will appear without difficulty, from other considerations, that the country of the Taurini was the first part of the plains which Hannibal entered after he had crossed the Alps. For, from the passage where the name of the Insubrians occurs, we may conclude, that, wherever it was that Hannibal emerged from the Alps, he descended from that point into the *plains*, κατῆρε τολμηρῶς εἰς τὰ περὶ τὸν Πάδον πεδία. That he should ever *afterwards* be close to the *Alps* is not likely. Yet, in the commencement of the 60th chapter, (the first part of the history relating to Hannibal after the digression beginning in the middle of the 56th chapter) he is spoken of as being encamped ὑπ' αὐτὴν τὴν παρώρειαν τῶν Ἄλπεων, under the very slope of the *Alps*, at the very roots of the mountains when they first spring from the plains. From this mention of the *Alps* we are led to conclude, that the encampment here spoken of was made *before* he descended into the *plains;* that it should, in fact, have been made when he *first* came out from the Alps, and previously to his entry into the Insubrian country. This becomes certain from a further examination of the

---

the Sesia lay the Libui or Libicii, who are distinguished by Polybius (Lib. II. c. 17), from the Insubrians.

[1] In order that the detailed narrative of a march may be clear, it is plainly necessary that its direction and object should be previously mentioned.

60th chapter; for there the encampment just mentioned is said to have been made, μετὰ τὴν εἰσβολήν, 'after the entry' (the entry into Italy, that is to say, as appears from the εἰς Ἰταλίαν just preceding). Yet this cannot refer to some indefinite date after the entry into Italy, but must mean the actual time when he first entered the country, the period when he reached the commencement of the plains. The account of the losses which the army had suffered, and the hardships that they had endured during the passage of the Alps,—this account, immediately following and connected with the statement of the encampment, also tends to fix the place of that encampment at the point of emergence from the Alps. Besides, as the army remained encamped for some time for the express purpose of recovering the strength it had lost in consequence of the hardships it had endured in the Alps, it seems to follow that this encampment should have been made as soon as they came out from the mountains.

Μετὰ δὲ ταῦτα, 'after these things,' as soon, that is to say, as the strength of the army was restored, and they were about to leave their encampment, and advance, their transactions with the Taurini commence. Now the Taurini are introduced as dwelling near the slope of the mountains, or at their foot, οἳ τυγχάνουσι πρὸς τῇ παρωρείᾳ κατοικοῦντες. What then was this particular παρώρεια? It was clearly the παρώρεια which is mentioned at the beginning of the chapter, and beneath which Hannibal encamped when he first issued from the mountains. That the expression, οἳ τυγχάνουσι, κ.τ.λ. should merely mean that they dwelt somewhere at the foot of the Alps, is out of the question. Besides incurring the objection of irrelevancy, such an interpretation would not even define the position of the Taurini; since they might, as far as that description of their country is concerned, have lived anywhere along the base of the Alps, from the southern frontier of Piedmont to the eastern extremity of Friuli. The phrase also, 'they *happened* to dwell at the foot of the mountains,' is clearly employed for the purpose of explaining how they lay upon the line of Hannibal's intended march, which was directed, as Polybius had before intimated, towards the country of the Insubrians. They happened to lie in his way : he could not avoid passing through their country, and having some transactions with them.

The παρώρεια, therefore, by which the position of the Taurini is defined, being necessarily identical with the παρώρεια beneath which Hannibal encamped; and this latter παρώρεια being situated at the point where Hannibal first emerged from the mountains; it may be concluded, that the Taurini occupied the plains into which Hannibal first entered after his passage of the Alps. This conclusion is also, as has been seen, strengthened by the fact of Polybius' employing the word τυγχάνουσι, as if expressly to intimate that the Taurini lay in the way of Hannibal as he marched towards the country of the Insubrians[1].

Indeed, had Hannibal first descended into the Insubrian territory, the attack on the Taurini would be very difficult to explain. That the Taurini were at war with the Insubrians, the allies of Hannibal, is no sufficient reason. This circumstance is mentioned by Polybius to account for the Taurini refusing the overtures of Hannibal, but would not be a sufficient cause to induce the Carthaginian general, when he had once arrived in the Milanese, and was about to march upon Southern Italy, to go so far out of his way as Turin, for the purpose of attacking, with an army ill adapted to bear further diminutions, a people with whom there was no necessity for hostilities. It is, however, unnecessary to dwell upon the unreasonableness of such a supposition. That Hannibal descended at once from the Alps into the country of the Taurini is sufficiently plain, without the aid of any such considerations : and the improbability of a contrary supposition need not be canvassed at any length.

The following, then, is the last condition for the determination of Hannibal's route over the Alps[2]:

'The plains into which the road over the pass enters, when it emerges from the mountains on the side of Italy, must anciently have been inhabited by the Taurini.'

---

[1] A country which we know he reached *after* leaving Turin, and probably never reached but *once*.

[2] Condition X.

The examination of Polybius' narrative of Hannibal's march, from the confluence of the Rhone and Isère to the commencement of the plains of Italy, being now concluded, all that remains to be done is, to present in one view the principal points which have been elicited from it: to give, in the first place, the journal of the march; and then to collect together the various conditions which have been deduced, for the purpose of assisting in the identification of the pass, by which Hannibal crossed the Alps.

Starting, then, from the confluence of the Rhone and the Isère (on the left bank of the latter river) the journal of the march will be as follows:

I.   The ten days' march to the town of the Allobroges, including the halt in that place.

1—7. Hannibal marches up the left bank of the Isère to the neighbourhood of the defile leading to the town: he finds that the heights commanding the defile are held by the Allobroges, and sends forward a party of Gauls to learn the plans of the enemy.

8. The Gauls having returned with the requisite intelligence, Hannibal advances to the entrance of the defile and there encamps: he seizes in the night the abandoned posts of the Allobroges.

9. The defile is passed with much loss, and the town captured.

10. The army remains in the neighbourhood of the town.

II.   The fifteen days' march across the Alps, from the town of the Allobroges to the commencement of the plains of Italy.

1. Hannibal begins his march from the town: he meets, either on this evening, or on the following morning, a deputation of the Alpine Gauls: he makes a treaty with them, and subsequently employs them as guides.

2, 3. Hannibal proceeds on his march under the guidance of the Alpine Gauls.

4. The Carthaginians are attacked by the Alpine Gauls, in front and rear, while passing through a defile: the attack on the rear is repulsed, but great loss is suffered in the van. Hannibal eventually gains possession of a commanding position on the heights, near a certain 'strong white rock.' He remains during the whole night upon these heights with half his army, apart from his cavalry and

baggage-animals, whose passage through the defile he thus
protects.

5. Hannibal rejoins his cavalry and baggage, and continues
his march towards the summit of the Alps.

6—8. The army proceeds on its march.   It is harassed at intervals, during the march from the Rock, by predatory
attacks on the part of the barbarians.

9. On this morning the summit of the pass is gained, and the
army encamps for the sake of rest, and in order to allow
stragglers to rejoin it.

10. The army remains encamped on the summit of the pass :
the troops become greatly discouraged. In order to remove
their despondency, Hannibal brings them to a point within
sight of the plains of the Po, and indicates to them the
quarter in which Rome itself lies.

11. The army begins to descend. The descent is precipitous,
and the path is concealed by the snow.   Multitudes, both
of men and animals, miss their footing, and are lost down
the precipices. A place is ultimately reached, where the
path is destroyed, and the march arrested.   Hannibal
attempts to continue his progress by making a circuit.
The attempt is frustrated in consequence of the snow.
Hannibal encamps about a ridge-back above the broken
path, which he begins to repair.

12. The construction of the new path continues.   On this
morning, or on the previous evening, it is made practicable
for horses and baggage-animals : they are brought down
and left to seek forage in the pasture-grounds which lie
below the broken path and are free from snow.

13. The path is made practicable for the elephants. They
are brought down, and the whole army is again collected
together.

14. The army marches towards the plains of Italy, exposed
only to slight and furtive attacks.

15. The army continues its march, arrives at the commencement of the plains of Italy, and encamps at the roots of
the Alps.

The conditions for the identification of the pass are
these :

I. The commencement of the ascent of the Alps must be
situated at a distance of about 100 Roman miles from
the junction of the Rhone and the Isère, reckoned along
the left bank of the latter river.

II. The length of the route over the Alps, beginning at the

commencement of the ascent of the mountains, and terminating at the commencement of the plains of Italy,
must be about 150 Roman miles.

III. At the commencement of the ascent of the Alps, a defile
must be found, the character of which, and of the surrounding country, is in accordance with the events related by
Polybius to have occurred in that place.

(Minor conditions included in the above.)

(1) The defile must be commanded by certain heights of considerable elevation.

(2) These heights must not be easily accessible from below
the defile.

(3) The way through the defile must skirt in some place the
edge of a precipice.

(4) Immediately below the defile must be found a place
where an army as numerous as that of Hannibal could
encamp.

(5) This place of encampment should be visible from the
heights commanding the defile.

(6) Above the defile, and near it, must be found an open district, where a town either stands or might have stood,
and where an army such as Hannibal's could have
encamped.

IV. At a place nearly half-way, in point of time, between the
town of the Allobroges and the summit of the pass, a
certain 'strong white rock' must be found; and the
adjacent country must be in accordance with the events,
which are recorded by Polybius to have taken place in
the neighbourhood of this rock.

(Features of the country in the neighbourhood of the
Rock.)

(1) A difficult and precipitous ravine, through which the road
must pass.

(2) A range of acclivities overlooking the road, and liable
to be swept, in one or more places, by rocks set in
motion from above.

(3) A large extent of practicable ground above these acclivities.

(4) A position on this ground, at some distance from the road,
where 20,000 men could be stationed, so as to protect
completely the flank of an army marching along the
road beneath, and such as would not expose themselves
to be attacked at any serious disadvantage, by an
enemy lying beyond them relatively to the road.

V. A place suitable for the encampment of Hannibal's army must be found at the summit of the pass.

VI. From a point, probably not far from the road over the summit of the pass, but yet not upon the ground where the Carthaginians would encamp when they first reached the summit, the plains of the Po, and, in all probability, the Apennines also, ought to be visible.

VII. The commencement of the plains of Italy must be less than three days' march from the summit of the pass.

VIII. The first part of the descent from the summit of the pass on the Italian side must be of a precipitous character.

IX. At a place, within half a day's march from the summit of the pass, on the Italian side, the path must lie along a precipitous mountain-side, liable to be broken up for a length of nearly 300 yards (English), and the country in the vicinity should be of a nature adapted to Polybius' account of the events which took place in the neighbourhood of the broken path.

X. The plains, into which the road over the pass enters, when it emerges from the mountains on the side of Italy, must anciently have been inhabited by the Taurini.

CHAPTER VI.

Improbability of Hannibal's having crossed the Alps by the Great or Little St Bernard, or by the Mont Genèvre.—Probability of his having crossed the Mont Cenis.—Determination of the point where Hannibal would have left the Isère.—The oldest line of road known over the Mont Cenis traced and described.—The Little Mont Cenis selected as the pass which Hannibal crossed, in preference to the Great Mont Cenis.

S EVERAL passes have been suggested as having each their claims to be considered as the pass which Hannibal crossed[1]. Four only, however, seem to have, even at first sight, any considerable probability in their favour: the Great and the Little St Bernard, the Mont Cenis, and the Mont Genèvre. The Great St Bernard might perhaps also be left out of consideration: but as the examination which leads to the rejection of three out of the four passes named will not be long, it has been thought better to include it among the number.

In the endeavour to identify the pass which Hannibal crossed, the first question to be asked is: What are its distinguishing characteristics? Are there any circumstances connected with it of an extraordinary nature, such as are rarely to be found on any of the passes of the Alps; and such as, if not found on any particular pass, raise great difficulties, if not impossibilities, against the adoption of that pass? Now, there are two circumstances of this kind, which have been deduced from Polybius' narrative, and are embodied in Conditions VI. and VII. That Italy should have been visible from the summit of the pass, and that the commencement of the plains of the Po should lie

---

[1] The names of these passes, and of the advocates for each, may be found in the Appendix on Hannibal's passage in Ukert's *Geographie der Griechen und Römer*.

within less than three days' march from the summit,—these are the prominent and distinguishing characteristics of the pass which Hannibal crossed.

But, of the four passes named, it is only from one, the Mont Cenis, that Italy can be discerned.   With respect to the other three, neither from the roads themselves, nor from any neighbouring eminence, would it be possible to see any part of Italy, as distinguished from the Alpine country.   Nothing but ranges of mountains, and perhaps some valley locked in on all sides by them, would meet the eye.   From the Mont Cenis alone could Hannibal have pointed out to his soldiers the plains of the Po[1].

The great proximity also to the plains of Italy of the summit of the pass which Hannibal crossed, its second distinguishing characteristic, is only to be remarked on the pass of the Mont Cenis.   The distance between the summit of the pass which Hannibal crossed and the commencement of the plains was less than three days' march. Now from the point where Hannibal left the banks of the river (the Isère) to the commencement of the plains, the distance is given as 150 Roman miles.   From the town of the Allobroges, therefore, from which the fifteen days' march across the Alps is reckoned, the distance to the commencement of the plains would be rather less ; perhaps 140 Roman miles or a little more.   Of the fifteen days which Hannibal employed in the passage of the Alps, only eleven were occupied in marching : nearly two were spent on the summit of the pass, and fully two lost, during the descent, at the broken path.   Consequently, as Hannibal marched 140 Roman miles, or perhaps a little more, in eleven days, his rate of marching in the Alps would be about thirteen Roman miles a day.   On his descent he might march rather more rapidly than on his ascent : but the difference would not be considerable, for the vigour of the army was then much diminished.   Three days' march,

---

[1] Der Cenis ist auch der einzige Berg, über welchen eine grosse Strasse führt, von dem man an mehren Stellen die Ebene Oberitalien's sehen kann, was weder vom grossen und kleinen Bernhard, noch vom Simplon möglich ist.—Ukert, *Geographie*, ii. 2, p. 600.   (The Genèvre should also have been mentioned by Ukert among these latter passes.)

at the rate of thirteen Roman miles a day, will be sufficient to allow for the distance between the summit of the pass and the commencement of the plains, especially as not quite three days were spent on the actual march. It may therefore be inferred, that the distance between the summit of the pass and the commencement of the plains of Italy did not exceed forty Roman miles.

The roads from the Great and the Little St Bernard into Italy unite at Aosta, and emerge into the plains of Italy near Ivrea, which may for these two passes be fixed upon as the commencement of the plains[1]. The roads over the Mont Cenis and the Mont Genèvre unite in like manner at Susa, and enter the plains nearly at Avigliana[2]; although Rivoli is sometimes fixed upon as the place where the plains may rather be said to begin. Yet the irregularities in the ground below Avigliana cannot be considered as parts of the mountains: the conspicuous Monte Pirichiano, crowned by the monastery of San Michele, and at the foot of which Avigliana lies, stands out plainly when seen from any point in the neighbourhood of Turin, as the last of the Alps. There is, besides, ample room about Avigliana for an encampment; and if Hannibal had advanced further with his enfeebled army, he would have lost the protection of the mountains behind him, and exposed himself to attack from the Taurini before he was well prepared for hostilities.

Ivrea, anciently Eporedia, was a Roman station, and lay, according to the Itineraries, at a distance of 46 miles from Aosta. From Aosta to the summit of the Great St Bernard (Summus Penninus) was a distance of another 15 miles[3]: so that the whole distance from Ivrea to the summit of the Great St Bernard was 61 Roman miles.

---

[1] See *Penny Cyc.* Art. 'Ivrea.' Blaev, *Theatrum Statuum Regiæ Celsitudinis Sabaudiæ Ducis*, Art. 'Eporedia.'

[2] See Murray's *Hand-Book for Northern Italy*, ' Avigliana.'

[3] According to the Roman Itineraries, 25. The Government Itinerary of the Sardinian States (1839) gives, however, 10 Piedmontese or 16½ Roman miles, as the distance from Aosta to the Hospice of the Great St Bernard, so that the xxv miles of the Roman Itinerary is probably a mistake for xv.

From Aosta to Arebrigium (generally identified with Pré St Didier, but perhaps rather Arpi on the road from Morgex leading to La Thuile and the Little St Bernard by the 'Camp of Prince Thomas'), the Itineraries give 25 miles. From Arebrigium to Artolica (La Thuile) is a distance of another 6 miles: and from La Thuile to the summit of the Little St Bernard (Alpis Graia) there are about 5 miles more. From Ivrea to the summit of the Little St Bernard is consequently, according to the Itineraries, a distance of 82 Roman miles.

Avigliana is the 'Ad Fines' of the Itineraries, and lay at a distance of 24 Roman miles below Susa. From Susa, taking the old road over the Mont Cenis, the distance to La Novalèse is about 5 English miles : from La Novalèse to La Grande Croix, at the southern extremity of the plateau of the Mont Cenis, the distance is about 6 English miles. To the centre of the lake of the Mont Cenis (which lies nearly in the middle of the plateau of the Great Mont Cenis, and from which the plateau of the Little Mont Cenis branches off at right angles to the other plateau[1]) the distance will be nearly 3 English miles more: so that, from Susa to the central point of the plateaux of the Mont Cenis, the distance is nearly 14 English, or about 15 Roman miles. From Avigliana, then, to the central point of the summit of the Mont Cenis, the distance is 39 Roman miles.

From Susa to Ad Martis, the modern Oulx, the Itineraries give 16 Roman miles, and 9 more to Gesdao or Cesanne. From Cesanne to the central point of the plain of the Mont Genèvre the distance may be taken at 4 Roman miles. From Avigliana to the summit of the Mont Genevre the distance is thus 53 Roman miles.

In all these cases it appears, by comparison with the

---

[1] There are two ways of ascending the Mont Cenis from the side of Savoy: (1) by the road over the great Mont Cenis, the present high road, which leaves the valley of the Arc at Lanslebourg; and (2) by the road of the Little Mont Cenis, a mule-path, which turns off from the valley of the Arc at Bramans. Both these passes are of nearly equal height. The two roads unite on the summit of the mountain, and the descent into Italy is the same for both.

present distances, that there is no material error in the Itineraries, excepting in the instance already noticed.

From the summits of the respective passes to the commencement of the plains the distances therefore are:

For the Great St Bernard	61	Roman miles.
For the Little St Bernard	82	„ „
For the Mont Cenis	39	„ „
For the Mont Genèvre	53	„ „
And the actual distance on the pass which} Hannibal crossed probably did not exceed}	40	„ „

The Mont Cenis seems here to be plainly indicated as the pass which Hannibal crossed. With respect to either of the St Bernards, the discrepancy in point of distance raises not merely a difficulty, but it may be said an impossibility to overcome. The fact also, already noticed, of the invisibility of the plains from their summits, opposes another obstacle, equally strong, to the adoption of either of these passes.

A third objection arises from the circumstance, that it was not the Taurini, but the Libui, who would have inhabited the plains into which Hannibal entered on his emergence from the Alps, had he crossed either the Great or the Little St Bernard. Yet the Libui, although a tribe known to Polybius, are never mentioned by him in his account of Hannibal's passage of the Alps, the narrative necessarily implying that the Carthaginians found the Taurini in their way as soon as they issued out from among the mountains, and began their march to the Insubrian territory.

These three objections seem fatal to the Great and the Little St Bernard. The argument from discrepancy of distance presses also strongly, though perhaps not conclusively, against the Mont Genèvre, from which the plains of Italy are, besides, invisible. The route of the Mont Genèvre is, in addition, at variance with Condition I; for Hannibal would, on the supposition of his having crossed the Genèvre, have to leave the Isère near Grenoble, and penetrate into the mountain-valley of the Drac. But the distance between Grenoble and Valence, which is of the same length as the distance between Grenoble and the

confluence of the Isère and the Rhone, is only 96 kilomètres, or about 66 Roman miles; a distance too widely
removed from the 800 stadia or 100 Roman miles of Polybius, to be admitted.

Of the four passes mentioned, three seem thus to be
excluded from consideration by strong improbabilities.
The Mont Cenis remains alone with likelihood in its favour.
The next thing, therefore, to examine is, whether the
characteristics of this latter pass are completely in accordance with the conditions derived from the narrative of
Polybius. Should they prove so, the adoption of the Mont
Cenis as the pass which Hannibal crossed, seems an inevitable conclusion; for the negative evidence in its favour,
arising from the great improbabilities with respect to the
other passes, is exceedingly strong. We shall consequently
now proceed to apply systematically to the Mont Cenis
all the conditions which have been deduced from the discussion of Polybius' account of Hannibal's passage of the
Alps.

For this purpose it will first be necessary to trace the
oldest line of road over the Mont Cenis, which rarely ever,
when the mountains are once entered, coincides with the
modern road. The marshes and defiles, which the modern
road has been enabled to traverse, by the aid of dykes to
restrain the rivers, or gunpowder to blast away the rocks,
were, in remote times, obstacles not to be directly overcome. They forced the road away from the river, which
flowed through the valley leading to the summit of the
pass, and compelled it to skirt or to ascend the flanks of
the mountains at the side of the valley, in search of practicable ground on which it might run.

From the confluence of the Rhone and the Isère as far
as Grenoble, there can be no doubt about the direction
taken by a road making for the Mont Cenis by the left
bank of the Isère. It must always have followed the river,
nearly in the line of the modern road, leaving it probably
a little to the left on approaching Sassenage and Grenoble, where there is some marshy ground which might
cause it to recede from the Isère. From Grenoble the
easiest way of proceeding to the Mont Cenis would still be

to pursue the broad vale of Graisivaudan, (as the French part of the Val Isère is called) and so gain the entrance of the valley of the Arc, the river which waters the Maurienne and leads to the Mont Cenis. A much shorter, though, at the same time, a much more difficult way would be, to cross the mountains, if possible, between Grenoble and St Jean de Maurienne, and thus avoid the great circuit which the easier road makes. There was a Roman road which took this shorter course. Remains of it have been found in the neighbourhood of the Col de la Coche, upon the mountains between the Graisivaudan and the valley of the Olle. It would, therefore, in all probability, strike off from the road along the left bank of the Isère, about twelve miles above Grenoble, and a short distance below Froges,—at the point where the stream descending from the Col de la Coche enters the Graisivaudan.

Having crossed the Col de la Coche, and entered the upper valley of the Olle, its subsequent course, if it was intended to lead into the Maurienne (and this was evidently, by its crossing the Col de la Coche, the ultimate design), would be most likely by way of the Col du Glandon. From the summit of this pass it would descend into the valley of the Arvan, and join the other line of road, leading to the Mont Cenis, at St Jean de Maurienne. It is said, and in all probability with justice, as will be seen in a subsequent chapter, that this road formed part of the route followed by Julius Cæsar, when he crossed the Alps in haste to intercept the Helvetii, who had broken into Transalpine Gaul[1].

---

[1] With this pass from the Graisivaudan to St Jean de Maurienne I am personally unacquainted. It is mentioned in the following note from Pilot's *Histoire de Grenoble*, p. 7. Grenoble, 1829.

Il y avait une autre route qui traversait les montagnes de Theys pour aller dans la Maurienne. On en trouve encore une partie considérable qui se dirige vers le Col de la Coche ; elle est pavée en blocs bruts de granit, et a près de dix pieds de largeur. On raconte communément que César est entré dans les Gaules par ce chemin, lorsqu'il partit d'Aquilée. *Ab Ocelo, quod est citerioris provinciæ extremum, in fines Vocontiorum ulterioris provinciæ pervenit : inde in Allobrogum fines.*

This route would not be that followed by Hannibal. It leaves the banks of the Isère too soon to be in accordance with the measurements of Polybius; and the length of the Alpine route would also be too short. Besides, we have no record of any mountains having been *crossed* by Hannibal, with the exception of the actual pass, 'the highest summits of the Alps.' An easier, but longer route, seems to have been the one followed by the Carthaginians, which must also have struck off from the Isère at a greater distance above Grenoble.

From Grenoble to the confluence of the Isère and the Arc, the valley of the Isère is bounded on the east by a range of hills, lying in advance of the Alps behind, and cut through by the lateral streams which descend to the Isère. At first, on leaving Grenoble, all these hills are connected with the mountains behind, but at Le Cheylas, about 20 miles above Grenoble, they become distinct. Passing through the gorge of Le Fay, which here breaks through the chain of hills, and affords a passage for the diligence-road to Allevard, a broad and rich valley is reached, lying between the hills and the Alps, and extending for a length of rather less than 20 miles, from St Pierre d'Allevard to the marshes where the Arc joins the Isère. The upper or French part of this valley is called the valley of Allevard; the lower or Savoyard part, divided from the upper by the river Brédaz, and a small tract of hilly ground to the north of that torrent, is called the valley of La Rochette. Through this valley, according to M. Albanis de Beaumont, a Roman road formerly ran : he also speaks of the former importance of La Rochette, and of the fertility of the surrounding country[1].

---

[1] A l'extremité de cette vallée est le bourg de la Rochette, autrefois très considérable, et ayant titre de ville; il est même connu, qu'anciennement ce bourg se trouvoit sur une des voies romaines qui conduisoit d'Ai-guebelle à Vienne, alors la capitale de l'Allobrogie; j'ai aussi été à même de voir plusieurs titres qui prouvent que cette ville étoit dans le douzième siecle très considérable, puisqu'Aymon, seigneur de Mont Maïeur, y leva à cette époque cinq cents lances et deux cent cinquante cavaliers. La situation de la Rochette est très agréable, et ses environs, qui sont très fertiles, offrent une quantité de sites aussi romantiques que pittoresques.— *Les Alpes Grecqus et Cottiennes*, Vol. II. p. 595. Paris. 1802.

At Pont Charra, four or five miles above Le Cheylas, the line of hills is again broken through, and the Brédaz issues forth. Through this defile a road runs by way of Moutaret to Allevard; but the defile does not afford a convenient access to La Rochette, the road to which place, from Montmélian, evades the defile by passing over the heights to the north. A road to Grenoble, from La Rochette, would be more likely to take the line of Allevard and Le Cheylas than that of Pont Charra.

There is also a path from Allevard over the mountains to St Jean de Maurienne. It crosses the Col du Merlet, and descends into a valley which joins that of the Arc at Ste Marie de Cuines. From this tributary valley of the Maurienne a path over a lateral ridge leads to St Jean de Maurienne. This route is probably of some antiquity, as immediately below the crest of the Col du Merlet, on the eastern side, a group of châlets is marked on the Government map of this country, as the 'Granges de la Vieille Route.' It is solely on this account that it is mentioned here; for it is not likely to have been the route followed by Hannibal.

The last line of route on the left bank of the Isère, by which the Maurienne could be reached from Grenoble, is the modern road, which follows the river over the frontier into Savoy. At a place called La Chavanne, about half or three quarters of a mile from Montmélian, it falls into the high road from Chambéry to Turin by the Mont Cenis, which leads by way of Maltaverne to the entrance of the valley of the Arc.

Two lines of road have therefore to be considered:

(1) The road which branches off from the Graisivaudan at Le Cheylas[1], and leads by way of Allevard and La Rochette to Aiguebelle.

(2) The road by Pont Charra, La Chavanne, and Maltaverne, to the same place.

It is the first of these two roads which is in accordance

---

[1] The oldest path probably left the Graisivaudan here. The modern diligence-road to Allevard branches off at Goncelin, and has been constructed, partly by the aid of gunpowder, along the southern side of the gorge of Le Fay.

with the requisitions of Polybius' narrative. The length of both routes is almost exactly the same; but the country through which the first route leads is more productive. It is, however, rather the more difficult of the two, though both are partially hilly. Yet the ascent which is requisite on the first road is not very important. The elevation of Allevard, which lies on the highest part of the road, is given as 170 mètres, or 560 English feet[1], above Grenoble, which would make it less than 500 feet above Le Cheylas, perhaps not more than 400.

There appear, however, sufficient reasons for supposing, that in former times, when the country was in its natural state, its barbarous inhabitants, when they wished to go from Grenoble to Aiguebelle, might not only have chosen, but may have been absolutely obliged, to take their way through Allevard and La Rochette. For the road which goes by way of Maltaverne twice crosses great tracts of marsh-land, which in ancient times must have been impracticable morasses. The first of these lies between Pont Charra and Montmélian, the second between Maltaverne and La Croix d'Aiguebelle. Neither is it possible to skirt these marshes and so avoid them, for they extend, in both cases, to a considerable distance on the right of the road, along the banks of two small streams, which have to be crossed. The first of these streams descends from Maltaverne, and joins the Isère between Pont Charra and Montmélian; the second is the Gellon, descending from the valley of La Rochette. In fact, with the exception of the part where the road keeps along the range of hills extending from Maltaverne to La Chavanne and also a little beyond each place, nearly all the route from Pont Charra to La Croix d'Aiguebelle is marshy. There are also small marshes by Maltaverne, on the heights, but they might have been avoided without difficulty.

The marshes between Montmélian and Pont Charra are thus mentioned in a short notice on the territory of La Rochette[2]:

---

[1] In a small book, called the *Guide du Visiteur au pays d'Allevard,* par P. A. Rigollot Delavaquerie.

[2] Richard, *Guide en Savoie et en Piémont.*

'L'étendue de ce territoire est d'environ 20 kilom. ou 4 lieues, sur 3 lieues de large. La partie qui longe l'Isère après le pont de Montmélian est composée d'une terre d'alluvion très fertile ; il se déploie ensuite sur les bords de l'Isère, en forme de *grands marais, une vaste prairie* qui descend jusque vers Pont Charas.'

M. Albanis de Beaumont, in his *Description des Alpes Grecques et Cottiennes*, also mentions these marshes, as they extend by St Hélène du Lac towards Coise and Maltaverne. Speaking of the road between Montmélian and Maltaverne along the crest of the ridge overlooking these marshes, he proceeds:

'Du hameau de la Chavane, (near Montmélian) la route, quoique légèrement montueuse, est très agréable, étant ombragée de chaque côté de gros noyers et divers arbres fruitiers. A une demi-lieue de ce hameau on commence à apercevoir çà et là des bancs de schistes feuilletés d'une espèce argilleuse mais très tendre ; ces schistes paraissent se prolonger jusqu'à la haute colline de mont Maïeur, située au sud-est du chemin, *dont elle n'est séparée que par une suite de belles prairies et de marais qui se prolongent jusqu'au lac de Ste Hélène; ces prairies ont visiblement été sous les eaux, et elles ont fait dans un temps partie de ce lac*[1].'

All these marsh-lands are now in a great measure reclaimed by means of drainage and embankments: but in ancient times they must have formed, as may be concluded from the passages above cited, and from the appearance of the country, a great swamp, which prevented all passage along the left bank of the Isère, between Pont Charra and Montmélian. In order to reach Aiguebelle from the Graisivaudan, it must have been necessary to pass by way of La Rochette; or else, (which is however a mere supposition, for no road is known to have adopted such a course) to have proceeded from Pont Charra, along the north-western flank of the ridge of Montmayeur.

But even if Maltaverne were reached, the same difficulties would occur again. Another large tract of marsh

---

[1] *Les Alpes Grecques et Cottiennes*, p. 591. The author speaks again (p. 596) of the lake of Ste Hélène, and the marshes adjoining it.

defends the entrance of the valley of the Arc. Bourgneuf is already on the fen, and from thence to La Croix d'Aiguebelle the road lies entirely over marsh-land. A great quantity of ground has indeed been reclaimed here; yet extensive swamps are still left on the banks of the Isère and the Arc, though both these rivers are now almost entirely confined by dykes; the vast undertaking of their embankment being nearly completed, down to the place where the Isère enters France[1]. Fifty years ago, M. Albanis de Beaumont remarked the great swamps then existing about the confluence of the Isère and the Arc[2]. M. Bertolotte also, in the year 1827, took notice of these morasses, 'le paludose lande ove l' Isera riceve le acque dell' Arco;' and mentions the swampy meadows, 'i prati paludosi,' as being found on the banks of the Gellon as far from the Arc as the neighbourhood of Bettonet[3].

It seems clear then that, in ancient times, a large marsh lay between Maltaverne and the entrance of the valley of the Arc; and it is not likely that any way ever lay across it, before the Romans, in all probability, (as will be seen in a later chapter) constructed a line of road here from the Maurienne to Montmélian. The barbarian inhabitants of the Maurienne, when seeking a way to the Graisivaudan,

---

[1] When these dykes are completed, the high road from Montmélian to Turin will be carried along them by the sides of the Isère and Arc into the Maurienne, and the present road by Maltaverne will be abandoned. The new road was indeed, in the spring of the present year (1853), nearly finished.

[2] A une demi-lieue de Maltaverne l'on traverse le Gelon; à droite la vue plonge dans la vallée du Beton, et à gauche dans celle de l'Isère, dont on suit les sinuosités de la rivière jusqu'à Conflans, situé à l'entrée de la vallée de Tarantaise. Bientôt l'on se trouve vis-à-vis du confluent de l'Isère et de l'Arc, où le voyageur sentimental voit avec regret les ravages que causent les eaux de ces deux rivières, particulièrement sur la rive gauche de l'Isère, *où il y a des marais d'une étendue de plusieurs lieues*, dont les exhalaisons ou miasmes qui s'en dégagent lors des grandes chaleurs, poussées par les vents nord-ouest, et remontant dans l'étroite vallée de Maurienne, y occasionnent annuellement des fièvres intermittentes, et plusieurs autres espèces de maladies également nuisibles aux habitants.— *Les Alpes Grecques et Cottiennes*, Vol. II. p. 600.

[3] *Viaggio in Savoia*, Lettera LXVI.

would, on their arrival at La Croix d'Aiguebelle, have followed the line of the valley of La Rochette.   The inhabitants of the Graisivaudan, in like manner, when wishing to penetrate into the Maurienne, would also, when the marshes beyond Pont Charra hindered their further progress up the Isère, have been induced, if not compelled, to strike into the same valley of La Rochette, either from Pont Charra or Le Cheylas.   But from La Rochette to Grenoble, the most natural line of route is by Allevard and Le Cheylas.   On this line, then, the old Gallic way would have been made; and here Hannibal would find his road when on his march from Grenoble to the Mont Cenis.

On this road the marshes present no obstacles.   There is a narrow tract of marsh on the plain between Allevard and St Pierre d'Allevard, the highest part of the route. This tract, however, the road can skirt without experiencing any difficulty, on the gently rising ground at the foot of the ridge of hills called Brame-Farine.   As to the marshes at the extremity of the valley of La Rochette, which extend from near Bettonet to the Arc, the road, being already on the ground lying on their south side, cannot, of course, be inconvenienced by them.

From the entrance to the valley of the Arc, at La Croix d'Aiguebelle, to the summit of the Mont Cenis, the way, lying in a valley confined on both sides by mountains, necessarily follows up the Arc, as closely as the difficulties of the ground will allow it.   Four lines of way up the Maurienne may be mentioned : (1) The present high road ; (2) the first carriage-road made under Napoleon ; (3) the mule-road of the last century ; and (4) the earlier mule-road, the oldest path known to have existed.   These roads are, in places, more or less coincident with one another : the first and the last have, however, an exceedingly small number of miles in common.   For the ancient road generally ran, and sometimes at a great height, along the flanks of the mountains, avoiding the marshes in the Lower Maurienne, and the deep defiles in the Upper Maurienne. An artificial line of causeway now carries the high road straight through the marshes; and the defiles of the Upper Maurienne have been laid open for its passage, either by blasting away the rocks which close in upon the river, or by means of artificial terraces which deprive it of a part of its channel.

It is necessarily along the most ancient path, the earliest mule-road, that we must seek for the route of Hannibal. Now, though this road is partially destroyed in several places, the whole line may be almost completely traced. From La Croix d'Aiguebelle, mentioned above, it skirts the bases of the mountains to Aiguebelle. Directly behind Aiguebelle, two hills rise from the bed of the valley, leaving between themselves and the mountains on each side only three narrow openings. Through the most easterly of these openings runs the high road, supported on a causeway occupying part of the old channel of the river, which it follows to the bridge of Argentine. The first carriage-road and second mule-road passed through the opening between the two hills; the oldest path of all passed through the opening between the western hill and the mountains, and fell into the line of the first carriage-road and second mule-road immediately behind the hill. This first carriage-road joins the present one shortly before reaching the bridge of Argentine, the junction taking place at the foot of a precipice, which in ancient times must have sprung directly from the river or the marshes, and, in all probability, have barred this line of way. The oldest road is thus, it may be supposed, if there was no passage here, represented for a short distance by a mule-road, which, after the hills previously mentioned behind Aiguebelle have been passed, strikes off from the second mule-road, into which the first has just fallen, and ascends along the heights towards the mines of St George. From this road, in a short time, a foot-path branches off to the left, and, keeping for some distance along the sides of the mountains, eventually descends through a hollow directly upon the bridge of Argentine. This, it may be conjectured, is the oldest route through the hills and defile of Aiguebelle.

From the bridge of Argentine the old line of way is known throughout by the inhabitants of the country as far as the summit of the Mont Cenis. It passes through Argentine to the left of the marshes and of the modern

6

carriage-roads (though Argentine itself is accessible in a carriage) and encounters no difficult ground until it approaches Epierre. Here there is a spur projecting from the mountains, and presenting towards the west a precipitous face, which rises from the marshes. On the crest of this spur is a tract of cultivated ground. Over this tract the old road passed, attaining it by a gradual ascent along the flanks of the mountains which stretch towards Argentine. On the northern side of this tract of ground the road has been destroyed, and its line is lost for a short time among the fields. On the summit of the spur it is again recovered, and descends in a well-preserved state upon Epierre, passing through the most ancient part of this village, where the church is situated. Continuing its course through Le Tardy it crosses another, but a lower spur of the mountains, and descends upon Tigny. From thence, having passed through La Chapelle, it quits, near Gondran, the large tract of fertile ground which extends into the marshes, and upon which Tigny, La Chapelle, and Gondran are situated; and then pursues its course along the mountain sides through Les Chavannes, till it arrives immediately behind the post-station of La Grande Maison[1]. From thence it reaches La Chambre, keeping along the side of a steep mountain, and coinciding probably with the earliest carriage-road now rapidly falling into complete ruin. From La Chambre it passes through St Avre to the bridge of Sainte Marie de Cuines, which is situated about a mile above the village of that name, at a point where a projecting edge of rocks formerly obliged the road to cross the river. It does not however seem unlikely, from the nature of the country, that the river may have been once crossed a little below this bridge, so that the way from La Chambre may have passed through Sainte Marie itself. At the bridge of Sainte Marie de Cuines, the great marshes of the Lower Maurienne may be said to terminate. A long defile bounded by precipices of vast height is then

---

[1] From La Grande Maison to St Martin de la Porte, a distance of about 15 English miles, the first three roads up the Maurienne deviate little from each other.

entered. The river is again crossed at Pontamafrey, and also a third time at the upper end of the defile. The valley then opens out, and the road emerges upon an open tract of country in which stands St Jean de Maurienne, the chief town of the province of the same name.

From St Jean de Maurienne to St Martin de la Porte, the way lies in the bottom of the valley, which has here for a time a considerable width. The river is again crossed between St Jean and St Julien. The present high road keeps close to the river, and leaves the villages of St Julien and St Martin on the left. Almost immediately beyond St Martin the valley is suddenly terminated. The great rock of Baune, several hundred feet in height, and about three quarters of a mile in length, stretches across the valley from side to side. Between the southern edge of this rock and the precipices on the opposite side of the valley, the Arc has cut itself a narrow passage between the cliffs. Through this passage the three most modern roads were conducted, the face of the precipice having been blasted away by the aid of gunpowder to make room for them. An entrance was thus gained into the little plain of St Michel, and into a series of defiles about ten miles in length, which extends as far as a village called Le Freney, some three miles below Modane.

No such course was practicable for the ancient road; nor, according to the report of the inhabitants, did any way exist, till within the last 150 or 200 years, by the southern extremity of the Rock of Baune. The old road passed by the northern extremity of that rock, penetrating through the narrow defile of La Porte, which separates the Rock of Baune from the rest of the ridge, of which it forms the prolongation into the valley. Having passed through this defile the road did not descend upon the plain of St Michel (in ancient times probably a morass[1]), but climbed the heights by Le Village de la Porte and Villard Bernond to a village called La Traverse; from whence it ran, nearly on a level, round a projecting moun-

---

[1] According to Bertolotti (*Viaggio in Savoia, Lettera* LXX.) perhaps a lake.

tain-shoulder, to Le Thyl d'en haut, the highest point of
this part of the route, and probably about 1500 feet above
the valley beneath.   Between Le Village de la Porte and
Villard Bernond there is only a foot-path now; and between Villard Bernond and La Traverse a considerable
portion of the former road is gone, though fragments of
the old rough paving sometimes appear.   The rest of the
way from St Martin de la Porte to Le Thyl d'en haut
is good.   From Le Thyl d'en haut, the old road rapidly
descends upon Le Thyl d'en bas and La Buffaz; from
whence, still descending, but less rapidly, along the mountain side through Basilières, it arrives on the banks of a
small tributary of the Arc, having almost reached the level
of that river.   From Le Thyl to this little tributary stream
the road is good; but, after the stream has been crossed,
nothing but a narrow and bad foot-path remains to indicate the course of the old road.   Before reaching Orelle
the road again becomes wide and good, the old track being
here followed by the present mule-road which branches
off to Orelle from the high road in the defile beneath.
From Orelle to Le Freney the old road is still in use and
in very good preservation.   It runs at a great height along
the mountains through the villages of Bonvillard and Le
Villaret[1].   From Le Villaret it descends upon St André,
through which the later mule-road and the first carriage-
road also passed; and another descent leads down to the
bridge of Le Freney, where all the lines of road again
meet, and where an open valley is once more reached[2].

---

[1] In a detached part of this latter village, called, as well as the sound
could be caught, La Paille, there is an old house with early Gothic
windows, which is reported by the inhabitants of the place to have been
formerly a post-house for mules or horses, when the old road passed
this way.

[2] The course of this old road, from St Martin to Le Freney, may be
frequently discerned from the high road by the side of the Arc beneath.
Between La Buffaz and Basilières it runs in one place along the face of a
precipitous mountain where its actual line is perceptible.   A similar
place occurs between Bonvillard and Le Villaret.   Where the line of road
itself cannot be seen, its course may be partially traced by means of the
numerous crosses along it, and by the villages, when visible, through
which it runs.

From Le Freney to Modane the valley is open, especially around Modane. The old road passes through the villages of Le Freney and Le Fourneau, to the right of the present high road. Above Modane the defile of Bramans or of l'Esseillon, a passage of great difficulty, is entered. The high road (the two carriage-roads are here identical) is cut out of the rock for the greater part of the way to the plain of Bramans. There seems also never to have been more than one line here for mules or horses. Leaving Modane, this track passes to the right of the carriage-road, being separated from it by an eminence, behind which the older road makes its way. Emerging from behind this eminence, it descends to, and cuts across the high road, and leads down to Villarodin. Mounting again from this village, and re-crossing the high road, it ascends the heights into a wood, rejoining after a time, but only for a moment, the high road, at the bridge which crosses a small stream opposite the great fort of l'Esseillon. The mule-road then again ascends the heights, and is lost in the pine-forests, and finally descends upon Bramans behind a ridge of some elevation, which intervenes between it and the carriage-road.

On the plain of Bramans the roads to the Great and Little Mont Cenis separate. The way to the Little Mont Cenis, the pass which agrees best with the accounts of Hannibal's passage, and which seems to have been the most ancient route by which the mountain was ascended[1], here strikes off from the valley of the Arc, and ascends the lateral valley of St Pierre. The old mule-road to the Great Mont Cenis passed from Bramans through Le Verney, Le Châtel, and Sollières, to Termignon; from whence, with the exception of a small portion on leaving Termignon, where the carriage-road makes a zigzag, it nearly coincided with the line of that road as far as Lanslebourg, a large village at the foot of the Great Mont Cenis. From Lanslebourg it forms what is called the 'Petite Route' by which the mountain is ascended. The high road is only

---

[1] *Histoire du diocèse de Maurienne,* par M. Le Chanoine d'Angley. See also below, Chap. XI.

able to accomplish this ascent by means of several zigzags. At La Ramasse, the northern extremity of the plateau of the Great Mont Cenis, the two roads unite, and follow nearly the same line to La Grande Croix, at the southern extremity of the plateau. This plateau is five miles long. The highest point of the passage, 6770 feet above the level of the sea, is situated about three-quarters of a mile to the south of La Ramasse. At La Grande Croix the old road from the Little Mont Cenis falls into the present line of route[1].

The road to the Little Mont Cenis has been already mentioned as diverging from the valley of the Arc at Bramans. It strikes thence up the valley of St Pierre, and, after a course of about five miles, reaches the foot of the Little Mont Cenis. A very steep ascent, of one hour in length, leads to the crest of the pass, 6820 feet above the sea-level. The summit of the Little Mont Cenis is a plateau of grass, of considerable width, and exceeding three miles in length. It is enclosed by mountains on both sides, and terminates towards the N. E. in a slope, which declines to the lake of the Mont Cenis. The path, on arriving at this opening above the lake, does not descend to it, but turns off towards the south-east, and enters a kind of short valley, having the mountains on the right, and on the left a range of hills, mentioned in the note as forming on the south-west the boundary of the plateau of

---

[1] There are three paths leading from the Little Mont Cenis to the high road which runs along the plateau of the Great Mont Cenis. The first lies along the northern side of the lake, and falls into the high road at Les Tavernettes. The second runs to the Hospice by the southern side of the lake, along the extremity of a range of hills which forms the boundary of the plateau of the Great Mont Cenis, from the lake to La Grande Croix. The third crosses these hills through a hollow in them, and descends directly upon La Grande Croix. This last, the shortest and most natural way, is the ancient line from the Little Mont Cenis into Italy. In the map given in Blaev's *Theatrum Statuum Regiœ Celsitudinis Sabaudiœ Ducis*, the roads from Italy over the Great and the Little Mont Cenis are marked as separating at La Grande Croix or even a little before. The road to the Little Mont Cenis seems to have skirted the base of the hills, and to have left the present hamlet of La Grande Croix some hundred yards or so to the right.

the Great Mont Cenis. Through a hollow in these hills, as there stated, the path finally passes, and rejoins, at La Grande Croix, the route of the Great Mont Cenis. The descent into Italy, which begins at La Grande Croix, is the same for both passes.

This descent is at first very steep. The road winds down a precipitous declivity, called the 'Fourmiguier,' by which the little plain of St Nicholas, lying perhaps about 500 feet below La Grande Croix, is at length reached. The face of this declivity is traversed from side to side by the several arms of the high road, which is cut in places out of the rock, and is only able to accomplish the descent by a zigzag route. By these arms of the high-road, rising one above another, the old mule-road seems to have been quite obliterated. The little plain of St Nicholas, once reached, is soon crossed. At the extremity of this plain the carriage-road (always the same from this point), separates from the common line of the old mule-roads, and is only joined by it again at Susa; the extreme steepness of the descent to La Novalèse rendering that line of route very ill adapted for a carriage-road. The first part of the descent from the plain of St Nicholas, by the mule-road, lay through a covered gallery, built for the protection of travellers, and now in a great measure buried beneath the fragments of rock which were detached from above, when the mountain-side was blasted away to afford a passage for the high-road. The rest of the descent, as far as La Ferrière, is rapid, but not excessively steep. At La Ferrière the first and second mule-roads separate, and unite again at La Novalèse. The second road, strongly constructed, and paved with large stones, was made under Charles Emmanuel III. (1730—1773) in consequence of the dangers which attended the oldest line of way. This second mule-path from La Ferrière keeps on the right or southern side of the Cenise or Cenischia: the old path lay on the northern side of the stream. The descent between La Ferrière and La Novalèse is very rapid, and in parts precipitous.

At La Novalèse the descent from the Mont Cenis is terminated. This village, though so near the summit of

the pass, lies at an elevation of no more than 2560 feet
above the sea.   From thence to the plains of Italy the
route presents no further difficulty, unless the passage of
a low ridge, immediately before reaching Susa, be considered as one.   Yet even this obstacle might, it should
seem, have been avoided, if necessary, by following the
Cenise from Venaus, on its left bank, down to its junction
with the Dora Susina in the valley, or Combe, of Susa.
From La Novalèse downwards, there is no further question
of mere mule-roads, as the country does not offer any im-
pediment to the construction of carriage-roads.   In such
a district it is not of much importance to determine the
oldest route.   From Susa to Bussoleno, on the way to
Turin, the northern side of the Dora affords the best line
of road, though the southern side may have been anciently
followed.   From Bussoleno to Turin the southern side has,
till late years, always been taken, though the river is now
crossed at Borgone, instead of Bussoleno.   The earliest
road seems to have passed, after leaving Bussoleno,
through the towns or villages of San Giorio, Sant' Anto-
niño, Vayes, Chiusa, Sant' Ambrogio, Avigliana, Buttigliera, Rosta, and Rivoli, and thus to have finally reached
the city of Turin.

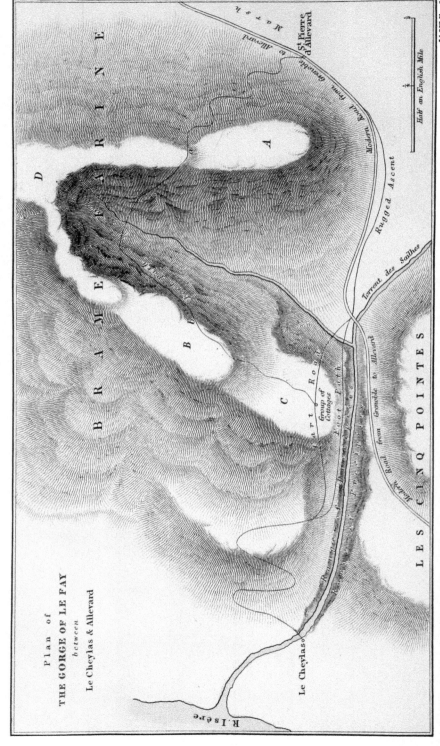

Plan of
THE GORGE OF LE FAY
between
Le Cheylas & Allevard

R. Isère

Le Cheylas

B R A M E F A R I N E

D

B

B

C

Cart Road

Group of
Cottages

Foot Path

St Pierre
d'Allevard

Modern Road from Grenoble to Allevard

Rugged Ascent

Torrent des Sailhes

Modern Road from Grenoble to Allevard

LES CINQ POINTES

A

Marsh

Half an English Mile

J.&C.Walker Sc.

CHAPTER VII.

Application of the conditions deduced from Polybius' narrative to the route of the Mont Cenis.—Accordance of the actual distances with those given by Polybius.—Identification of the defile at the commencement of the ascent of the Alps with the gorge of *Le Fay.*—Probable identity of the town of the Allobroges and the modern *Allevard.*—Identification of the "strong white rock" with the *rock of Baune.*—Arrival at the *Col of the Little Mont Cenis.*

THE first two conditions for the determination of Hannibal's route relate to two distances; (1) the distance from the junction of the Rhone and Isère, (or from Valence) to the point where Hannibal would have left the Isère; and (2) the distance from this latter point, across the Alps, to the commencement of the plains of Italy. It will therefore be necessary to compute: (1) the length of the road along the left bank of the Isère from Valence to Le Cheylas; and (2) the length of the Alpine route across the Little Mont Cenis from Le Cheylas to Avigliana.

Now from Valence to Grenoble the distance is 96 kilomètres; and from Grenoble to Le Cheylas the distance is 33 kilomètres. The total distance, therefore, from Valence (or from the junction of the Rhone and Isère) to Le Cheylas is 129 kilomètres or 87½ Roman miles[1].

The following table will give the distances between the different places in succession on the way from Le Cheylas[2]

---

[1] A Roman mile is equal to 1475 mètres.

[2] The name *Cheylas* is probably identical with *chalà*, a word existing in the pâtois of Dauphiné, and signifying a footpath. (" *Chalà*, petit sentier, particulièrement celui qu'on fait sur la neige." Champollion-Figeac, *Nouvelles recherches sur les pâtois.*) *Chalà*, however, of which another form is *chal*, seems to be a corruption of the Latin *scala*, and would have signified originally an ascending path, and thence a mountain path generally. " Il est à presumer que la montée de Chalemont (a place by Grenoble) fut ainsi nommée du vieux mot *chal*, qui signifie *route*, c'est-à-dire, *route de la montagne*. Nous avous trouvé dans un manuscrit *scala montis.*" Pilot, *Histoire de Grenoble.* In the Val. d'Orca, also,

to Avigliana. The government Itinerary of the Sardinian
States, published in 1839, gives the distances on the road
then existing between La Rochette and Bramans in Piedmontese miles.   On the older road the distances are of
course somewhat different : but, with the exception of the
part between St Jean de Maurienne and Modane, the dif-
ferences must be slight, and the distances of the Itinerary
may, with that exception, be adopted.   The distances
between Le Cheylas and La Rochette, between St Jean de
Maurienne and Modane, and between Bramans and Susa
by the Little Mont Cenis,—distances for which no table
could be consulted,—have been estimated with considerable care, principally, but not solely, by observing the time
occupied in walking between different points, and may be
relied upon as free from all material error.   The distance
of 24 Roman miles between Susa and Avigliana (Ad fines)
is taken from the Roman Itineraries.

A Piedmontese mile is equal to 2466 mètres, and a
Roman mile is equal to 1475 mètres, or 1614 English yards.
Five Roman miles will consquently be almost accurately
equivalent to three Piedmontese miles, and twelve Roman
miles will be equivalent to eleven English miles.

---

there is an ascent called the *Scalare di Ceresol*. The use of the German
word, *Steg*, in the Swiss Alps, seems to correspond to the use of *chalà* in
the Alps of Dauphiné.   The meaning of *Steg* is given as simply *path*,
but it is derived from *Steigen, to mount,* and, under the forms *Steg,
Steig*, or *Gsteig*, is found in several places where ascents begin.   (Ex.
Gsteig, Sanetsch pass, N. side, and Simplon pass, S. side; *Am-steg*, St Gothard road; *Steg*, entrance to Lötsch Thal.)   The terms *Monta, Montets,
Montée*, are used in some districts of the Alps where French is spoken
to designate similar places.   The word ἀναβολή seems quite identical
in meaning with such terms as Monta and Gsteig, and with the term
Chalà in its primitive signification.   As there are in the Alps at the
present day, so also there would have been in the time of Hannibal,
several places known and designated as points where ascents began.
All such points might be called ἀναβολαί by a Greek writer.   *The ἀναβολή*, of which Polybius speaks, would be one of these points, and, as
is evident from the context, the first point where the road into Italy
from the banks of the Rhone ascended into the mountains.   Le Cheylas
is accurately in this position, and probably derives its name from its
situation, as being what Polybius calls the ἀναβολὴ τῶν Ἄλπεων ἡ εἰς
Ἰταλίαν, or, in another place, the ἀναβολὴ πρὸς τὰς Ἄλπεις.

			Pied. Miles.	English Miles.	Roman Miles.
From Le Cheylas	to	Allevard	......	$5\frac{1}{2}$	6
Allevard	,,	La Rochette	......	$6\frac{1}{2}$	7
La Rochette	,,	Chamoux	$4\frac{1}{2}$	......	$7\frac{1}{2}$
Chamoux	,,	Aiguebelle	$3\frac{1}{2}$	......	$5\frac{5}{6}$
Aiguebelle	,,	La Chapelle	$5\frac{1}{2}$	......	$9\frac{1}{6}$
La Chapelle	,,	La Chambre	$4\frac{1}{4}$	......	7
La Chambre	,,	St Jean de Maurienne	$4\frac{1}{2}$	......	$7\frac{1}{2}$
St Jean	,,	St Martin de la Porte	......	6	$6\frac{1}{2}$
St Martin	,,	Orelle { to Villard Bernond $1\frac{1}{4}$,, La Traverse ...... $1\frac{1}{4}$,, Basilières? .... 2 ,, Orelle .... $1\frac{1}{4}$ }	......	7	$7\frac{2}{3}$
Orelle	,,	St André	......	5	$5\frac{1}{2}$
St André	,,	Modane	......	$3\frac{1}{2}$	$3\frac{5}{6}$
Modane	,,	L'Esseillon	3	......	5
L'Esseillon	,,	Bramans	2	......	$3\frac{1}{3}$
Bramans	,,	Col of Little Mont Cenis	......	7	$7\frac{2}{3}$
Col	,,	Grand' Croix	......	$6\frac{1}{2}$	7
Grand' Croix	,,	La Novalèse	......	6	$6\frac{1}{2}$
La Novalèse	,,	Susa	......	5	$5\frac{1}{2}$
Susa to Avigliana or "Ad Fines"			......	......	24
Total distance from Le Cheylas to Avigliana					$132\frac{1}{2}$

The first two conditions are these:

I. The commencement of the ascent of the Alps must be situated at a distance of about 100 Roman miles from the junction of the Rhone and the Isère, reckoned along the left bank of the latter river.

II. The length of the route over the Alps, beginning at the commencement of the ascent of the mountains, and terminating at the commencement of the plains of Italy, must be about 150 Roman miles.

Instead of the 100 Roman miles of (I.) the route gives $87\frac{1}{2}$
,, ,, 150 ,, ,, (II.) ,, ,, $132\frac{1}{2}$

The actual distances thus fall, in both cases, a little below those given by Polybius. This is exactly what ought to occur when the distances are estimated, as they are by Polybius, in *stadia*: for the estimated distances in stadia always exceed the real distances[1]. It has also been pre-

[1] "The principal argument for a variety of *stadia* is that of Major Rennell, (*Geog. of Herod.* s. 2.); namely, that when ancient authors have

viously noticed, that Polybius measures distances by lengths of 200 stadia, or 25 Roman miles.   Now 100 is the lowest multiple of 25 which exceeds $87\frac{1}{2}$; and 150 is also the lowest multiple of 25 which exceeds $132\frac{1}{2}$.   The argument, therefore, drawn from the comparison of distances, could not be more favourable than it is to the route of the Little Mont Cenis.

———

We now proceed to the consideration of Condition III.

III.   At the commencement of the ascent of the Alps, a defile must be found, the character of which, and of the surrounding country, is in accordance with the events related by Polybius to have occurred in that place.

The chain of lofty hills, which bounds the valley of Graisivaudan on the east, has been already mentioned. At Le Cheylas, there is a gap in this chain, affording a passage to a small stream, called the Torrent des Sailhes, which rises in the elevated valley behind the hills.   This gap or defile is called the gorge of Le Fay.   It is compressed on the north by the extremity of the ridge of Brame-Farine, and on the south by a very elevated hill crowned by five sharp summits, and bearing, on that account, the name of Les Cinq Pointes.   Through the gorge of Le Fay, which divides these hills, admission is gained from the Graisivaudan into the valley of Allevard.

The road from Allevard to St Pierre d'Allevard lies over a plain, enclosed between the ridge of Brame-Farine and the higher Alps.   This plain is marshy in the middle : the road leaves the marsh on the east, and skirts the steep slopes of Brame-Farine on the west.   At its southern extremity the ridge of Brame-Farine forks, as will be seen by the plan, into two spurs.   From St Pierre d'Allevard, the road to Le Cheylas begins to descend, and winds round the base of the eastern spur of Brame-Farine.   The descent eventually becomes rugged, and the base of the hill, 'Les Cinq Pointes,' begins to approach the road.   The old path

———

stated the distances between known places, and a comparison is made between their statements and the actual distances, *the distances stated by them are invariably found to be too great, never to small.*"—*Penny Cyc.* Art. " Stadium," which see.

here lies immediately to the left of the carriage-road, which is partly cut out of the rock. After the bridge over the Torrent des Sailhes is reached, the defile becomes very contracted. The modern road here crosses the torrent by a bridge, and pursues its course to Goncelin, the rocks having been blasted to gain a passage for it. After passing under this bridge the torrent begins to sink in a rift, and is soon lost in a deep and narrow trench, bounded on both sides by sheer precipices, between which it flows for a full mile, until it emerges into the Graisivaudan at Le Cheylas. Two roads branch off, along the extremity of the western spur of Brame-Farine, from the bridge over the torrent. The first and most direct is a footpath, which keeps along the edge of the precipices; the second, a cart-road, constructed higher up the face of the declivity, and avoiding, at the expense of a slight ascent and subsequent descent, the dangers of the precipices. The foot-path, the shortest and most natural way, would be the earliest road. For about a quarter of a mile from the bridge it lies over a small tract of nearly level ground, crossing a little stream on its way. The projecting edge of the western spur of Brame-Farine then forces it to the edge of the precipices, and for half a mile it is obliged to skirt them closely, and frequently to run along their very brink. At length it is enabled to turn away from this dangerous vicinity, and to descend, by a long and winding course, down the western slopes of Brame-Farine, to Le Cheylas.

Here, then, in the gorge of Le Fay, we find a defile existing at the first commencement of the ascent to the Alps. Its character also, and the nature of its vicinity, will prove, upon examination, to be in accordance with the requisitions of Polybius' narrative. For

(1) The defile must be commanded by certain heights of considerable elevation.

These heights are those of Brame-Farine[1]. The general character of this ridge is that of an exceedingly steep slope, partly covered with brush-wood, and partly with

---

[1] The heights commanding the defile are called by Livy "tumuli," (i. e. hills as distinguished from mountains.) It will be seen that the heights of Brame-Farine are of this nature.

grass. Some more level tracts than usual are, however, under cultivation. The ridge, as previously mentioned, forks, at its southern extremity, (marked D on the plan) into two spurs. From D, the ridge-line of the eastern spur descends to a, and then expands into a small level tract A, the most commanding portion on the heights. The ridge-line of the western spur also eventually expands into a similar tract B ; but this tract is considerably lower than A, and is commanded by it. A rapid descent intervenes between the tract B, and another piece of level ground C, on which stands a group of cottages. From C, short steep slopes descend to the foot-path running along the edge of the precipices beneath.

These heights are accessible by various tracks. One of them is traced upon the plan. By this path it is a walk of about three quarters of an hour, up a steep ascent, from St Pierre d'Allevard to the point a, the northern extremity of the level tract A. From a it is a descent of nearly half an hour, along the sides of rapid slopes, to b, on the edge of the tract B. From b to the group of cottages is another descent of about twenty minutes. The old foot-path through the defile lies at a short distance below this group of cottages.

From these measurements of time it will be seen, that the heights A and B, commanding the defile, are of considerable elevation. The level tract A, the most important of the two positions A and B, can, indeed, hardly be less than 1500 feet above the Graisivaudan.

(2)   These heights must not be easily accessible from below the defile.

From the side of the Graisivaudan these heights are certainly not easily accessible, especially the more commanding of the two posts, that marked A. But from the valley of Allevard this post is much more readily gained, both as being nearer, and as requiring an ascent, of which the perpendicular elevation is considerably less.

(3)   The way through the defile must skirt in some place the edge of a precipice.

It has been already mentioned, that the foot-path from Le Cheylas through the gorge of Le Fay skirts the edge of a precipice for a distance of about half a mile.

(4) Immediately below the defile must be found a place where an army as numerous as that of Hannibal could encamp.

The Graisivaudan, from Grenoble to Pont Charra, is a broad and level vale throughout. On the ground between Le Cheylas and Goncelin, Hannibal might encamp without difficulty.

(5) This place of encampment should be visible from the heights commanding the defile.

From the heights A, a large part of the country between Goncelin and Le Cheylas is visible, as well as the western part of the Graisivaudan down to Grenoble. From the position B the rest of the eastern side of the Graisivaudan is visible in addition.

(6) Above the defile, and near it, must be found an open district, where a town either stands, or might have stood, and where an army such as that of Hannibal's could have encamped.

Such an open district is the valley of Allevard. Its length, reckoning from St Pierre d'Allevard to the Savoyard frontier, is nearly six miles. Its breadth is about half an hour's walk from side to side[1]. The town which Hannibal took would probably be where Allevard, the chief place in the district, now stands. Polybius calls this town πόλις, which would lead us to infer that it was a place of some importance in the country of the Allobroges, where Hannibal then was. Livy mentions it as being the capital of the district. It would therefore either be the chief town of the Allobroges, then perhaps a smaller tribe than that which afterwards bore this name, or else the chief town of one of the districts into which their country was divided, the capital of one of the smaller tribes which together composed the whole people. That the chief town of an Allobrogic district should have been situated at Allevard seems probable, both from the present importance of the place, and from its appearing to preserve, in its own name, that of the Allobroges[2].

---

[1] *Guide du Visiteur au pays d'Allevard.*

[2] The root of the latter part of the name of the Allobroges, called

Having now shewn the accordance of the character of
the gorge of Le Fay, and of its neighbourhood, with the
requirements of Polybius' narrative, it may be advisable,
before proceeding further, to obviate an objection which
might be raised against considering Le Cheylas as lying
at the commencement of the ascent of the Alps. It might
be said that as, from the extremity of the Graisivaudan,
near Voreppe, a point about 30 miles below Le Cheylas, the
road has lain through a valley bounded on both sides by
mountains, the commencement of the ascent of the Alps,
ἡ πρὸς τὰς Ἄλπεις ἀναβολή, ought to be fixed there. Yet
'the commencement of the ascent of the Alps' need not
signify the geographical commencement of that mountain-
system, but the point where the route first begins to ascend
the mountains. Indeed, the term is much more applicable
to a locality of the latter kind. Now the route up the
wide and level vale of Graisivaudan has nothing of a mountainous nature. It is at Le Cheylas, where Hannibal is
supposed to have left the Isère, and turned off to Allevard,
that the character of the way changes abruptly from level
to mountainous; so that the commencement of the ascent
is here definitely marked. Besides, the mountains on the
right bank of the Isère are not properly the Alps, but the
Chartreuse mountains, a group perfectly isolated from the
Alps by the valley of Chambéry and the Graisivaudan.
Neither does Polybius seem to have considered them as a
part of the Alps; for, having occasion to mention them in
his description of the Island, he speaks of them indefinitely
as ὄρη, and as if they were unconnected with the Alps and
the Alpine route. In fact, the mountains to the east
or south-east of the valley of Allevard are at present

Allobriges by Polybius, is the frequently recurring Celtic word *brig,*
which, under the forms *briga,* or *brica,* appears as the termination of the
names of a great number of ancient towns in Gaul and Spain. That
Allevard should be a corruption of Allobriga or Allobrica, or some
similar word, is not improbable. The ancient name of Briançon, *Brig-
antio,* or *Brig-antium,* is found in Ammianus Marcellinus as *Virg-antia,*
or *Verg-antium.* The name of the ancient *Tala-brica,* also, has become
corrupted into the modern *Tala-vera;* and the ancient *Baudo-brica,* (or
Bonto-brica) on the Rhine, is now identified with the modern *Bop part.*

spoken of as being the 'first' of the Alps, 'les premières montagnes alpines¹;' so that when Hannibal ascended, by the gorge of Le Fay, to the valley of Allevard, through the chain of hills intervening between that valley and the Graisivaudan, it might be said of him, with perfect accuracy, that he then ἤρξατο τῆς πρὸς τὰς Ἄλπεις ἀναβολῆς.

When Hannibal first entered, or approached, the country of the Allobroges, they were afraid of attacking him, partly on account of his cavalry, and partly on account of the escort of the men of the Island, who guarded the rear of the Carthaginians. Now the vale of Graisivaudan, from Grenoble to Le Cheylas, being perfectly level, is quite adapted throughout to the action of cavalry, so that the Allobroges would never venture to descend from the hills, and fall upon Hannibal's line of march. The ambuscade they projected in the defile leading to Allevard was a surer method of destroying the Carthaginians. From the difficulties of the road, and the manner in which it winds, throughout the whole distance from Le Cheylas to Allevard, either up, or along the base of the acclivities of Brame-Farine, with steep slopes, precipices, rugged ground, or marshes on its other side;—on account of these disadvantages, and the centrical position and unassailable nature of the commanding heights of Brame-Farine, an army, marching from Le Cheylas to Allevard, would have been brought into imminent danger of destruction by an attack from the heights, every point in the long line of march being exposed to assault.

Such a destructive attack was projected by the Allobroges: but Hannibal had become aware of their plans, and took measures to frustrate them. On the evening of the eighth day after leaving the confluence of the Rhone and the Isère, the Carthaginians, having advanced from their previous position, in full view of the Allobroges on the heights, encamped on the plain between Le Cheylas and Goncelin, before the entrance of the defile. As night drew on, the camp-fires were lighted, and were observed

¹ *Guide du Visiteur au pays d'Allevard.*

7

by the Allobroges from their posts on the hills, who, concluding that no further movement was meditated by Hannibal, withdrew from the heights to the neighbouring town
of Allevard. But Hannibal, previously aware that the
Gauls would withdraw, selected a body of active and lightly-
equipped men, passed through the gorge, along the edge
of the precipices, in the dead of night, and seized upon
the heights which the Allobroges had abandoned. Hannibal himself would probably choose for his own post the
eastern heights[1], from whence Allevard is seen, and the
most comprehensive view of the route obtained. Having
thus gained possession of the heights, the Carthaginians
took up their position upon them, and waited for the day.

When morning dawned, the Allobroges prepared to
return from Allevard to their former posts, but were
seized with dismay for a time, when they perceived that
they had been occupied during the night by the Carthaginians. Nothing, however, would have prevented the
Gauls from advancing towards the defile, and watching the
progress of events. They might, without incurring much
danger of molestation on the part of Hannibal, have
occupied the ground to the south-east and south of the
road, from St Pierre d'Allevard to Les Cinq Pointes, or
even have advanced along the lower slopes of the eastern
spur of Brame-Farine, and have collected to the north of
the road leading through the defile. For Hannibal, besides being at a considerable distance from the Allobroges,
could not fall upon them from above without leaving the
heights open to recapture from the side of Allevard.

At length the leading columns of the Carthaginian
army, the cavalry and baggage-animals, began to appear,
making their way in a long line through the defile, and
much embarrassed by the difficulties of the ground. The
Allobroges were unable to resist the opportunity which
the defenceless state of their enemy seemed to afford
them, and fell upon the line of march at many points. By
these attacks the Carthaginians sustained severe losses.
A number of horses and baggage-animals, as well as the

---

[1] Those marked A in the Plan.

men with them, fell into the hands of the Allobroges, and were carried off to their town. Nearly all, probably, became captive, who had passed the line of precipices, and were ascending the rugged ground towards St Pierre d'Allevard. Attracted by the hopes of spoil, the greater part of the inhabitants of the town issued out to join in the attack, and the town itself was left with comparatively few occupants.

The foremost columns of the Carthaginian army having been thus cut off, the Allobroges attempted to destroy the rest in detail, as they made their way along the edge of the precipices. Taking possession of a small plateau immediately above this part of the road[1], they directed their attacks upon the Carthaginians beneath. Numbers of the baggage-animals were thus destroyed, rolling with their burdens down the precipices by the side of the road. The loss was much increased by the horses of the cavalry, which, becoming unruly in consequence of the wounds they received, created great confusion in the line of march, and threw the whole column into disarray.

Hannibal saw from above the gradual destruction of his army, and determined to charge down from the heights upon the Allobroges, and attempt to preserve the remainder of his baggage, on which the subsequent safety of the army depended. Accordingly, accompanied by the men who had seized the heights in the night, he descended from above, and fell upon the enemy[2]. Attacked at a disadvantage, in consequence of Hannibal's charging them from the heights, the Allobroges were defeated, and obliged to give way. Borne back towards the precipices, they were thrown upon the Carthaginian column of march beneath them, and involved them in their own fate. The success of Hannibal was thus inevitably attended with the destruction of part of his own army. By no other means,

---

[1] Marked C in the Plan.

[2] The group of cottages on the plateau marked C would be the point about which the contest was hottest. Hannibal would probably descend in a direction represented by the footpath marked on the Plan along the heights.

however, could the safety of the remainder have been assured, and the sacrifice was therefore made. The greater part of the Allobroges were either slain by the sword, or driven down the precipices: the few survivors of the conflict turned and fled to their own town, or dispersed themselves among the surrounding mountains.

Hannibal, however, gave his enemies no time to recover themselves. No sooner was the battle terminated, than he collected together as many of his scattered troops as he could, and marched directly upon the town of the Allobroges, while the rest of his army was making its way through the defile. The town was enabled to offer no effectual resistance, (for it was very nearly empty) and fell at once into the hands of Hannibal. By its capture he recovered possession of his own horses, baggage-animals, and men, who had been carried off by the Allobroges at the commencement of the contest, and obtained a supply of provisions for his army, sufficient for two or three days' consumption. The fugitive Allobroges also, dispersed in the neighbouring districts, diffused such terror among the inhabitants by the story of their defeat, as to make them very cautious of molesting the Carthaginians. When Hannibal was next attacked, it was not by open hostility, but by a previously concerted system of treachery[1].

The fourth condition which has been deduced from the history of Polybius, is the following:

IV. At a place nearly half-way, in point of time, between the town of the Allobroges and the summit of the pass, a certain 'strong white rock' must be found; and the adjacent country must be in accordance with the events which are recorded by Polybius to have taken place in the neighbourhood of this rock.

In point of distance, St Jean de Maurienne lies half-way between Allevard and the lake on the summit of the

---

[1] A good general view of the supposed scene of the contest with the Allobroges is gained from the modern road between Goncelin and Allevard, shortly before it arrives at the bridge over the Torrent des Sailhes, on its way from Goncelin.

Mont Cenis, being about 40 English miles from each. In point of time, however, the half-way point must be placed somewhat above St Jean, as the difficulties of the way are much greater above than below, and Hannibal would have marched most quickly in the Lower Maurienne and the valley of La Rochette, where, in addition to the comparative easiness of the ground, his march was also unimpeded by any aggression on the part of the inhabitants. The 'strong white rock,' consequently, being nearly, but not quite, half-way, in point of time, between the town and the summit of the pass, must be sought, either in the immediate neighbourhood of St Jean de Maurienne, or a little above.

It is found accordingly between six and seven miles above St Jean, immediately beyond St Martin de la Porte, being, in fact, the great rock of Baune, already mentioned, (p. 83) as putting a sudden termination to the open valley extending from St Jean to St Martin. This rock seems to possess the characteristics of the λευκόπε-τρον ὀχυρόν of Polybius, that is to say, to form a prominent feature in the country, and to be remarkable for its whiteness and (military) strength[1].

The rock of Baune is first seen, from a distance of about seven miles, on the approach to St Jean de Maurienne from the lower valley; and it forms the great feature in the neighbourhood of St Michel and St Martin de la Porte. From the old road by La Traverse its appearance is also particularly striking. It owes this conspicuous character, not only to its great size, but also to its singularly isolated character. It projects, as before observed, for a length of about three-quarters of a mile, from the sides of the mountains on the north of the valley, across which it completely extends, only leaving between the cliff in which it terminates and the mountains opposite, a narrow gorge, or 'étranglement,' just

---

[1] The subject of this λευκόπετρον might possibly be illustrated, if an accurate description of the promontory of Leucopetra, now Capo dell' Armi, in Calabria, could be obtained. I have not been able to meet with one.

sufficient for the passage of the Arc. Its height is probably about 500 or 600 feet, the summit being a kind of long irregular plateau, about 200 yards broad. Its southern extremity is a lofty precipice, springing naturally from the river, but now blasted to afford a passage for the road. Its eastern and western faces are likewise abrupt, both being long ranges of absolute precipice, which render the summit of the rock completely inaccessible from either side. On the north it is also inaccessible, except at one point. Here the defile of La Porte perfectly isolates it in its upper part from the sides of the mountains on the north, to which its lower part is attached. Towards this defile the Rock of Baune presents a fourth precipitous side. It is only from the north-eastern corner of the rock, after having gained the highest point of the defile, marked by a cross, and elevated perhaps 300 or 400 feet above the Arc, that it is possible to reach the plateau on the summit of the rock.

It will easily be seen, from these details, that the Rock of Baune forms a great feature in the country, and is of a particularly inaccessible nature. Indeed its adaptation for a stronghold renders the term ὀχυρόν particularly applicable to it. Had it stood in ancient Greece it might have sustained an acropolis. Its claim to the title of a λευκόπετρον, though more liable to be disregarded, is no less well founded; for its whiteness, if not a striking, is a peculiar and distinctive characteristic of this rock. It is, indeed, only the northern half of its eastern face which is composed of rock either absolutely white, or of a tint so nearly approaching to whiteness that it may be called white[1]. In the southern half of the eastern face of the rock, and in the whole of the western face, the colour is grey. The presence of the white portion of the rock is also the more liable to escape notice, in consequence of its being considerably discoloured by the weather, and partially concealed by vegetation. It might only be from

---

[1] Specimens of this rock, submitted to examination, have proved it to be gypsum. Some of it is perfectly white; other portions are of a pinkish white.

certain situations, La Traverse for instance, that the lightness of its colour would be so remarkable as to strike particularly the attention of an ordinary traveller. Yet, though the greater part of the Rock is not white, its whiteness is, nevertheless, one of its peculiarities. The reason is this : all the surrounding mountains are composed of grey rock of a dark hue. The white stratum, which crops out here through the grey, only appears in the Rock of Baune, and in the eminence immediately on the other side of the defile of La Porte. But this eminence is of an unimportant character, and forms no feature in the country. The only one of the great masses of rock in this neighbourhood, distinguished from the rest by its whiteness, is the Rock of Baune. Some of the surrounding mountains exhibit enormous surfaces of naked rock. The precipitous mountain rising from the valley directly to the north of St Martin de la Porte, is one pile of crag, of vast height, from base to summit. The bare precipices on the other side of the Arc are scarcely less remarkable. All these rocky masses are of a sombre grey. The Rock of Baune, though also in a great measure of that colour, is distinguished from them in a singular manner by its containing the white rock, which protrudes through the grey[1].

---

[1] The rupture of the upper strata here, and the protrusion of the lower, a convulsion signalized by the formation of the Rock of Baune, is noticed by Prof. A. Sismonda, in his "Memoria sui terreni stratificati delle Alpi," published in the "Memorie della Reale Accademia delle scienze di Torino" for the year 1841. The author, after having spoken of the calcareous rocks which compose the mountains of the Upper Maurienne nearly as far down as Modane, thus proceeds: (p. 30)

'Cessando il calcare, viene di nuovo l'arenaria modificata, che mi parve superiore ad esso, quindi si entra in mezzo a monti coperti delle roccie già altrove in questo scritto indicate come le rappresentanti l' *Oxford clay*, ossia il terreno antracitoso superiore. Consistono esse in psammiti, in calcare scistoso, arenarie e poddinghe generalmente con tinta bigia intensa, e racchiudono depositi d'antracite che si scava in varii punti. Le roccie di questo terreno sono rotte sotto *S. Michel*, e ne esce il calcare, che forma poi il monte collocato al N. N. O. del paese; la sua posizione, ed i suoi caratteri assicurano che è la continuazione del potentissimo banco di *Villet*. Ho molto detto sull' ordine di soprapposizione dei differenti terreni fin qui nominati; tuttavia credendo

The nature of the country in the neighbourhood of the Rock of Baune must now be considered.

The precipitous mountain to the north of St Martin de la Porte has already been noticed. This mountain forms the extremity of a short chain, extending northwards from St Martin to the Mont des Encombres, where it joins the chain dividing the Tarentaise from the Maurienne. This principal chain, after having stretched in length, first E. and then S. E. to the Roche Château Bourreau, sends out a lateral chain in the direction of St Michel. The

---

ciò cosa utilissima, non posso proseguire senza fermarmivi ogni qual volta pel metodo impiegato in questa descrizione me ne viene l'occasione. Ho tuttora ricordato che li psammiti, certi calcari scistosi, le arenarie, e infine anche certe poddinghe soprastanno al calcare di *Villet*, il quale è superiore al liasse.'

M. Albanis de Beaumont, in his 'Description des Alpes Grecques et Cottiennes,' notices the closing of the valley of the Arc by the Rock of Baune, and conjectures that Hannibal was attacked here by the Allobroges and their allies. He speaks, however, only of the modern way by the side of the Arc, and not of the older way through the defile of La Porte. The following is the passage alluded to :

'A peu de distance de l'entrée de cette vallée, (La Combe de Valoires) commence une chaîne de rochers calcaires, dont les faces sont abruptes, et qui compriment de nouveau la vallée de l'Arc, au point qu'il y a à peine de la place pour le chemin et le cours de la rivière ; chaque fois que j'ai traversé ce défilé, qui a environ un mille de long, je me suis rappelé ce passage de Tite-Live *ad castrum quod erat caput ejus regionis*, etc. etc. Dans cette supposition, la ville de S. Jean seroit le *castrum* dont Annibal (qu. Tite-Live,) fait mention, et le défilé dont je viens de parler, celui où les Allobroges et leurs alliés se mirent en embuscade pour attaquer l'arrière-garde de ce général ; les rochers qui bordent ce défilé sont, ainsi que j'ai déjà observé, en partie calcaires, et en partie schisteux, ils offrent même une grande variété dans ces deux espèces de pierres ; les unes ont des couches très dures et fort épaisses, d'autres tendres, fissiles, et poreuses ; des troisièmes contiennent des paillettes de mica verdâtre ou gris foncé, ainsi que des rognons de petrosilex, leurs couches sont inclinées à l'horizon sous un angle de soixante degrés ; les matières calcaires qui composent ces rochers sont séparées par des couches argilleuses d'une grande dureté, qui se décrépitent en petits feuillets d'un pouce d'épaisseur ; celles qui sont schisteuses se montrent en grande masse du côté de la rive gauche de l'Arc, elles reposent sur une roche compacte et très dure, qui ne fait effervescence que très lentement avec les acides.' (Vol. II. p. 625.)

three chains, extending in this manner from St Martin de la Porte to St Michel, enclose a large extent of habitable ground, divided into two parts by a small stream, sunk in a gully, and flowing into the Arc through the plain of St Michel, which lies to the east of the Rock of Baune. Another small stream, the source of which is in the Mont des Encombres, flows down from that mountain in a deep impracticable gorge, with precipices on both sides, and forms the impassable western boundary of the habitable ground on the mountains. This gorge terminates immediately behind St Martin de la Porte, below which place the stream may be passed without any difficulty. To facilitate the description of the country, it will be convenient to give names to the two divisions of this tract of mountain-ground. The western portion, comprised between the two streams, may be called 'the Ridge of Baune;' the eastern portion may be designated 'the Slope of La Traverse.'

A path, leading from the valley of the Arc into the Tarentaise, runs along the Ridge of Baune, and crosses the chain which separates the two provinces by the Col des Encombres, a pass which is considerably frequented. The first descent from this pass into the Maurienne is steep, though the pasturages reach nearly to the summit of the Col. The steep descent subsides before reaching Plan Villard, the first village on the road. From thence to Baune the descent is gradual, lying along the back of the ridge, here from about half a mile to a mile broad. At Baune the ridge separates into two branches, divided by a hollow. The first and shortest extends towards St Martin de la Porte. The descent between these two places is quick, through a series of cultivated fields. The longer branch of the Ridge of Baune terminates in the Rock of Baune, which is cut off from the upper half of this arm of the ridge by the defile of La Porte. On these upper heights there stands by itself a conspicuous chapel; a circumstance from which the heights may be conveniently spoken of as 'the heights of the chapel.'

The slope of La Traverse declines at first very rapidly from the crest of the chain on the east; but, after a long descent, the steepness abates, and a plateau or terrace of considerable breadth is presented, extending in length from La Traverse nearly to Villard Putier. The path between these two places is on a level almost all the way. There is a slight ascent required on leaving Villard Putier, and an equally slight descent before arriving at La Traverse. This long plateau between La Traverse and Villard Putier, may be called the ' Terrace of La Traverse.' From its western edge, the slope declines steeply again to La Simbran and Villard Bernond. A narrow strip of ground is then left, along which the path ascends from Villard Bernond to Villard Putier. On the west this strip of ground is abruptly cut short by the gully, which forms the channel of the stream already mentioned.

It is at St Martin de la Porte that the old road was obliged to leave the valley and ascend the mountain-sides. From St Martin it leads along the slopes with a gradual rise for above half a mile, directing its course towards the entrance of the defile of La Porte. After crossing the hollow which divides the two arms of the Ridge of Baune, it runs upon the abrupt side of the Heights of the Chapel for about 200 yards: it then reaches the entrance of the defile, the ' Porte ' itself, a passage between the rocks only a yard or two in breadth. The defile within the ' Porte ' is wider, though still very narrow. Its length is about 300 yards; the path through it rises all the way; and the eastern or upper extremity of the defile is nearly as contracted as the western. For the 300 yards through the defile, and the previous 200 along the side of the Heights of the Chapel, the path is exposed throughout to be swept by rocks rolled down upon it from the abrupt declivities of those heights. On the side of the Rock of Baune the acclivity is precipitous or very steep, and the defile equally dangerous. On emerging from the defile, the path turns to the left, and passes through Le Village de la Porte along the sides of a slope, eventually crossing the gully, a task of some little difficulty, to Villard Bernond. From St Martin to Villard Bernond, the distance is about a mile and a half. It is about the same distance from Villard Bernond to La Traverse, a great ascent being requisite between the two places. For nearly half the distance the mountain-side is very steep, and might be swept from above by rolling rocks. From La Traverse to Le Thyl the way is nearly on a level, and crosses the shoulder of the lateral chain extending from the Roche Château Bourreau towards St Michel. From Le Thyl the path descends, having ceased to be flanked by practicable ground after leaving the neighbourhood of La Traverse. Beyond this last village, which is also the termination of the ascent, no enemy could easily collect in any force on the mountain-sides above the road. The perpendicular elevation of La Traverse above the Arc is probably about 1500 feet.

Now the features of the country in the neighbourhood of the 'strong white rock,' as deduced from the narrative of Polybius, are:

(1) A difficult and precipitous ravine, through which the road must pass.

This is found in the defile of La Porte, a narrow passage to which the expressions χαράδρα, and φάραγξ δύσβατος καὶ κρημνώδης, are perfectly applicable.

(2) A range of acclivities overlooking the road, and liable to be swept, in one or more places, by rocks set in motion from above.

For about three miles, from St Martin to La Traverse, the road is flanked by acclivities, a considerable part of which, as mentioned just above, might be swept by rolling rocks.

(3) A large extent of practicable ground above these acclivities.

This has been already shewn to be the case in the description of the country.

(4) A position on this ground, at some distance from the road, where 20,000 men could be stationed, so as to protect completely the flank of an army marching along the road beneath, and such as would not expose themselves to be attacked at any serious disadvantage, by an enemy lying beyond them relatively to the road.

The position indicated in the Plan would be such a position. A line extending across the back of the Ridge

of Baune, through the village called Le Mollard, would
not be exposed to attack at any important disadvantage
from the side of Plan Villard.   The continuation of this
line through Villard Putier, and along the Terrace of La
Traverse, would also be exposed to no serious danger of
attack from above, if the position were held by a sufficient
force.   The whole length of this position, from behind La
Traverse to the gorge on the west of the Ridge of Baune,
would exceed two miles, and might well require 20,000
men for its occupation.   The whole length of the road
from St Martin to La Traverse is, it will be at once seen,
completely protected by it.   Its distance from the road is
also considerable, being, except near La Traverse, more
than a mile.

When Hannibal had broken up his encampment in the
neighbourhood of Allevard, he proceeded on his march for
three days without experiencing any hindrance, but was
attacked on the fourth day at the Rock of Baune.   The
third night would probably have been spent at St Jean de
Maurienne.   On the first night after leaving Allevard, he
would reach the neighbourhood of Chamoux; on the
second, that of La Chapelle.   Now the entrance of the
valley of the Arc is at La Croix d'Aiguebelle: at this point
Hannibal would, in all probability, leave the country of the
Allobroges, and enter that of another tribe[1].   Accordingly,
we find that it was on the evening of the first day's march,
or the morning of the second day's march, that Hannibal
met the deputation of the Alpine Gauls; so that the first
night would naturally have been spent upon their frontier,
which they might either have crossed to meet Hannibal, or
else have awaited his arrival within their borders.   As the
night, passed by the Carthaginians near Chamoux, was the
third after the capture of Allevard, ample time would have
been given for the news of the defeat of the Allobroges to
have reached the Lower Maurienne, especially if the intel-

---

[1] The lower valley of the Arc seems to have been inhabited, in the
time of the Romans, by a tribe called Garoceli or Medulli.

ligence was brought by fugitives across the mountains.
The approach of the Carthaginians might easily have been
known at St Jean de Maurienne, probably the chief town
of the tribe, in the middle of the day during which Hannibal remained at Allevard.   On that day the Gauls might
have determined on their measures, and resolved to send
the deputation to meet Hannibal.   The following day
Hannibal began his march from Allevard, and the Gallic
deputation, probably, left St Jean.   On the evening of the
same day, the Gauls and Carthaginians perhaps met near
Chamoux, about 27 English miles from St Jean de Maurienne, and 14 from Allevard; or else, as seems more probable, the conference may have taken place on the following
morning.   At this meeting a treaty was made between the
two parties, and Hannibal began to enter into the lower
valley of the Arc, the territory of the Gallic tribe whose
envoys he had received.

In two days more Hannibal reached St Jean de Maurienne; and, on the morning of the fourth day after
leaving Allevard, began his march from St Jean through
St Julien towards the defile of La Porte.   A band of Gauls
led the way in the van, and other bands followed in the
rear, where a large number of men was now collected.
The gathering together of these last bands had made
Hannibal extremely suspicious of the intentions of the
Gauls, and he therefore placed his heavy infantry in the
rear, to repel any attack in that quarter.   His apprehen-
sions for the safety of the van of his army do not seem to
have been great.   Perhaps the band of Gauls which led the
way was a small one; and Hannibal would not have been
able to see that there were others, as was probably the
case, waiting to join them on the heights towards the Col des
Encombres.   Had all the Carthaginian infantry been in the
van and centre, and the baggage and cavalry in the rear, the
line of march might have been cut through by an attack
from the heights of Baune and La Traverse, the van of the
army isolated from the rear, if not overwhelmed, and all
the cavalry and baggage probably taken or destroyed.

The result of the attack was not, however, so disastrous
to the Carthaginians.   When the Gauls at length fell upon

the rear, which they probably did between St Julien and St Martin de la Porte, they were able to make no impression on the heavy infantry of Hannibal. The valley is here open, though rather broken and irregular; so that the heavy infantry would fight at no great disadvantage on account of the ground, while their superior weapons and military skill would be sufficient to turn the scale in their favour. The position they took up would perhaps be a little to the east of a small hamlet called Crozat. Here their left might rest on the Arc, and their right upon the side of a mountain rising in sheer precipices, along which it would be impossible for an enemy to move and turn their position. Drawn up thus across the valley, they would resist with success all the efforts of the Gauls in the rear.

While the Carthaginians thus repulsed the enemy upon their rear, the leading columns, composed of cavalry and baggage-animals, were destroyed by an attack on their flank. How far the Gauls allowed the Carthaginians to proceed along the mountain-road between St Martin and La Traverse is uncertain. All that left St Martin were probably overwhelmed, either crushed beneath rocks rolled down the steep declivities, or killed by great stones, which the Gauls, descending the more gentle slopes, would be enabled to hurl at them from a distance of a few yards. The rest of the horses and other animals would be obliged to remain at St Martin de la Porte, until the passage of the defile, and the road along the mountains, could be made secure.

The safety of the rear being by this time assured, Hannibal was enabled to execute in person an attack upon the heights near the defile of La Porte. An attack directed immediately upon the defile was not likely to have been attended with success, the 'Porte' being merely a narrow gap in a very steep ridge. The first point to be captured would be the ground about the village of Baune, where the arm of the ridge, which forms the Heights of the Chapel and the Rock of Baune, branches off from the main heights. Though it is a continuous ascent from St Martin to Baune, yet the ground is not difficult, and Hannibal's

light infantry, being in great force, would eventually succeed, though not without loss, in driving back the Gauls.
The capture of Baune would give Hannibal possession of
the Rock of Baune and the Heights of the Chapel; for
neither of these positions, lying below Baune, could be
defended against a superior force with any chance of success.
The Gauls, who had previously held them, would be
obliged to retreat in the first instance to Villard Bernond,
and then to Villard Putier or La Traverse; for Villard
Bernond lies below Baune, and the gully in front of it
would not be a sufficient protection against the Carthaginians. The Gauls, whom Hannibal had driven from
Baune would probably retire towards Le Mollard.

The capture of Baune would ensure a safe march for
the rest of the army from St Martin to the gully. To
protect the rest of the line of road, from the gully near
Villard Bernond to La Traverse and Le Thyl, the possession of the Terrace of La Traverse is also necessary. The
way to carry this terrace from Baune seems evident. It
would be necessary to advance along the Ridge of Baune
as far as the neighbourhood of Le Mollard, then to cross
the gully, not difficult of passage in this place, to Villard
Putier, and finally to march from Villard Putier towards
La Traverse, thus taking possession of the Terrace. To
this movement from Baune, the Gauls could have offered
no effectual opposition. They would have been obliged to
evacuate Le Mollard, Villard Putier, and La Traverse, as
Hannibal approached, and retire towards the higher ground.
All the heights commanding the road having been thus
gained by the Carthaginians, Hannibal would encamp
along the line represented in the Plan, having the Gauls
above him, and completely protecting the road beneath
from any attack on their part. In this position on the
heights, more, as already mentioned, than two miles in
length, the half of the Carthaginian army may be supposed
to have been stationed.

By the time the heights had been carried, the evening
had probably almost fallen: but Hannibal did not wait for
day to withdraw the rest of his army from the valley to the
high ground. During the night the Carthaginians passed

through the defile of La Porte, and by the morning of the
next day, but not before, they had all ascended to La
Traverse, the first columns having perhaps proceeded further
on their way.   The safety of the Carthaginians was now
assured : the Gauls had no longer any opportunity or incli-
nation of offering them further molestation, and retired
from the contest.   They may, perhaps, seeing their positions lost, have retreated in the night.   On the fifth day
Hannibal rejoined the rest of his army, and resumed
his march[1].

During the remainder of the march to the summit of
the pass, the mountaineers never attacked the Carthaginians in any force.   Small bands, watching their opportunity, fell at times upon the army at different points in
the line, and carried off part of the baggage.   Where the
elephants were found, no attack was ever made, their
appearance striking the Gauls with terror and astonish-
ment.   The march seems here to have lain (as might have
been anticipated when Hannibal was approaching towards
the summit of the pass) through a country thinly peopled,
and inhabited by a wild race of men.   There are indeed
plausible reasons for conjecturing, that these Gauls were
a different tribe from those who dwelt in the Lower Maurienne : for they appear to have had no share in the battle
of the Rock, nor to have had any previous acquaintance
with the Carthaginians, or connexion with the other
Gauls[2].

After the toils of the battle, and the subsequent night-
march or watch, the progress of the Carthaginians might
be expected to be a little retarded.   The evening and
night of the sixth day would probably be spent around
Modane : the seventh day would bring them to Bramans ;
and on the eighth night a large part of the army would

---

[1] The supposed scene of this contest, and of the operations connected
with it, is very well observed from the summit of the rock of Baune.

[2] This conjecture is probably well founded.   In the Roman times
the Upper Maurienne was inhabited by the Cottian Caturiges, whose
lowest village seems to have been Orelle, situated four miles above La
Traverse.   See below, Chap. xi.

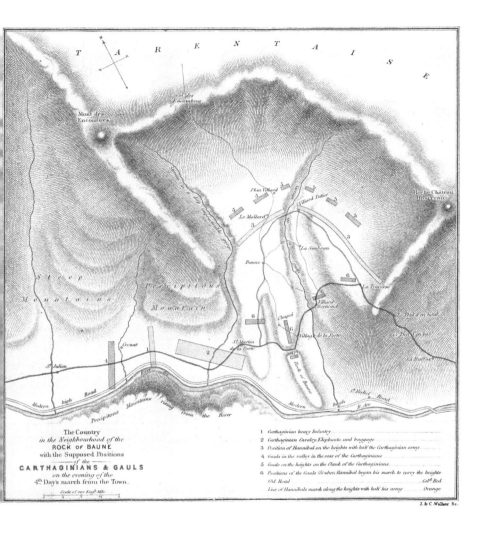

The Country
in the Neighbourhood of the
ROCK OF BAUNE
with the Supposed Positions
— of the —
CARTHAGINIANS & GAULS
on the evening of the
4th Day's march from the Town.

Scale of one Engl.h Mile

1 Carthaginian heavy Infantry
2 Carthaginian Cavalry, Elephants, and baggage
3 Position of Hannibal on the heights with half the Carthaginian army
4 Gauls in the valley in the rear of the Carthaginians
5 Gauls on the heights on the flank of the Carthaginians
6 Positions of the Gauls (5) when Hannibal began his march to carry the heights
Old Road . . . . Col.d Red
Line of Hannibals march along the heights with half his army . . . . Orange

J. & C. Walker Sc.

The material originally positioned here is too large for reproduction in this reissue. A PDF can be downloaded from the web address given on page iv of this book, by clicking on 'Resources Available'.

most likely have gained the summit of the Little Mont Cenis.   On the following morning the rear-guard would arrive, and all the army, with the exception of the stragglers who afterwards rejoined them, would have accomplished the ascent of the Alps.   The transactions which took place on the summit of the pass, and during the descent, will be considered in the next chapter.

CHAPTER VIII.

Application of the conditions deduced from Polybius' narrative to the route of the Mont Cenis concluded.—Encampment of Hannibal on the *Plateau of the Little Mont Cenis.*—Point from which the plains of Italy were most probably seen.—Precipitous character of the descent from the Mont Cenis into Italy.—Probable situation of the place where the path was destroyed.—Arrival at the commencement of the plains of Italy.—Siege and capture of Turin.

THE summit of the Mont Cenis has already been partly described. It consists of two large plateaux, between 6000 and 7000 English feet above the sea-level, surrounded by mountains elevated, in some instances, more than 4000 feet above the plateaux beneath. The longest of the two plateaux is that of the Great Mont Cenis, extending five miles in length from La Ramasse to La Grande Croix. On the left, towards the east or north-east, this plateau is bounded all the way by the bases of the mountains; on the right it is bounded, first by the mountains, then by the lake, and finally by a range of hills, running from the lake to the neighbourhood of La Grande Croix, and terminating towards the south in a precipice of great height, which rises from the little plain of St Nicholas. This latter plain lies about 500 feet below La Grande Croix, and is separated from it by the precipitous descent called the Fourmiguier. To the W. or S.W. of the lake, extends the plateau of the Little Mont Cenis, about three miles and a half in length, and bounded on both sides by ranges of mountains. The two plateaux form, in a manner, three of the arms of a cross, which meet in the lake. Besides these two plateaux, there is a small valley or hollow upon the mountain. It is enclosed between the hills which run from the lake to La Grande Croix, and the mountains on the west. A small stream flows down this valley into the lake. The path from the Col of the Little Mont Cenis, which is at the furthest extremity of the plateau of the same name, leads along the plateau nearly to the lake. It then turns to the right and follows the little valley behind the hills, which conducts it to a depression in that range of heights, through which it descends upon La Grande Croix, at the extremity of the plateau of the Great Mont Cenis.

The first condition relating to the summit of the pass is this:

V. A place suitable for the encampment of Hannibal's army must be found at the summit of the pass.

The plateau of the Little Mont Cenis perfectly satisfies this condition. Its great length and ample width would afford abundant room for the encampment.

The next condition is the following:

VI. From a point, probably not far from the road over the summit of the pass, but yet not upon the ground where the Carthaginians would encamp when they first reached the summit, the plains of the Po, and, in all probability, the Apennines also, ought to be visible.

The ground where the Carthaginians would encamp, when they first reached the summit of the pass, would be the plateau of the Little Mont Cenis. From thence no part of Italy, nor even any opening in the encircling ranges of mountains, can be perceived. It seems completely shut in by the Alps on every side. On leaving the plateau of the Little Mont Cenis for La Grande Croix, the path turns sharply to the right, and eventually passes over the hills often mentioned, at a point where there is a depression in the chain. Turning to the south, along the crest of the heights, from this point, so as to ascend out of the hollow through which the path runs, and thus arrive upon the long summit of the ridge, the traveller will gain a prospect of Italy in the course of some five minutes. The view is better seen from the southernmost extremity of these eminences, a walk of a few minutes further. The part of the hilly range from whence this prospect is gained, and which lies to the south of the depression through which the path runs, forms a ridge about half a mile in length, without any definite head rising above the general level of its summit. It presents a very steep slope towards La Grande Croix, and terminates, as before mentioned, above the plain of St Nicholas, in a very lofty precipice.

From the crest of this ridge it may be conjectured that Hannibal pointed out Italy to his army. Great numbers might have collected on the long summit, so that many hundreds of men might have looked upon Italy at once. There is no difficulty whatever in arriving here, and the view is seen from a point so close to the path, that the fact of such a prospect being visible could hardly be unknown to those who were acquainted with the pass. It is indeed only a very small portion of Italy that is descried; but the existence of any extensive prospect does not seem to be required by the narrative. In fact, if we suppose the action, intimated by the word ἐνδεικνύμενος, to have been a natural, and not merely an oratorical, gesture, we should be led to imagine that only a small part of the plains was visible; for to any very large expanse it would have been superfluous to direct attention. Besides, any prospect of Italy, however limited, would have been sufficient for Hannibal's purpose. It would have proved to the Carthaginians, by visible demonstration, that their extrication from the Alps was at hand, that the mountains were about to terminate, and that the plains of Italy were almost gained.

It is towards the S. E. that the view is open. The country seen would thus be the district to the east of the Po, and the south of the Tanaro, where the cities of Alba and Acqui are situated. This part of the plains is intersected by several ranges of hills, one of which may be discerned from the point of view on the Mont Cenis, even after the hazes, so prevalent in the plains of the Po during a great part of the day, especially in summer, have effaced the prospect of the flat country. In the extreme distance the chain of the Apennines closes the view, and would have offered to Hannibal, as previously explained, the means of indicating the position of Rome[1].

---

[1] Another point on the Mont Cenis, from which the plains of Italy are visible, is mentioned by M. Grosley, who wrote in the middle of the

On the morning of the ninth day the whole Carthaginian army had gained the summit of the Little Mont Cenis. During the remainder of that day, and during the following night, they remained encamped on the plateau of the Little Mont Cenis. On the morning of the tenth day Hannibal found them in a state of great despondency. One resource only, but that an effectual one, and such as could never have been anticipated by the Carthaginians, offered itself to Hannibal, as a means by which he could restore the courage and fortitude of his army. He had become aware, probably by the report of the Cisalpine Gauls who then accompanied him, and who had previously crossed the pass to meet him on the Rhone, that there was a point on the mountain, by the side of the path, some two or three miles from the plateau of the Little Mont Cenis, from which the plains of Italy could be discerned. To this point, accordingly, Hannibal led his army, or a part of it, and pointed out to them the plains of the Po, and the range of the Apennines, behind which, as he stated, lay the city of Rome itself. He dwelt also upon the friendly disposition towards them of the inhabitants of the country then lying beneath their feet, and succeeded eventually, to a certain extent, in dispelling the gloom which had fallen upon their spirits. By this movement to obtain the prospect of Italy, the position of the Carthaginian encampment on the tenth day would be a little altered from what

last century on the subject of Hannibal's route across the Alps. The passage is given by Ukert in his *Geographie*, II. 2. p. 600.

L'espèce de coupe que forme le plateau du Mont Cenis, est bordée de falaises très élevées, et ainsi il n'occupe pas, au pied de la lettre, le sommet de la montagne. C'est a mi-côté d'une de ces falaises, à la hauteur du Prieuré, qu'on découvre les plaines du Piémont, et c'est de là qu'Annibal put les montrer à son armée.

I believe this point of view to be a remarkable kind of shelf on the eastern side of the mountain which lies S. W. from the lake. It is easily recognized from the high road over the Mont Cenis. This shelf is distinctly seen, by the aid of a telescope, from La Loggia, a village about seven miles to the south of Turin. The path from the Little Mont Cenis runs at the base of the mountain, on the side of which it is situated. The ascent to the shelf is steep, and in time of snow almost, if not quite, impracticable.

it was on the ninth : for, from the summit of the hills
from which Italy was seen, it is not likely that the Carthaginians would have been led back to the plateau of the
Little Mont Cenis, but would rather have descended to
La Grande Croix.   On the tenth night the army probably
lay encamped on the eastern extremity of the plateau of
the Little Mont Cenis, around La Grande Croix at the
southern extremity of the plateau of the Great Mont Cenis,
and on the ground between these two positions.   On the
eleventh morning they began, from La Grande Croix, their
descent into Italy, and left the summit of the Mont Cenis,
on which they had spent two days and nights.

The accordance of the pass of the Mont Cenis with the
seventh condition, that ' The commencement of the plains
of Italy must be less than three days' march from the summit of the pass,' has already been shewn in an earlier
chapter (p. 72).   We pass on therefore to the eighth condition.

VIII.   The first part of the descent from the pass on
the Italian side must be of a precipitous character.

The precipitous character of the descent into Italy by
the old road over the Mont Cenis, has been already mentioned (p. 87).   It is one of the most remarkable features
of the pass, and is particularly noticed in many descriptions of it[1].   Between La Grande Croix, where the descent

---

[1] Enfin, à l'extrémité de la plaine est l'auberge de la *Grande-Croix*,
où les voyageurs s'arrêtent souvent pour se reposer ou se réchauffer.
C'est de là que commence la descente du côté du Piémont.   La pente
de l'ancien chemin qui passait par *Ferrières*, et aboutissait à la *Novalaise*,
où l'on faisait remonter les voitures, était si rapide, que plusieurs voyageurs ont fait la peinture la plus effrayante des dangers qu'elle présen-
tait.—Richard, *Guide en Savoie et en Piémont.*

Dalla Novalesa ultimo villaggio del Piemonte, tale era l'antica strada ;
per una rapida e spaventosa salita, a svolte serpeggianti si giungeva al
villaggio delle *Ferrières*, d'onde oltrepassato il piccolo piano di S. Niccolò
ove ancora si vedono i limiti che segnavano i confini della Savoia e del
Piemonte, montate le erte rampe a zig-zach dette il *Fourmiguier,* si veniva
alla Gran Croce, povero e scarso abituro, e traversatone il piano si met-
teva capo alla Ramassa, d'onde scorrendo pel dorso del monte si calava
a Lanslebourg.—*Itinerario Postale degli Stati Sardi.*

begins, and the village of La Novalèse, near which it terminates, the road falls, in the course of six miles, more
than 3600 feet; so that the rapidity of the descent must
necessarily be considerable and long-continued[1].
We now come to the ninth condition.

IX. At a place, within half a day's march from the
summit of the pass, on the Italian side, the path must lie
along a precipitous mountain-side, liable to be broken up
for a length of nearly 300 yards (English); and the country
in the vicinity should be of a nature adapted to Polybius'
account of the events which took place in the neighbourhood of the broken path.

A remarkable passage in a geographical work of the
last century seems to indicate clearly the situation of this
place, where Hannibal's path had been destroyed by a
landslip[2]. The passage in question runs thus[3]:

'From the inn, called La Grand' Croix, on account of
the wooden cross which stands by its side, and which forms
the boundary between Savoy and Piedmont, the descent
begins. On descending, there is found a plain, enclosed

M. Deluc also (*Histoire du Passage des Alpes par Annibal,* p. 280,)
notices the precipitous character of the descent from the Mont Cenis, a
circumstance which he brings forward as an argument *against* the supposition of Hannibal's having crossed this pass. See below, Chap. X.

[1] Height of La Grande Croix above the sea, 6211 English feet; of
La Novalèse, 2577.

[2] Büsching's Geography of Italy, enlarged and improved edition.
Venice, 1780. Vol. I. p. 78.

[3] Dall' osteria, detta *la Grand' Croix,* dalla croce di legno, che v'è
accanto, e che forma il confine tra la Savoja ed il Piemonte, incomincia
la scesa. Nello scendere ritrovasi una pianura rinchiusa fra' monti, detta
la Plaine de S. Nicola, passata la quale v'è una scesa, che tempo fà i
macigni, ed i sassi talmente rendevano impraticabile, che coloro, i quali
solevano portar in sedia i viandanti, eran costretti a scender da' sassi a
salti, come da tanti gradini. In questa discesa inevitabile, presso il Novalese nel Piemontese v'erano 3 o 4 luoghi, ove il sentiero fiancheggiato
da precipizj altissimi era strettissimo, e l'acque talmente aveano smosso
il terreno, che la sedia colla persona portatavi, per la metà pendeva in
aria sul precipizio. Ma sotto il regno di Emmanuele III. fu fatta una
strada nuova, ove non c'è pericolo alcuno; nondimeno v'è uno spazio di
circa 16 miglia, ove il passaggiero è obbligato a farsi portare in sedia.

by the mountains, called *La Plaine de S. Nicola;* this plain being passed, there is a descent, which, at one time, the stones and rocks rendered impracticable to such a degree, that those who were accustomed to transport travellers in chairs, were obliged to descend by leaping from rock to rock, as it were down so many steps. *Upon this inevitable descent, towards La Novalèse, there were three or four places, where the path, flanked by very lofty precipices, was exceedingly narrow, and the waters had broken away the ground to such an extent, that the chair, with the person carried in it, hung half in air over the precipice.* But under the reign of Emmanuel III. (1730—1773), a new road was made, upon which there is no longer any danger; nevertheless there is a distance of about sixteen miles where the traveller is obliged to be carried in a chair.'

This part of the old road is again referred to in the same work. It is said, in the description of La Ferrière, that the path leading down to La Novalèse was sometimes contracted by the precipices to a width of no more than one foot[1].

Here then we have direct evidence that, between La Ferrière and La Novalèse, the path over the Mont Cenis, a century ago, lay along a precipitous mountain-side liable to be broken up by the falling away of the ground. In the English translation of Büsching (London, 1762) it is mentioned that these three or four dangerous places were only a few paces in length: they would no doubt be the worst parts of the crumbling precipice, where it was not possible to construct any solid road.

The mule-road of Emmanuel III., a broad and strongly-constructed way, runs from La Ferrière to La Novalèse on the right bank of the Cenise: the old road, abandoned on account of the dangers caused by the landslips, ran on the left bank of the stream. This last path is still partially

---

[1] *Ferrière, Ferrera, o Ferrara,* borgo che giace alla metà della strada fra *la Grande Croix,* e la città di Novalese, cioè nelle falde del Monte Senis. La strada fra questo luogo, e fra Novalese in più luoghi è molto ristretta fra' dirupi, e passa talvolta in mezzo a' precipizj, che non lasciano più d'un piede di larghezza.

used by the inhabitants of the country. It is a distance of
about three miles from La Ferrière to La Novalèse. For
the first mile on the road there was no difficulty, or none
of any importance : but with the second mile the dangers
began. The Cenise had previously flowed through a series
of fields, at no great distance below the path. It now sank
in a narrow gorge, and left the path high above it, running
along the face of an abrupt declivity composed of earth
intermingled with rocks, and continually liable to crumble
away. Here the old road, still remaining, forcibly recalls
to mind the narrative of Polybius, where he relates how
Hannibal found his path destroyed by a landslip, and was
eventually obliged to reconstruct it, *by building up the precipice*. For the old road is here, in many places, supported
on terraces, such as Hannibal must have raised along the
mountain-side[1]. These have, however, fallen away in many
places, the path being now only partially used by the inhabitants, and having been long abandoned by travellers.
From the point where it first begins to skirt the precipice,
about a mile below La Ferrière, it runs nearly in a straight
line, gradually descending, for about three hundred yards.
It then meets with a gully, laying open the mountain-side,
and quite impassable where the path first encounters it, on
account of the sheerly precipitous character of its eastern
face. Repelled at this point, the path makes an angle,
and returns for above a hundred yards along the precipice
towards La Ferrière, thus gaining a lower level. It then
resumes its original direction, and, after a course of about
three hundred yards more, reaches the gully again, and
succeeds in crossing it. At the point where the gully is
crossed, and for a considerable distance beyond, the path,
never used now, is quite destroyed. Nothing but a mere
cattle track is left, though fragments of the old terrace-
walls may still be perceived where the path has been
destroyed. Proceeding towards La Novalèse, the mountain-side, though steep, becomes less precipitous, and the
path is well preserved. Rather more than half a mile
beyond the gully, the head of the valley of La Novalèse is

---

[1] See above, pp. 55—57.

reached, and another mile across the fields brings the
traveller to the village itself[1].

It would be on the first part of this descent that Hannibal's path was broken up. The length of the first arm
of the ancient zigzag road, about 300 yards, seems to
identify this part of the mountain-side with the crumbling
precipice, recently broken up, which Polybius mentions as
nearly a stadium and a half across. The whole of the
ground on the west of the gully was, in all probability,
more or less broken up by the landslip which had taken
place[2]. The distance from La Grande Croix to the commencement of this precipice is about four English miles.
It was, therefore, within half a day's march from the summit of the pass, the hamlet of La Grande Croix, at the
southern extremity of the plateau of the Mont Cenis, being
the point from which Hannibal commenced his descent.
The first part of Condition IX. is thus fully satisfied: the
latter part, relating to the events which took place in this
neighbourhood, now requires consideration.

These events have been already discussed (pp. 57—60).
When Hannibal first found that the path was destroyed, he
attempted to continue his march by taking a circuit. He
arrived however eventually, on making this attempt, upon
a very steep slope of old snow, thinly covered with snow
which had lately fallen. It has been conjectured above,
from this circumstance, and also because such a line
of descent would be natural, that Hannibal attempted to
bring his army down by some gully; for in such hollows
the old snow frequently lingers, when the ground in the
neighbourhood is quite clear. These gullies also form the
channels of avalanches, by which, on extraordinary occasions, old snow is sometimes found at a very low level, even
in the heat of summer. Such a circumstance may be

---

[1] The whole course of this ancient path is well seen from the later
mule-road. The old line of way may still be followed throughout on
foot, though with some little difficulty where the path has been destroyed.

[2] The cause of this landslip was, perhaps, the series of heavy rains,
which, as may be gathered from Livy's account of the swelling of the
'Druentia,' had prevailed in the Alps about three weeks before Hannibal
arrived at the broken path.

alluded to by Polybius in the words ἴδιον καὶ παρηλλαγμένον (Chap. 55), though it is not absolutely necessary to make such a supposition. For, although no permanent snow is now found anywhere near the path between La Ferrière and La Novalèse, or indeed upon any part of the Mont Cenis road; yet, in ancient times, the climate of Europe must have been much severer than it is at present, and permanent snow would have been found on the passes of the Alps at a considerably lower level than where it is now met with. Indeed, we should be led to conclude, from what Polybius says, not only that the summits of the passes were continually covered with snow, but that the fields of snow even reached half-way down the declivities, on both sides of the Alpine passes, towards the level country; so that not only patches of snow might be found at a considerable distance below the summits of the passes, but even the great snow-field itself may have extended to a distance of several thousand feet below the present line of perpetual snow[1]. It seems, however, necessary to understand these statements of Polybius with some modification, and to suppose that he speaks, not of fields of snow, but rather of isolated patches, which are found, at the present day, in many instances, two or three thousand feet below the snow-line, and, in some places, even more[2].

It may thus be supposed, without violating probability, that, at the time of Hannibal's descent, the gully on the precipitous way between La Ferrière and La Novalèse was filled with old snow, compact and hard; and that fresh snow may have lain upon it to the depth of a few inches. Now, if all the ground to the west of the gully was broken up, but the path, as appears to have been the case, remained uninjured on the east of the gully; then the way by which Hannibal would naturally have attempted to

---

[1] Τῶν γὰρ Ἄλπεων τὰ μὲν ἄκρα καὶ τὰ πρὸς τὰς ὑπερβολὰς ἀνήκοντα τελέως ἄδενδρα καὶ ψιλὰ πάντ᾽ ἐστὶ διὰ τὸ συνεχῶς ἐπιμένειν τὴν χιόνα καὶ θέρους καὶ χειμῶνος, τὰ δ᾽ ὑπὸ μέσην τὴν παρώρειαν ἐξ ἀμφοῖν τοῖν μεροῖν ὑλοφόρα καὶ δενδροφόρα καὶ τὸ ὅλον οἰκήσιμά ἐστιν.

[2] On the subject of the greater severity of the climate of Europe in ancient times, see Gibbon's *Roman Empire*, Chap. IX., and Arnold's *History of Rome*, Vol. III. p. 89, and Note M, p. 485. See also below, Chap. X.

rejoin the path where it was undestroyed, would have been down the gully itself. From the point where the path from La Ferrière first begins to run along the precipice, it would not be very difficult, (for men alone it would be easy) to pursue a directly straight course (represented by the broken line in the sketch) as far as the gully. A great part of the ground which would be traversed is now covered with grass, and quite unlike the crumbling face of the precipice beneath. Hannibal's army however could not cross the gully, for its eastern face is quite precipitous, but would be obliged to attempt to descend by its channel. The calamitous results which Polybius mentions would then naturally follow. For the fresh snow, which, by its yielding character, seemed to give a firm hold to the foot which penetrated it, was only a few inches in depth, and had not adhered to the hard snow beneath. This hard snow the feet of the men did not penetrate; they slipped and fell, attempted in vain to save themselves by clinging to some support, probably to their companions, rolled down the snow with whatever they had clung to, and were lost down the precipices. The animals, however, heavily laden, struck their feet into the old snow in their efforts to save themselves when they slipped, and remained fixed without the power of extricating themselves, being held fast by the tenacity of the hard-compacted snow. Hannibal, seeing from these misfortunes that it would be impossible to effect his descent, excepting by the line of the old road which had been destroyed, abandoned his attempt to descend by the gully, and determined to reconstruct the broken path.

When Hannibal had thus relinquished his first project, ἐστρατοπέδευσε περὶ τὴν ῥάχιν, διαμησάμενος τὴν ἐπ᾽ αὐτῇ χιόνα, he encamped about the back (or crest) of the ridge, having cleared away the snow from it[1]. Now the descent from the plain of St Nicholas to the head of the valley of La Novalèse is effected down a steep hollow, sloping to the east, and bounded on the north and south by very lofty mountains. This hollow, however, is not single, but is

---

[1] See above, p. 59.

divided into two minor parallel hollows by a ridge extending from west to east, and originating a little below the plain of St Nicholas. In the northern of these hollows flows the Cenise ; in the southern, and at a distance of about half a mile from the Cenise, runs a small rill of water, which joins the Cenise near La Novalèse. It seems probable that it is this ridge, which is alluded to by Polybius under the name of the ῥάχις. Its crest or back, at its eastern extremity, is a nearly level tract of ground, raised on very high precipices above the valley of La Novalèse, and having on one side the deep gorge of the Cenise, where the path was destroyed, and on the other a very steep gully, through which the rill of water, previously mentioned, falls down into the valley beneath[1]. This tract of ground is now almost entirely covered with great blocks of rock, the results, apparently, of some mountain-fall. These heaps would at present disqualify it from being the site of an encampment ; but their fall may have been subsequent to the time of Hannibal. The fields through which the Cenise flows, between La Ferrière and the commencement of the broken precipice, would have afforded in themselves a considerable space of ground for the encampment. Yet the whole army could hardly have found sufficient room here, so that Hannibal would have been obliged to pitch part of his camp on the ridge to the south of these fields. If there were no heaps of fallen rocks at that time on the ground at the eastern extremity of the ridge, it would be there that the most eligible position would have been found for a part of the camp.

In one day, the path which Hannibal constructed along the precipice, by means of terraces, was sufficiently wide and strong for the passage of the horses and baggage-animals. They were immediately brought down from the encampment above, another encampment was made below, on ground perfectly free from snow, and the animals were then left to find pasturage for themselves in the country round. This second encampment would be made near La

---

[1] When Hannibal attempted to descend by taking a circuit, he may possibly have tried to bring his army down by this gully. The gully, however, on the broken precipice itself, seems the more likely place.

Novalèse, immediately at the foot of the precipitous and broken descent; and in the broad fields at the head of this open valley, the animals would be let loose, and left to seek the fodder, of which they were so greatly in need. The upper and lower encampments would probably be less than two miles apart; and that near La Novalèse would be in sight of the one above.

On the evening of the thirteenth day, the road was completed for the passage of the elephants, who were by this time almost starved[1]. They were accordingly brought down, and the whole army was again collected together. In two days more the Carthaginians reached Avigliana, at the commencement of the plains of Italy. The tenth and last condition relates to this point in the route, where the Alpine march was at last brought to a conclusion.

X. The plains, into which the road over the pass enters, when it emerges from the mountains on the side of Italy, must anciently have been inhabited by the Taurini.

Avigliana is generally identified with the 'Ad fines' of the Roman Itineraries, the boundary between the district of the Taurini and the Cottian tribe of the Segusini. Hannibal would therefore be, at Avigliana, on the frontier of the Taurini, and at the commencement of the plains which they occupied.

No part of Hannibal's passage of the Alps was attended with such disasters as the descent into Italy. Although the Carthaginians encountered no hostility on the part of the inhabitants, (for the furtive aggressions mentioned by Polybius seem to have been too insignificant to merit such a name,) yet their losses, in consequence of the snow and the precipitous character of the descent through the uninhabited country, were nearly as great as they were upon the ascent from the banks of the Isère to the summit of the pass. Between La Grande Croix and La Novalèse, a distance of only six miles, nearly 10,000 men, or one-fourth of the whole army which encamped on the summit of the

---

[1] It should seem that fodder might have been brought up to the elephants from below. Nothing of the kind however is mentioned by Polybius.

mountain, must have perished without meeting a living enemy. Nothing but the extremely precipitous character of the descent from the Mont Cenis can explain this enormous loss. Whole hosts, indeed, must have been destroyed by the precipices of the Fourmiguier, between La Grande Croix and the plain of St Nicholas. All this abrupt declivity, probably some 500 feet in perpendicular elevation, would have been, at the time of Hannibal's passage, completely covered by the snow, which had lately fallen, and beneath which the path was lost. A vast and trackless precipice of snow, which there was no possibility of avoiding, presented thus the only way by which the army could descend. On this slippery declivity, nothing that fell escaped destruction. Multitudes must have been carried down the precipice, before the survivors succeeded in reaching the plain of St Nicholas. On the descent from this plain, similar losses, but probably on a much smaller scale, would have been experienced. The army, however, it is said, bore all these disasters with fortitude, because they had already encountered calamities of a like nature. Perhaps, on the steep ascent to the Col of the Little Mont Cenis, the path may have been partially concealed by the snow, and some losses have ensued in consequence. It was, however, the fresh snow which seems to have fallen while they remained for two days on the summit of the pass, by which the dangers of the descent were so terribly increased.

At length the progress of the Carthaginians was completely arrested. The path by which they hoped to have descended had been destroyed by a landslip, and they found themselves condemned, in their reduced and starving condition, to fix their encampment in the midst of the snow. Their despair at this calamity, and the bold, and, as it might seem at first, the even rash attempt of Hannibal to bring the army down by a new and untrodden route, can readily be understood. They looked down on the broad fields of La Novalèse immediately below them. No snow was there to be seen, and no danger or difficulty was afterwards to be encountered. Could they but succeed in effecting this last descent, all their calamities and privations would be at once greatly mitigated, if not entirely terminated. To gain this end, it was well to risk the dangers of an uncertain descent, before embracing the only alternative which remained, of halting amidst the snow, till the broken path could be reconstructed.

This latter course, however, was found inevitable ; and it was only on the thirteenth evening that the elephants descended to La Novalèse, where all the army was again collected together. No events of importance characterized the rest of the march to the plains of Italy. Indeed, no effectual opposition could have been offered to Hannibal here, on account of the nature of the country. For the valley of the Dora, below Susa, is perfectly open : there are no defiles which might be defended, or which would offer opportunities for any serious attack. On the fourteenth night, Hannibal would probably reach the neighbourhood of the village of S. Giorio, and on the fifteenth, all the army would encamp, at the foot of the Alps, about Avigliana. Here Hannibal remained for some time, during which his exhausted forces recovered their strength and condition. He then advanced into the plains and laid siege to Turin, (16 Roman miles from Avigliana[1]) the chief town of the Taurini, who had rejected his overtures of amity and alliance. After three days' siege, the town was taken and all that offered opposition put to the sword. This example of severity brought all the neighbouring people to Hannibal's feet. The other Gallic tribes, also, who inhabited the plains, shewed themselves favourably inclined to the Carthaginian alliance ; and Hannibal prepared to advance, and strike some great blow, which might fix them permanently to his side, and induce them to join with him in attempting the overthrow of Rome.

---

[1] In the Roman Itineraries, one measurement (that generally adopted) gives 24 miles as the distance from *Segusio* to *Ad Fines,* and 16 miles as the distance from *Ad Fines* to *Augusta Taurinorum.* Another measurement gives 33 (a plain mistake for 23) miles in the first instance, and 18 in the second. If Avigliana stands accurately on the site of *Ad Fines,* the latter (corrected) measurement would perhaps be nearest the truth. By the roads of 1839, according to the Sardinian Itinerary published in that year, the distance from Turin to Avigliana is $9\frac{3}{4}$ Piedmontese miles ($16\frac{1}{4}$ Roman miles); and the distance from Avigliana to Susa is 12 Piedmontese miles ($20\frac{1}{2}$ Roman miles.)

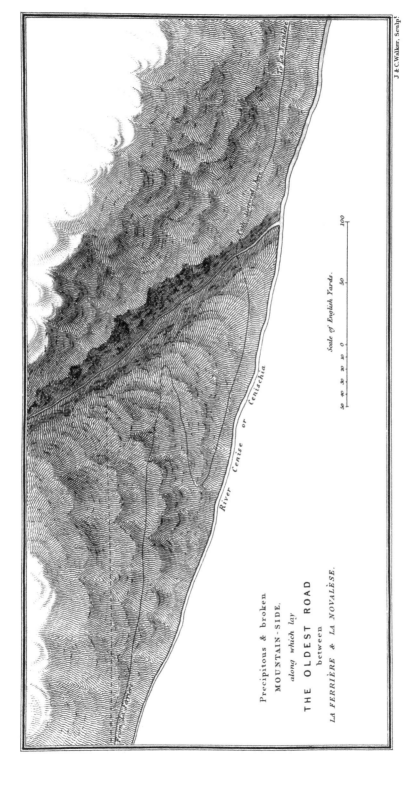

Precipitous & broken
MOUNTAIN - SIDE,
along which lay
THE OLDEST ROAD
between
LA FERRIÈRE & LA NOVALÈSE.

River Cenise or Cenischia

Scale of English Yards.

100   50   0   10 20 30 40 50

J & C.Walker, Sculpt.

CHAPTER IX.

IT will not be necessary to examine Livy's account of Hannibal's passage of the Alps at the same length as that of Polybius, the greater importance and accuracy of the Greek narrative being sufficiently evident. Indeed, Livy had none of the peculiar advantages of Polybius. He flourished about a century and a half after the earlier historian, and had therefore no communication with the contemporaries of the expedition. Neither had he examined the scene of Hannibal's passage, as Polybius had, but appears ignorant, not only of that particular pass, but also of the general nature of the Alpine country. The authority of Livy's narrative is also much weakened by his extremely careless mode of composition. He seems to have collected his materials from various sources, and then to have reported them almost in their crude state, without examining their bearing on one another or digesting them into a consistent story. He also relates some events of a strange and improbable nature, and is glaringly incorrect with respect to dates. Carelessness and love of the marvellous are the chief causes of his errors; his aim is to produce effect, rather than to ensure accuracy and truth.

Notwithstanding, however, Livy's faults, his narrative cannot be totally disregarded, or set aside as entirely false. Some true materials must be worked up in it. Indeed, the chief materials are clearly furnished by Polybius, though some additional and independent matter is introduced. A part, at least, of this additional matter, is probably authentic, however disfigured and alloyed by carelessness and extravagance. But, although whatever is clearly extravagant must be either rejected or modified, and whatever contradicts Polybius must be set aside, a considerable part of the history will still be left, and cannot well be neglected. A body of new facts will thus be obtained. Yet, even with respect to these facts, further precautions may be necessary; for, in the case of such a writer as Livy, the arrangement of his materials, even when the facts they contain may be true, is very likely to be faulty, and may demand re-adjustment. When the materials, on which a history is founded, are collected from various quarters, and arranged by a careless historian, it is not unreasonable to imagine that they may sometimes be wrongly disposed, and that the order in which events actually happened may thus be inverted. The first passage in Livy which will require consideration seems to be vitiated by an error of this nature, and is inexplicable as it stands. In examining his account, it will be necessary partly to undo what he has done; to resolve his ill-digested narrative into its component parts, and to arrive in this manner, through the history, at a knowledge of the materials from which it has been made up.

There seems to be nothing that calls for notice in Livy's account of the expedition, until he brings the Carthaginians to the district called the Island. The river designated by Livy the Arar, Bisarar, or Isara, is no doubt the modern Isère. Hannibal, having crossed the Rhone near Orange, would find himself, after his passage, in the country occupied in the Roman times by the Cavares, and a few miles from the southern frontier of the Tricastini. Marching subsequently up the Rhone through the country of the Tricastini and Sego-vellauni or Segalauni, he would arrive at the Isère, the boundary of the district called the Island. The Segalauni are not mentioned by Livy: they are perhaps included by him among the Tricastini. Both these tribes are included by Strabo among the Cavares[1]: it is by Ptolemy that they are mentioned as distinct tribes[2]. These three tribes occupied the level country along the Rhone from the Durance to the Isère. On their east, and extending in like manner from the Durance to the Isère, the Vocontii lived among the Alps bordering on the plain.

---

[1] Lib. IV.   [2] Lib. II.

Vaison[1] and Die[2] were two of their towns; and their territory along the Durance reached, according to Strabo[3], as far as Embrun, where the Cottian land began. Among the Vocontii must therefore be comprised a tribe called the Caturiges, one of whose towns was Caturiges, or Caturigæ, now Chorges. It is necessary to distinguish this tribe carefully from the Cottian Caturiges, who bordered on the Salassi. Some other small tribes may also have been included among the Vocontii. The eastern, or north-eastern, boundary of the Vocontii seems to have been the river Drac. Their frontier could not well have been far from that river, on whichever bank it may have lain.

Before proceeding further with the consideration of Livy's narrative, it will also be advisable to define, in this place, the position of two other tribes, the Medulli and Tricorii. The Medulli are mentioned in the list, given by Pliny, of the Alpine tribes subdued by Augustus (Hist. Nat. III. 20.)[4] Their name occurs there between the Acitavones and the Uceni. Now the Acitavones seem clearly to be the same tribe as the Centrones. For the name of the Centrones does not appear in the list, and the name of the Acitavones is found where that of the Centrones, who dwelt in the Tarentaise, should occur; (i. e.) after the Nantuates, Seduni, Veragri, and Salassi. The Uceni inhabited the Pays d'Oysans, the valley of the Romanche. The Medulli would thus naturally be sought between the Tarentaise and the Pays d'Oysans, (i.e.) in the Maurienne. According to Ptolemy[5], they lived above the Allobroges, a statement which would also fix them in the Maurienne, or, at any rate, the Lower Maurienne, as being the only district bordering on the territory of the Allobroges not

---

[1] Ptol. Lib. II.   [2] Dea Vocontiorum.   [3] Lib. IV.

[4] Gentes Alpinæ devictæ: Triumpilini, Camuni, Vennonetes, Isarci, Breuni, Naunes, Focunates; Vindelicorum gentes quatuor, Consuanetes, Virucinates, Licates, Catenates, Abisontes, Rugusci, Suanetes, Calucones, Brixentes, Lepontii, Viberi, Nantuates, Seduni, Veragri, Salasi, Acitavones, Medulli, Uceni, Caturiges, Brigiani, Sogiontii, Ebroduntii, Nemaloni, Edenates, Esubiani, Veamini, Gallitæ, Triulatti, Ectini, Vergunni, Eguituri, Nementuri, Oratelli, Nerusi, Velauni, Suetri.

[5] Lib. II.

occupied by some other tribe. We should be led also, from Strabo's account[1], to place the Medulli in the Maurienne. 'Above the Cavares,' Strabo says, 'are the Vocontii, the Tricorii, the Iconii, the Medulli.' He states again further on; 'Beyond the Vocontii are the Siconii, the Tricorii, and beyond these the Medulli, who inhabit the most lofty mountains.' This description again tends to fix the Medulli in the Maurienne, the Iconii or Siconii being probably the Uceni. The position of the Medulli being thus ascertained, that of the Tricorii is easily found. They dwelt between the Vocontii and the Medulli, bordering also, in all probability, upon the Uceni. Their territory would thus lie to the east of the Drac, and would extend towards the Lower Maurienne and the Pays d'Oysans. How far they reached to the south is uncertain; perhaps about as far as the present boundary of the department of the Isère.

The Medulli, then, were the inhabitants of the Lower Maurienne[2]. The Upper Maurienne, it will afterwards appear, was occupied by another tribe. The Tricorii dwelt to the south-west of the Medulli, and to the south of the

----

[1] Lib. IV.

[2] The mountains of the Maurienne are very high; a century ago, they were thought, erroneously, to be the highest of the Alps. Büsching says that "in Maurienne, more than in any other part (i.e. of the Alps) are found mountains of immense height." This agrees with what Strabo says of the position of the Medulli.

Strabo speaks also in this place of a pass from the country of the Medulli into that of the Taurini; but his account is very deficient in accuracy. The pass, however, which he speaks of, seems clearly to be that of the Little Mont Cenis. The length of the ascent, he says, is stated to be 100 stadia; and the descent to the frontiers of Italy is said to be of the same length. Now the valley of the Arc is left, and the ascent to the Little Mont Cenis begins, at Bramans; from which place to Susa, the frontier town of Italy, (it is named as such in the Itinerary from Bourdeaux to Jerusalem) the distance is very nearly 200 stadia, the lake on the summit of the Mont Cenis being about half-way. Indeed, as will afterwards be shewn, the distance from Bramans to Susa, by the Little Mont Cenis, is given in the Peutingerian Table as 25 Roman miles, or exactly 200 stadia.

The great lake which Strabo mentions must be that on the Mont Cenis. The exaggeration, by which this small lake is spoken of as a

country of Allevard, and extended probably to Grenoble and the river Drac.

Having followed up the Rhone, and arrived on the banks of the Isère, Hannibal reached the confines of the district called the Island. Livy's account of the transactions in this country rather differs from that of Polybius. According to Livy, Hannibal was chosen as arbitrator between the two brothers who were contending for the sovereignty; while Polybius states that the assistance of the Carthaginians was requested by the elder brother alone, and that the younger brother was expelled in consequence of Hannibal's joining his forces with those of the elder. The discrepancy, however, is of no importance with regard to the present question.

Livy calls the inhabitants of the Island, Allobroges. They were such in his time, but not in that of Hannibal, as is perfectly clear from the narrative of Polybius. Livy indeed says at first, with respect to the Island, that the Allobroges live near it. He should have said that they lived near it in the time of Hannibal. It was subsequent to that period that the Island was comprised in the territory of the Allobroges, their name being probably applied in the course of time to all the tribes they absorbed in succession[1].

---

great one, may lead us to infer that Strabo was not personally acquainted with this country. Gray, however, in his letters, speaks of the lake on the Mont Cenis as a 'great lake.' Considering its position, it perhaps is so. It is also a great inaccuracy to speak of the sources of the Durance and the Dora Baltea, the Salassian Dora, as being near one another, and on the same mountain as the lake. Strabo has probably confounded with one another the Dora Susina and the Dora Baltea, and combined together, as if the two were but one pass, the features of the Mont Cenis and the Mont Genèvre. As both these roads cross the Cottian Alps, unite at Susa, and lead into the country of the Taurini, the mistake may have occurred. A similar error, as will afterwards appear, is made in the Peutingerian Table, the 'Alpis Cottia' and the 'Alpes Cottiæ' being there confounded. It is perhaps from this lake, the 'Ceann-uisg,' or 'river-head,' that the pass has taken the name of the Mont 'Cenis.'

[1] Something analogous to the probable extension of the name of the Allobroges may perhaps be found in the case of the modern Switzerland, the district so called originally comprising scarcely more than one-half of the present Canton of Schwyz.

The account which Livy gives of the march of Hannibal from the Island to the Alps is attended with considerable difficulty : indeed, as previously mentioned, it is inexplicable without alteration. The passage runs thus: ' Sedatis certaminibus Allobrogum, cum jam Alpes peteret, non recta regione iter instituit, sed *ad lævam* in Tricastinos flexit; inde per extremam oram Vocontiorum agri tendit in Tricorios, haud usquam impedita via priusquam ad Druentiam flumen pervenit.'

When Hannibal had arranged the affairs of the Island, (the inhabitants of which Livy here erroneously calls Allobroges,) he would resume his march to the Alps, as we have previously concluded from Polybius, from the confluence of the Rhone and the Isère. But if from this point he turned to the left, he would be going away from, instead of approaching, the country of the Tricastini. Besides, if Hannibal struck into the territory of the Tricastini, and then proceeded along the Vocontian frontier till he reached the Tricorii, his movements would be quite inexplicable. He would, on this supposition, have retraced his steps down the Rhone, or nearly so, and then have gained the country of the Tricorii by the very circuitous route of Vaison, the Durance, and the valley of the Drac: for it was along the Vocontian frontier, and not through the Vocontian territory, that Hannibal directed his march towards the Tricorii. It is quite clear that this route is inadmissible, and that Livy's account is erroneous.

A single correction, however, grounded on the conclusions previously drawn from Livy's character, seems to remove the difficulty. All the facts in the passage cited are true, but one of them is misplaced. The transactions at the Island occurred, not before, but after, the passage through the country of the Tricastini. When Hannibal had crossed the Rhone, he had the Alps immediately before him: their passage was the next act of the expedition: then it was ' cum jam Alpes peteret.' Now had he made directly for the mountains, he would have gone to the east. This, however, he did not do: 'non recta regione iter instituit.' Instead of proceeding in this direction, Hannibal, being then near Orange, almost on the northern frontier of the Cavares, 'ad lævam in Tricastinos flexit,' turned to the left (the north) into the country of the Tricastini, and thus arrived, marching along the side of the Rhone, at the point where the Isère joins it. The disputes of the men of the Island were then settled, and the march resumed from the confluence of the two rivers. 'Inde per extremam oram Vocontiorum agri tendit in Tricorios,' he directed his march along the left bank of the Isère, the northern boundary of the Vocontian territory, and thus reached the country of the Tricorii, who dwelt beyond the Drac. This seems to be the course indicated by Livy as that which Hannibal followed. It is the same as that which has been deduced from Polybius, and is clearly the only route by which the statements of both historians can be reconciled[1].

Another difficulty now results from Livy's narrative. He speaks of the Durance (Druentia) as lying on Hannibal's way to the Alps. This, however, is not possible. In order to reach the Durance from the neighbourhood of Grenoble, Hannibal must have followed up the valley of the Drac, crossed the mountains to Gap, and thus arrived at the Durance. But, after crossing the Durance, Livy says that Hannibal's route lay through a country of a level character, which certainly would not be found beyond the Durance, or in the valley of that river. Neither could Hannibal arrive by this route in the country of the Allobroges, the first tribe, according to Polybius, by whom Hannibal was attacked. Livy does not, it is true, call this tribe Allobroges, but Polybius's authority is conclusive upon the subject, and Livy speaks of the attack as being subsequent to the passage of the Druentia.

There seems to be little doubt that Livy has made another error here, and has mistaken some river of similar name for the Durance; and, under the influence of this deception, has introduced the description he gives of the Durance, of which river it is a sufficiently correct account.

---

[1] It is conjectured by the author of *A Dissertation on the passage of Hannibal over the Alps, by a member of the University of Oxford,* (p. 95), that the text of Livy is corrupt in this place. There seems however no sufficient reason for adopting this supposition. The fault is Livy's, rather than his transcriber's. The text is probably correct, but the historian has fallen into an error.

Now the name Durance, a term of Celtic origin, is applied, under different forms, to more than one Alpine river[1]. In the Chablais and the Vallais, it occurs under the contracted form Dranse, a name so nearly resembling Drac, as to render it not improbable, that it was the Drac which was mistaken by Livy for the Durance[2]. The Roman name of the Drac is not known: but, as the word Drac, or Dur-ac, is unquestionably Celtic, the river must have borne among its inhabitants, in the Roman times, a name not greatly different from that which it bears at present, and therefore one having a considerable resemblance to Dranse and Durance. It is thus not unreasonable to suppose, that, misled by the similarity of names, Livy mistook, in the accounts given him, the Drac for the Durance, called in consequence the Drac, Druentia, and applied to it the description he gives, which he no doubt intended for the Durance. It will be seen at once, on reference to the map, that an army, marching up the left bank of the Isère into the country of the Tricorii, would find the Drac directly in their way. This river is at all times a considerable mountain-stream: when swollen with rain, as Livy states it to have been when Hannibal crossed it, the passage would have presented sufficient difficulty to be of the importance he assigns to it[3].

Having crossed the Drac, Hannibal's future march must have lain up the Graisivaudan; for, according to Livy, the country through which he passed was of a level character. 'Hannibal ab Druentia campestri maxime itinere ad Alpes cum bona pace incolentium ea loca Gallorum pervenit.' This cannot be said of the valley of the Drac or of the valley of the Romanche, through which lie the two routes to the Mont Genèvre. It was not then the Mont Genèvre which Hannibal crossed; but, as far as appears from this portion of the narrative, the Mont Cenis, or else the Great or Little St Bernard, all which passes

---

[1] The first syllable is the word 'dur' or 'dwr,' 'water.' The second element is found in the Anza, the name of the river of the Val Anzasca.

[2] Strabo calls the Dora Baltea, 'Δρουεντία,' Lib. V.

[3] The Drac, and the Druentia of Livy, have been previously concluded to be identical by M. Larauza. See Ukert's *Geographie*, Appendix on *Hannibal's Passage of the Alps*.

might be reached by the way of the Graisivaudan. But Hannibal eventually arrived, after crossing the Alps, according to Livy, as well as Polybius and Strabo, in the country of the Taurini; so that he must have passed the Mont Cenis, and not either of the St Bernards, both of the latter roads leading through the country of the Salassi into that of the Libui or Libicii.

After noticing the Tricorii, no proper names occur in Livy till the Taurini are mentioned. The historian loses himself among the Alps, a region of which he appears not only personally ignorant, but also to have failed in forming any tolerably accurate conception. Having brought the Carthaginians to the foot of the Alps, he speaks as if the view of the mountains had then for the first time burst upon them, and transplants the features of the high Alps to the country at the commencement of the mountains, which would have been of an entirely different character. 'Tum, quanquam fama prius, qua incerta in majus vero ferri solent, præcepta res erat, tamen ex propinquo visa montium altitudo nivesque cœlo prope immixtæ, tecta informia imposita rupibus, pecora jumentaque torrida frigore, homines intonsi et inculti, animalia inanimataque omnia rigentia gelu, cætera visu quam dictu fœdiora, terrorem renovarunt.' This description, eloquent and picturesque as it is, and however graphic it may still be[1], when applied to the high valleys in the Alps, is quite out of place where it stands.

Livy's account of the contest with the Allobroges, and the attack made upon Hannibal at the 'strong white rock' of Polybius, may be passed over. Polybius has clearly furnished here the main groundwork of the Latin narrative: and it would have been well if Livy had adhered more closely than he has done to his principal authority. For his accounts of both battles are very confused, and cannot be correct. His explanation of the separation of the Carthaginian army into two parts near the Rock is exceedingly faulty, and quite at variance with the narrative of Polybius, though clearly drawn from it. Livy does not seem to

---

[1] See Gray's *Letters.*

have understood how the separation of the army into two bodies could have ensured its safety. He therefore abandons his authority, and makes the Carthaginian line of march cut in two by the Gauls, who descend from the mountains into the valley, interpose themselves between the two divisions of the army which they have thus broken through, and remain in this position all night. Yet from this important stroke, which must inevitably have brought on a severe contest on the following day, nothing results; and the two divisions of the Carthaginian army are represented as being reunited on that day with little or no difficulty, the opposition of the Gauls being much relaxed. The heat of the conflict thus subsides, according to Livy, exactly at the time when it ought, as far as can be judged, to have risen to the highest pitch[1].

There must be considerable exaggeration in what Livy relates, of the Carthaginians having been led astray by their guides, and of their endeavouring to find a way for themselves, by following up certain valleys at random. The Cisalpine Gauls, who were with Hannibal, would have been able to act as guides to the Carthaginians sufficiently well to prevent them making any important deviations from the right course. In certain local difficulties they may, however, have had recourse to the inhabitants of the country, and have pressed some of them into their service as guides. By such guides, if they employed them, they might have been led a little out of their way in places; but that they should have gone astray to any important extent is not likely. As to their seeking a way for themselves by entering into different valleys on conjecture, the supposition is very improbable, and can hardly be entertained for a moment.

Livy's account of Hannibal's exhibiting to his soldiers, from the summit of the pass, the prospect of Italy, seems partially drawn from some other source than Polybius,

---

[1] Livy speaks of the first meeting with these Gauls, and their subsequent attack upon Hannibal, as if both events occurred on the same day, (i.e.) the fourth day after leaving the 'town.' He omits the two days of guidance mentioned by Polybius.

and presents us with some additional circumstances. Two days, Livy says, the Carthaginians remained encamped at the summit of the pass. With this circumstance Polybius supplied him: what next follows appears to have been derived from another quarter. At the first dawn of day (the narrative proceeds) the standards were advanced, (apparently leading the way down into Italy). The marching columns followed slowly and without spirit through the snow, while an expression of sluggish and hopeless dejection was stamped on the faces of all the men. Hannibal, seeing this, passed on before the standards, and ordered a halt to be made *at a certain promontory*, which commanded a very extensive view, and from whence he pointed out Italy to his soldiers[1]. 'Per omnia nive oppleta cum signis prima luce motis segniter agmen incederet, pigritiaque et desperatio in omnium vultu emineret, praegressus signa Hannibal *in promontorio quodam*, unde longe ac late prospectus erat, consistere jussis militibus Italiam ostentat subjectosque Alpinis montibus Circumpadanos campos, mœniaque eos tum transcendere non Italiæ modo sed etiam urbis Romanæ.'

The place from which it has been concluded that Hannibal pointed out Italy to his soldiers, has been already mentioned[2]. It is a narrow ridge about half a mile long, nearly level at the summit, and separated on the north from the rest of the hilly range to which it belongs by the hollow through which runs the road from the Little Mont Cenis. It presents a very steep slope towards the plain of La Grande Croix on the east, and terminates on the south, above the plain of St Nicholas, in a sheer precipice many hundreds of feet in height. An eminence of this kind is accurately defined as a promontory : and it is very remarkable, that the consideration of Polybius' narrative alone, who is quite silent as to the nature of the point from which Italy was seen, should have led to the conclusion, independently of Livy, that it was from this pro-

---

[1] This circumstance renders the adoption of any pass but the Mont Cenis irreconcileable with Livy's narrative.

[2] P. 115.

montory that Hannibal pointed out to his soldiers the plains of the Po.

According to Polybius, Italy was seen while the Carthaginians remained on the summit of the pass. According to Livy, it would appear that it was seen at the commencement of the descent. The conclusion, which has been drawn, that it was seen from the road, or close to the road, between the plateau of the Little Mont Cenis and La Grande Croix, reconciles this apparent disagreement. For the descent from this pass into Italy is considered to begin from La Grande Croix, all the ground above, though varying considerably in level, being included in the plateaux which form the summit of the Mont Cenis. Hannibal, therefore, when on the promontory, or at La Grande Croix, would still be correctly spoken of by Polybius as being on the summit of the pass. Yet he might naturally be mentioned by another author as having begun his descent, when on his way from the plateau of the Little Mont Cenis to La Grande Croix. For La Grande Croix is 600 feet below the Col of the Little Mont Cenis, and not less than 400 below the general level of that plateau; so that the route from the plateau of the Little Mont Cenis to La Grande Croix is, strictly speaking, a descent. It would be very singular, if the Mont Cenis were not the pass crossed by Hannibal, that it should afford so obvious and simple an explanation of what at first sight appears a direct contradiction between the two authors.

Livy has not observed, that, if the day on which Italy was seen be included among the days of descent, two days cannot be allowed for the encampment at the summit of the pass. He should therefore have diminished to one the two days he mentions, and which he found given in Polybius. By these means he would have made his narrative of the events at the summit of the pass quite consistent in itself, and completely in accordance, though at first sight apparently at variance, with the account of the Greek historian.

Livy's statement, that the descent from the Alps, on the side of Italy, is shorter and more rapid than it is on the other side, is quite correct. On the pass of the Mont

Cenis this is particularly remarkable; Susa being more than 5000 feet below either of the Cols of the Great or Little Mont Cenis.

In relating the events which occurred at the place where the path was destroyed, Livy has introduced some additional circumstances. It was by the falling away of the earth, Livy says, that the path was broken up. This is no doubt correct: but when he mentions that the effect of this landslip was to produce a precipice a thousand feet high, he has plainly fallen into an error by misinterpreting Polybius. The broken ground, along which the path ran, was a thousand feet *across*: the measurement has nothing to do with the height of the precipice, which the path skirted.

This precipice, along which the path lay, was, according to Livy, so steep, that a light-armed soldier could only manage with difficulty to accomplish the descent, by availing himself of the bushes and stumps which presented themselves here and there upon the declivity. The mountain-side between La Ferrière and La Novalèse, which has been previously mentioned as the place where Hannibal was most probably stopped, is a precipice of exactly this kind. There are several bushes scattered about its surface, by which an unencumbered man would be greatly assisted in an attempt to get down, and by the aid of which he might succeed, without much difficulty, in effecting a descent.

The ' glacies ' of Livy is identical with the ' vetus nix ' he mentions just before. It was old snow, which had become hard and solid, and not real ice. It might be merely the want of a word to express this old snow, which induced Livy to call it ' glacies ' or ' ice[1].'

---

[1] In Smollet's *Travels through France and Italy*, Letter xxxvii., he speaks of the hard snow covering in March the Col de Tende as ' ice.' Latrobe, also, in his *Alpenstock*, speaks of ' ice' in summer on the Great St Bernard. Ice is likewise spoken of on the passes of the Splügen, and of the Monte Tonale, in the account of Macdonald's expedition in the year 1800. (Alison's *Europe*, Chap. xxxii.) Indeed, in this latter work, even *glaciers* are mentioned as existing on passes perfectly free from them, as on the Susten, the Nüfanen, and the Wörmser Joch.

Hannibal, having been defeated in his attempt to effect a circuitous route, by the difficulties which the old snow presented, was at length obliged to encamp above the broken path.

'Tandem nequicquam jumentis atque hominibus fatigatis, castra in jugo posita, ægerrime ad id ipsum loco purgato : tantum nivis fodiendum atque egerendum fuit. Inde ad rupem muniendam[1], per quam unam via esse poterat, milites ducti, cum cædendum esset saxum, arboribus circa immanibus dejectis detruncatisque struem ingentem lignorum faciunt, eamque, cum et vis venti apta faciendo igni coorta esset, succendunt, ardentiaque saxa infusa aceto putrefaciunt. Ita torridam incendio rupem ferro pandunt, molliuntque amfractibus modicis clivos, ut non jumenta solum sed elephanti etiam deduci possent.'

This story seems very extravagant. Polybius makes no mention of this method of breaking up the rock, nor even of cutting a way through the rock at all. Besides, it is certain, both from Polybius and even from Livy himself, that there were no great trees, nor even any trees whatever, in this neighbourhood. Nothing but some bushes would have been found to make a fire with : the vast pile of trees mentioned by Livy could never have been constructed. And even if the materials could have been found for it, it is difficult to say where it could have been placed on the face of a precipice, which seems to be the position Livy assigns to it. The liquid mentioned as 'acetum' or 'vinegar' would probably be the thin acid wine, which the soldiers may have had with them, and which might have been used because there was little or no water to be found in that snow-covered neighbourhood. They would hardly, however, have had a sufficient quantity of this vinegar to have been employed in making a long zigzag route down a precipice, or even perhaps to have broken up the rock to any extent.

Yet it is only snow which could have been found on any of these passes. On the Col de Tende and the Monte Tonale the snow is not even permanent through the summer. A word is in fact wanting for this old and hardened snow : the use of the word 'névé' is confined to the upper and snowy parts of glaciers, and is not applied to hard snow generally.

[1] Τὸν κρημνὸν ἐξῳκοδόμει, Polyb.

Yet, although this story is clearly extravagant, it is not satisfactory to reject it as a pure invention. Such tales are generally exaggerations or perversions of something true, and are seldom quite groundless. The foundation of this story is, however, difficult to be discovered, or its omission by Polybius to be accounted for. This omission, indeed, seems of itself to prove that it was not a very important or singular event. The true explanation of the origin of the story must always remain very doubtful, and it seems impossible to offer a conjecture on the subject with any confidence[1].

---

[1] There is perhaps some room for a suspicion, that it was not the rock, but the old snow hardened almost to the consistency of rock, which was cut through by Hannibal. The want of a proper word for old snow, by which it might have been distinguished from fresh snow, may partially have conduced to such an error, by vitiating the story as it came down from hand to hand till it reached Livy. The manner in which the event is related by Appian gives some colour to this surmise. He says : ' As there was a great quantity of snow, and it had been rendered hard by frost, (this seems the force of κρύους here) Hannibal cut some wood near and burnt it, and then poured water and vinegar on the ashes: and the rock being by these means decomposed, he broke it up with iron hammers, and made a way.' χιόνος τε πολλῆς οὔσης καὶ κρύους, τὴν μὲν ὕλην τέμνων τε καὶ κατακαίων, τὴν δὲ τέφραν σβεννὺς ὕδατι καὶ ὄξει, καὶ τὴν πέτραν ἐκ τοῦδε ψαφαρὰν γιγνομένην, σφύραις σιδηραῖς θραύων καὶ ὁδοποιῶν.—Appian, Lib. VII. De Bello Annibalico.

There is of course no doubt about Appian's meaning here, the breaking up of the *rock* being plainly stated : indeed he immediately afterwards expressly mentions a particular cutting in the rock as being known by the name of the δίοδος Ἀννίβου ; a groundless tradition probably, but alluded to in such a manner, as to make Appian's own opinion on the subject perfectly clear. Still, though there can be no question about Appian's meaning in the passage quoted, its strikingly inconsequent character tends to raise a doubt as to his right apprehension of the accounts from which he composed his narrative. For there could be no reason why Hannibal should have broken up the *rock*, on account of the presence of *snow solidified by frost:* and yet we can hardly help inferring from Appian's words, that it was this snow which was the *cause* of the cutting, in whatever substance that cutting may have been made. If, however, the words τὴν πέτραν could be referred to the solid snow, all would be easy and consistent. Hannibal found his way obstructed by it in some place, and was obliged to cut through the hardened mass, decomposing it

According to Livy, four days were spent in making the
new road. This error arises from his misinterpreting
Polybius, as will easily be seen on reference to that histo-

---

first by the aid of fire, and the percolation of some warm liquid, and thus
enabling himself to break it up with greater facility.

Instances are found in modern Alpine campaigns of roads being cut
through hard snow. In the winter campaign of Macdonald in the
Rhætian Alps, the best illustrative parallel to Hannibal's expedition, two
cases are mentioned. The first relates to the passage of the Splügen.
'In the narrow plain between the glaciers, (i. e. on the summit of the
pass, beneath the higher glacier-bearing peaks of the ridge crossed)
however, they found the road blocked up by an immense mass of snow,
formed by an avalanche newly fallen; upon which the guides refused to
enter, and in consequence the soldiers returned, unanimously exclaiming
that the passage was closed. . . . . Put to shame by such an example, the
troops and peasants redoubled their efforts; *the vast walls of ice and snow
were cut through,* and although the hurricane increased with fearful rapidity, and repeatedly filled up their excavations, they at length succeeded
in rendering the passage practicable.'—Alison's *Hist. of Europe,* iv. 431,
432, 5th Edit. Jomini, however, says nothing of ice or avalanches in this
place, but only speaks of the great depth of the snow on the plateau at
the summit of the pass, and of the fresh snow continually falling, (i. e.
from the sky). In the account of the passage of the ridge of San Zeno,
a pass among the low mountains between the lakes of Iseo and Idro,
bordering on the Lombard plain, another instance occurs. 'The difficulties of the ridge of San Zeno, however, had almost arrested the
soldiers whom the snows of the Splügen had been unable to overcome;
a few horses only could be got over *by cutting through blocks of ice*
(compact snow) *as hard as rock* at the summit, (après avoir taillé un
chemin dans la glace vive, *Jomini*) and the greater part of the cavalry
and artillery required to descend by the smiling shores of the Lago Isea
(Lago d'Iseo) to Brescia, and ascend again the vine-clad banks of the
Chiesa.'—Alison's *History of Europe,* iv. 446.

On the declivity between La Ferrière and La Novalèse, where Hannibal's path was broken up, he may possibly have been obliged to cut
through the mass of solid snow, which, it has been conjectured, filled at
that time the gully which penetrates into the mountain-side. For, after
the path had been reconstructed along the precipice above (i. e. to the
west of) the gully, it would then have been necessary to cross the gully
itself. But the snow, however solid, which filled the gully, would probably not have been capable of supporting the elephants; for even the
beasts of burden had become fixed in it, when the circuitous route was
attempted. It might consequently have been necessary to make a lane
through the snow, and perhaps to penetrate to the ground beneath. Yet

rian. Had Livy attended to the words ἐν ἡμέραις τρισὶ κακοπαθήσας, he would not have fallen into this mistake, which would lead us to imagine that the first day spent in the midst of the snow was one of comfort, and that the hardships the army suffered only began on the second day, since there were but three days of hardship in all.

The three days (which must be reduced to two) during which the men and baggage-animals, (the cavalry horses should be included) enjoyed an interval of rest, and were enabled to recruit their strength a little, were not, as

---

this lane would not have been long, as the gully is not wide, and as it was probably only in the gully that the old snow lay.

An operation of this nature would not have been of any great importance, and might have been passed over by Polybius, or not have come to his knowledge. That he had received no such intimation is perhaps most likely. He does, however, when he first speaks of the ῥάχις, (a word he introduces as if he had mentioned an equivalent for it before) employ the expression διαμησάμενος τὴν ἐπ' αὐτῇ χιόνα. Now, if ῥάχις could mean the side of a ridge or mountain, the words διαμησά-μενος, κ. τ. λ. might signify 'clearing a way through the snow upon it.' The proper meaning of ῥάχις is, however, the top, and not the side of a ridge; and the removal of the snow is spoken of in connexion with the encampment περὶ τὴν ῥάχιν, and cannot well be supposed to refer to the construction of the path. It is true, indeed, that Polybius' information may have been somewhat defective on this point, or his comprehension of what was related to him not quite perfect. In his account of the encampment at the summit of the pass, where there must have been snow, nothing is said of its removal.

If Hannibal really cut a path through the solid snow, it may possibly have been effected in the following manner.

The workmen, perhaps, first levelled the surface of the snow a little, on the line of the intended cutting; and then, collecting the bushes near, arranged them along it, and set them on fire. The surface of the snow would thus be partially melted, and the water produced would sink down through the snow beneath. A quantity of liquid thrown on the hot ashes would also have helped to dissolve this snow to some extent. By these means, the mass, originally hard and firm, would be decomposed and softened on the line of the projected path, and might have been broken up with pickaxes or similar instruments without great difficulty. To cut a way through old and solid snow, without taking any measures to soften it, would be a tedious and laborious task.

This supposition may possibly explain Livy's story. It must, however, be looked upon as nothing more than a mere conjecture.

10

might be at first supposed from Livy's account, days subsequent to the passage of the elephants, but the two days which succeeded the passage of the horses and baggage-animals, and during which the elephants were detained in the higher encampment.

Nothing is related by Livy as having occurred, after the new road was completed and passed, during the rest of the descent to the plains of Italy. Hannibal there entered into the country of the Taurini, a fact which Livy says was universally agreed upon. He then proceeds to mention two passes by which it had been erroneously supposed that Hannibal crossed the Alps: the Pennine Alp or Great St Bernard, and the ' Cremonis jugum,' probably the Little St Bernard, the ancient name being apparently preserved in the neighbouring peak of the Crammont. Neither of these, as Livy observes, could have been crossed by Hannibal, as they both lead, not into the country of the Taurini, but through that of the Salassi into the territory of the Libui. The name of the Salassi, indeed, although a large tribe, is never found at all in Polybius; and the name of the Libui, although mentioned by him elsewhere, does not occur in his account of Hannibal's passage of the Alps.

CHAPTER X.

Examination of objections brought against the Mont Cenis.

WE have now examined the narratives of Polybius and Livy, the two chief historians of Hannibal's expedition. Both seem to point to the Mont Cenis, as the pass by which the Carthaginian general effected his descent into Italy. To complete the evidence in favour of this pass, it will now be requisite to take some notice of the objections which have been brought against it.

Nearly all the objections which can be adduced, are collected together, in his *Histoire du passage des Alpes par Annibal*, by M. Deluc, one of the advocates for the pass of the Little St Bernard. The sixth chapter of the second book of his work is entitled a 'Réfutation des auteurs qui conduisent Annibal par le Mont Cenis,' and in it we find the following summary of the objections against this pass.

'Ce qu'il y a de très-remarquable dans la première route (the route of the Little St Bernard) c'est qu'elle ne traverse pas une seule fois l'Isère, la vallée n'étant nulle part aussi resserrée pour forcer à établir des ponts sur cette rivière; dans la vallée de l'Arc, au contraire, il y a un si grand nombre d'obstacles, que l'on est forcé de passer dix fois d'une rive à l'autre pour les éviter. "Il serait trop long de détailler," dit M. de Saussure, "les nombreux défilés que l'on passe dans cette route, et de noter combien de fois les étranglemens de la vallée et les sinuosités de l'Arc forcent à passer d'une rive à l'autre."

Cette vallée offrait donc de trop grandes difficultés pour que, dans les temps reculés, on y eût fait passer une route pour traverser les Alpes. La descente du Mont Cenis, du côté de l'Italie, était aussi un trop grand obstacle, car les rochers y sont presque à pic, et ce n'est qu'en taillant le chemin dans le roc avec un grand nombre de zigzags, qu'on a pu rendre cette descente praticable.

10—2

C'est sans doute à cause de ces difficultés naturelles
que la route du Mont Cenis n'a été ouverte que dans les
temps modernes, comparés à l'ancienneté de la route du
Petit Saint-Bernard ; aussi la première ne se trouve point
dans les itinéraires romains, qui, cependant, ont été faits
dans le 4ᵉ et 5ᵉ siècles de notre ère, ou six à sept siècles
après l'expédition d'Annibal.

La route du Mont Cenis n'était donc pas celle que les
Gaulois suivaient pour descendre en Italie, ni celle qu'Annibal, en marchant sur leurs traces, prit pour entrer dans
le même pays; nous ferons aussi observer qu'elle n'était
pas une des quatres routes qui seules etaient connues du
temps de Polybe.   Cet auteur, en décrivant la route d'Annibal, la même qu'il parcourut cinquante ou soixante
années après, ne peut décrire qu'une route qui était connue
de son temps.

Nous observerons encore qu'à la descente du Mont
Cenis, il est impossible qu'on pût rencontrer, à la fin d'octo-
bre, de la vieille neige conservée depuis l'hiver précédent ;
car, outre que ce passage est plus abaissé d'au moins 100
toises que celui du Petit Saint-Bernard, sa descente est
tournée vers le sud-est, exposition où la neige fond plus
vite que dans celle du Petit Saint-Bernard, qui est tournée
vers le nord est.'

The objections embodied above amount to the following :

(1)   The passage of the Mont Cenis must have been
very difficult in the time of Hannibal.

(2)   The road to the Mont Cenis crosses the Arc a
great many times.

(3)   The descent into Italy is very precipitous and
difficult.

(4)   The route of the Mont Cenis is not found in the
Roman Itineraries.

(5)   It was not one of the four routes known to Polybius.

(6)   It would have been impossible for Hannibal to
have found old snow on the descent from the Mont Cenis.

(1)   The fact of the passage of the Mont Cenis having
been very difficult in the time of Hannibal may be readily

granted. Such must inevitably have been the case with every Alpine route in the Gallic period. Yet, although the Mont Cenis must have been then a difficult pass, that difficulty can scarcely be considered sufficient to disqualify it for being received as the scene of the passage, described as 'toilsome, and excessively difficult, although not impossible,' ἐπίπονον μὲν καὶ δυσχερῆ λίαν, οὐ μὴν ἀδύνατον: for such are the epithets which are applied in Polybius to the pass which Hannibal crossed. Indeed, at the very commencement of the Alpine route, we read of τὰς δυσχωρίας. Between the town of the Allobroges and the 'strong white rock,' we are told again of τὰς ἑξῆς δυσχωρίας. By the Rock itself, also, we read of a φάραγγά τινα δύσβατον καὶ κρημνώδη. All these expressions certainly imply difficulty; and, as to the descent into Italy, many thousands of men were lost, ὑπὸ τῶν τόπων καὶ τῆς χιόνος, in consequence of the snow and the difficult or dangerous character of the descent.

To shew, then, that the Mont Cenis was a difficult pass in the time of Hannibal, proves nothing against it : for the pass which Hannibal crossed was also difficult. In order to exclude the Mont Cenis on this ground, it would be necessary to bring against it an amount of difficulty insuperable in ancient times. But this certainly cannot be concluded of a pass, which, however difficult, must rank, relatively to Alpine passes generally, among the easiest known ; a pass which may be shewn to have been always a thoroughfare through the Alps, and which is now, what it seems to have been for some centuries, the great highway from France into Italy.

(2) The road from the Valley of the Isère to the Mont Cenis certainly crosses the Arc very often : the old road to the little Mont Cenis would have passed the river six times. Once also, on the descent into Italy, it would have to cross the Dora Susina. But, although the modern road from Chambéry to the Little St Bernard never crosses the Isère, yet the older road, the Roman way from Lemincum, probably crossed that river four times, and the Arc once. For, of the Roman stations, Axima, Darantasia, Oblimum, Mantala, and Lemincum, each lay, in all pro-

bability, as will afterwards be shewn[1], on a different side of the Isère from the following station. Besides, on the descent from the Little St Bernard, even the modern road crosses the Dora Baltea three times : and it cannot be conceived, why the Arc should have offered such a great obstacle to Hannibal's progress, and the passage of the Dora Baltea have presented little difficulty.

But, in point of fact, the passage of these mountain-streams, at the end of October, would have been attended with no great difficulty, unless, as in the case of the Drac, they were swoln with rain. They would probably have contributed but little to the losses, which Hannibal is said by Polybius to have incurred in crossing rivers. For all these torrents are fed by the melting of the snows and glaciers, and present, during the long Alpine winter, no resemblance to the full and turbid streams, which sweep down the valleys in the summer months. At the end of the month of September, the last summer month, (the Alps, at least the high Alps, may be said to have no autumn) the action of the sun on the snow and ice begins rapidly to diminish in power, and the torrents to shrink in volume. Throughout the winter, little or no water is supplied by the glaciers to the mountain-rivers[2], which become

---

[1] See Note A. at the end of the book.

[2] Si, comme je l'ai montré par les tableaux du jaugeage de l'Aar, il existe un rapport direct entre l'état atmosphérique et le débit des torrents, *il doit arriver un moment en automne, où toutes les rivières subissent une baisse notable,* à raison de la fonte moins considérable qui a lieu à cette saison. Par la même raison, elles doivent tarir complétement en hiver, du moment que toute fonte a cessé à la surface. Voulant m'en assurer par l'observation directe je n'ai pas hésité à entreprendre dans ce but un voyage hivernal dans les glaciers. Au commencement du mois de mars 1841, par conséquent à une époque où l'hiver règne encore d'une manière absolue dans les Hautes-Alpes, je me rendis avec M. Desor au glacier de l'Aar que je remontai jusqu'à l'Hôtel des Neuchâtelois (le 12 Mars) [A great rock on the glacier of the Aar was called by this name]. Après avoir séjourné deux jours au Grimsel, nous visitâmes ensemble le glacier de Rosenlaui (le 14 Mars.)

A Meyringen déjà je trouvai l'Aar beaucoup plus faible qu'en été; à mesure que je montai, je la vis diminuer toujours plus, si bien qu'à la Handeck elle était réduite a un très-petit filet d'eau, à peine comin general clear and shallow streams, with a comparatively gentle current.   At the end of the month of October, two thousand years ago, Hannibal would have found no great difficulty in fording the Arc, or any other of the Alpine rivers.

(3)   The precipitous character of the descent from the Mont Cenis, brought by M. Deluc as an argument against that pass, is in strict accordance with what is related by Polybius with respect to Hannibal's descent from the Alps, and is one of the distinctive features by which the Mont Cenis is identified with the pass which Hannibal crossed. Certainly, not only is the descent of the Fourmiguier precipitous, but, in order to make a path of commodious width down it, it would most probably have been necessary to cut the rock away in places.   Nothing but a rugged and narrow path could have existed, in barbarous times, in such a situation.   Yet this precipitous and narrow way is precisely what we find mentioned by Polybius.   Οὔσης γὰρ στενῆς καὶ κατωφεροῦς τῆς καταβάσεως, τῆς δὲ χιόνος ἄδηλον ποιούσης ἑκάστοις τὴν ἐπίβασιν πᾶν τὸ παραπεσὸν τῆς ὁδοῦ καὶ σφαλὲν ἐφέρετο κατὰ τῶν κρημνῶν.   It has been noticed before, that nothing but the very dangerous character of the old descent from the Mont Cenis can explain the immense losses which the Carthaginians suffered on their way down into Italy, and which amounted, in men alone, to one fourth of the whole number that had gained the summit of the pass.

(4)   It is true that the route of the Mont Cenis is not

---

parable aux ruisseaux qui circulent sur le glacier en été. Plus haut, elle disparaissait complétement sous la neige, et je ne vis plus que quelques endroits de son lit, où la neige était imbibée. Je rencontrai les dernières traces d'eau près des châlets qui sont situés à l'extrémité du glacier, et sa présence en cette localité me fit supposer qu'elle provenait selon toute apparence de quelque source voisine. En revanche, je ne découvris aucun vestige du torrent de l'Aar, à l'endroit où il coulait l'été précédent, ni sur aucun point du talus terminal. La cascade du lac de Trübten et le torrent de l'Oberaar, dont le bruit en été se fait entendre de loin, avaient aussi complétement disparu. On ne reconnaissait leur emplacement qu'à quelques gigantesques glaçons qui etaient suspendus aux rochers.—Agassiz, *Etudes sur les Glaciers,* p. 373.

found in the Roman Itineraries. It will be shewn, how-
ever, in the next Chapter, that the route of the Little Mont
Cenis is laid down in the ancient map or table of the
Roman roads called the Peutingerian or Theodosian Table.
Other arguments will also be brought forward there, to
shew that this pass was known to the Romans.

(5) That the Mont Cenis was not one of the four
routes known to Polybius may be strongly questioned. It
will be seen, in fact, in the next Chapter, that it has a
stronger claim than the Mont Genèvre to be considered as
the ὑπερβάσις διὰ Ταυρίνων, ἣν Ἀννίβας διῆλθεν, mentioned
by Strabo on the authority of Polybius. Certainly, neither
the Great nor the Little St Bernard can have any right to
this designation. If Strabo has cited Polybius' words correctly, and Polybius was not mistaken as to the pass which
Hannibal crossed, (and there is no reason for doubting
either of these facts;) then the question, as to the locality
of Hannibal's passage of the Alps, resolves itself into the
consideration of the respective probabilities in favour of
the Mont Genèvre and the Mont Cenis, for no other pass
leading through the country of the Taurini, such as the Col
de l'Argentière or the Col de la Croix, can have much
likelihood on its side[1].

(6) It may be conceded, with respect to the last objection, that it would be quite impossible now to find any old
snow on the descent from the Mont Cenis in the month

---

[1] This passage in Strabo has necessarily embarrassed the advocates
for the Little St Bernard. The principal of them, M. Deluc, in his discussion of the passage in question, (p. 19) evades the difficulty by taking
no notice whatever of Strabo's assertion (derived from Polybius), that
Hannibal crossed the Alps by the road through the country of the Taurini.
The author of *A Dissertation on the Passage of Hannibal, by a member of
the University of Oxford*, attempts to overcome the difficulty in the following manner : ' It seems but fair to state, with regard to this passage
in Strabo, that it contains a positive assertion, that Hannibal took the
second road, εἶτα τὴν διὰ Ταυρίνων, ἣν Ἀννίβας διῆλθεν, and therefore has
been brought forward against the hypothesis here supported. But if we
prove that Polybius takes Hannibal by another pass, it will follow, that
these words are to be ascribed to Strabo, and not to Polybius. Strabo,
who wrote in the time of Livy, would probably adopt the opinion of
that historian.—p. 19.

of October. Yet it cannot be concluded from this, that it would have been impossible for Hannibal to have found any, for the greater severity of the climate at that time might have caused old snow to be found far below the level within which it is now confined. The statement of Polybius, Τῶν γὰρ Ἄλπεων τὰ μὲν ἄκρα καὶ τὰ πρὸς τὰς ὑπερβολὰς ἀνήκοντα, τελέως ἄδενδρα καὶ ψιλὰ πάντ᾽ ἐστὶ, διὰ τὸ συνεχῶς ἐπιμένειν τὴν χιόνα καὶ θέρους καὶ χειμῶνος· τὰ δ᾽ ὑπὸ μέσην τὴν παρώρειαν ἐξ ἀμφοῖν τοῖν μεροῖν, ὑλοφόρα καὶ δενδροφόρα, καὶ τὸ ὅλον οἰκήσιμά ἐστιν,—this statement is not true when applied to the present state of the principal Alpine passes. No such barrenness is now observed, and the encroachments of the snow are far less than is here represented. In Polybius' time the snow must have reached much lower than it does now.

In a previously mentioned note upon this subject in Dr Arnold's *History of Rome*, a reference is given to *Evelyn's Memoirs*, by which large tracts of snow are satisfactorily shewn to have existed two hundred years ago, in places where there is now none whatever. Evelyn appears to have crossed the Simplon pass in the first week in September 1646[1]; a time of year when there is perhaps less snow upon the mountains than at any other, for during the month of September the snow recedes little, if at all. The height of the Simplon pass above the sea-level is 6580 English feet, about 200 below the Great, and 240 below the Little Mont Cenis. The whole of the Simplon road, in the beginning of September, and indeed during the summer months, is now entirely free from snow, the line of

---

[1] Evelyn merely says that it was in September, but it appears to have been in the first week in that month. On the day he crossed the Simplon he reached Brieg; thence to Sion, one day; to Beveretta (Boveret), one day; to Geneva, one day; at Geneva, six weeks; (if exact, forty-two days) to Lyons, two days; to Farrara (Tarare) one day; to Rohan (Roanne) one day; to Orléans, two days; at Orléans, one day; to Paris one day : total, fifty-three days. Evelyn would thus reach Paris the fifty-fourth day after crossing the Simplon. But it was still October when he arrived in Paris; so that it would be in the first week in September that he crossed the Simplon.

perpetual snow being about 2000 feet above the summit of the pass.

Speaking of the house, where he passed the night, in the hamlet of Simplon[1], 4850 English feet above the sea-level, Evelyn says: ' The house was now, in September, half covered with snow, nor is there a tree or bush growing within many miles.' Yet there are, at the present day, numbers of pines about the village of Simplon, and no snow exists in the neighbourhood in the beginning of September.

After getting into a dispute with the inhabitants of the village about a goat, Evelyn's party resumed their journey on the next morning. Alluding to the circumstances under which they left the village, he proceeds:

' This was cold entertainment, but our journey after was colder, *the rest of the way having ben as they told us cover'd with snow since the Creation; no man remember'd it to be without;* and because by the frequent snowing the tracts are continualy fill'd up, we passe by severall tall masts set up to guide travellers, so as for many miles they stand in ken of one another like to our beacons. In some places where there is a cleft between 2 mountaines the snow fills it up, whilst the bottome being thaw'd leaves as it were a frozen arch of snow, and that so hard as to beare the greatest weight; for as it snows often, so it perpetualy freezes, of which I was so sensible that it flaw'd ye very skin of my face.

' Beginning now to descend a little, Capt. Wray's horse (that was our sumpter and carried all our baggage) plunging thro' a bank of loose snow slid downe a frightfull precipice, which so incens'd the choleriq cavalier his master that he was sending a brace of bullets into the poore beast, least our guide should recover him and run away with his burden; but just as he was lifting up his carbine we gave such a shout, and so pelted ye horse with snow-balls, as with all his might plunging through the snow he fell from

---

[1] Although Evelyn mentions this place as being on the summit of the mountain, it is plain that he is speaking of the present village of Simplon, and that the highest point of the pass was further on.

another steepe place into another bottome near a path we were to passe. It was yet a good while ere we got to him, but at last we recover'd the place, and easing him of his charge hal'd him out of the snow, where he had been certainly frozen in if we had not prevented it before night. *It was as we judg'd almost two miles that he had slid and fall'n,* yet without any other harme than the benuming of his limbs for ye present, but with lusty rubbing and chafing he began to move, and after a little walking perform'd his journey well enough. All this way, affrited with the disaster of this horse, we trudg'd on foote driving our mules before us; *sometimes we fell, sometimes we slid through this ocean of snow,* which after October is impassable. Towards night we came into a larger way, thro' vast woods of pines which clothe the middle parts of these rocks[1].'

It is sufficiently clear, from this account of Evelyn's, compared with the present state of the Simplon, that the snow has lost an immense quantity of ground in the Alps within the last two centuries: and it cannot be concluded, especially when the statement of Polybius as to the general character of the Alps and the Alpine passes is taken into the account, that it would have been impossible, because the descent from the Mont Cenis is now in summer entirely free from snow, that Hannibal should have found permanent snow in that place when he descended into Italy.

Having now answered the objections of M. Deluc against the Mont Cenis, it will be necessary to notice one from another source. This objection is brought forward in the work, entitled *A Dissertation on the Passage of Hannibal over the Alps, by a member of the University of Oxford;* a book written, like M. Deluc's, in advocacy of the Little St Bernard. In p. 52, the author observes:

'The great size of the army, drawing as it evidently did its resources from the country through which it passed, sufficiently proves, that this country must have been well cultivated, *and consequently full of inhabitants;* and this

---

[1] Evelyn's *Memoirs*, Vol. I. pp. 220, 221.   London, 1819.

latter circumstance is confirmed by the host of barbarians, who hung upon his rear, and attacked him on his passage from Scez[1]. *No other of the known passages of the Alps can be at all compared with this one* (i. e. the Little St Bernard) *in these two essential qualities;* and it is only necessary to have passed through the Maurienne or Mont Cenis road, and the road from the Mont Genèvre, along the Romanche to Grenoble, to be convinced, that a large army without magazines must have been starved in any attempt to get through them. *It is upon this fact, which has never been sufficiently considered before, that I am inclined to lay the greatest stress,* and when united with the agreement of distances, it becomes almost irresistible.'

It will not be necessary to examine whether this objection is pertinent or not: for, at least as far as regards the Mont Cenis, it has no foundation. The question is merely one of statistics, and may therefore be exactly determined without difficulty.

The road of the Little St Bernard traverses the provinces of Tarentaise and of Aosta. It enters the province of Tarentaise near a place called Cevins, about half-way between Albertville (L'Hôpital Conflans) and Moutiers: it leaves the province of Aosta at the bridge of St Martin, about eleven miles above Ivrea.

The road, from La Rochette, over the Little Mont Cenis, traverses the provinces of Maurienne and of Susa. It enters the province of Maurienne about two miles from La Rochette: it leaves the province of Susa between Buttigliera and Rosta, about four miles below Avigliana.

The length of the road through the Tarentaise and the province of Aosta is nearly the same as that of the road through the Maurienne and the province of Susa, the latter being only about six or eight miles longer. The question therefore rests upon the comparative density of population, in the provinces of Tarentaise and Aosta, and

---

[1] Had this attack happened on the pass of the Little St Bernard, as is here taken for granted, it would not have been at Scez, but at a great distance below, that it was made. This mistake, as previously shewn when discussing the narrative of Polybius, has arisen from a mis-interpretation of that author's words.

in the Maurienne and the province of Susa. This, however, may be previously observed in favour of the Mont Cenis: the mountain route is much shorter by this pass than by the pass of the Little St Bernard, the commencement of the Maurienne being about twenty-five miles below the commencement of the Tarentaise. Hannibal would thus have saved about two days of mountain marching by taking the route of the Little Mont Cenis, in preference to that of the Little St Bernard; for the frontier of the province of Susa is beyond Avigliana, the commencement of the plains, while the frontier of the province of Aosta is about eleven miles above the similar position of Ivrea.

The statistical table of the population of the Sardinian States on the mainland of Italy, in the year 1846, gives the number of inhabitants to a square kilomètre in every province. It appears from this table, that, of all the thirty-nine Sardinian provinces on the mainland of Italy, that of Aosta is the most thinly populated. Next in order comes the province of Ossola; and the third is the Tarentaise [1]. The Maurienne certainly comes fourth, and is, no doubt, thinly populated. It surpasses, however, by one-sixth, in density of population, the province of Tarentaise; while the population of the province of Susa is more than twice as great, in point of density, as that of the Tarentaise, and, *a fortiori*, as that of the province of Aosta.

The following are the numbers of inhabitants to a square kilomètre, given by the statistical table:

Pass of Little St Bernard.
Province of Aosta 24.45
Province of Tarentaise 25.83
Pass of Mont Cenis.
Province of Maurienne 30.16
Province of Susa 55.91

It appears then, that the provinces through which the Mont Cenis road passes, support a much thicker population than the corresponding provinces traversed by the road of the Little St Bernard. An argument, however, can hardly

[1] The Tarentaise can thus hardly be called 'a very populous country.' See *Dissertation on the Passage of Hannibal*, p. xvii.

be drawn in favour of the Mont Cenis from this circumstance: for Hannibal, beyond all doubt, followed a known path across the Alps, without being influenced by any considerations of population or fertility.   Besides, the Carthaginians carried some provisions with them, and are also said to have suffered from the failure of their supplies. They clearly did not depend entirely for provisions upon the productions of the districts through which they passed.

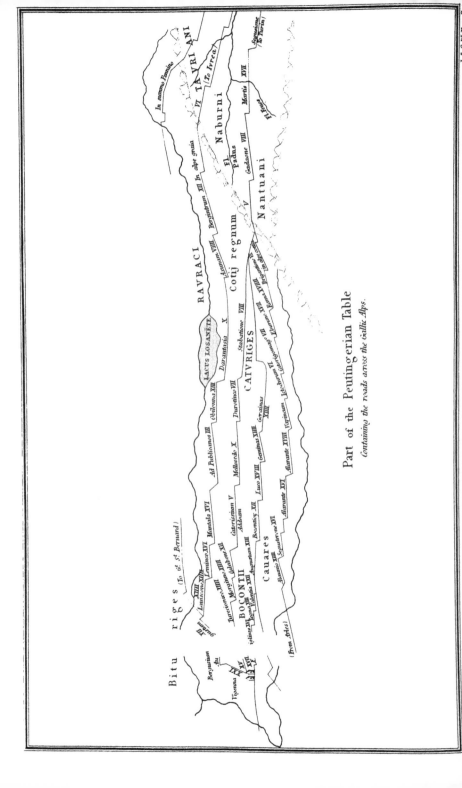

Part of the Peutingerian Table

Containing the roads across the Gallic Alps.

L. & C. Walker Sc.

CHAPTER XI.

Antiquity of the Pass of the Mont Cenis.—First mentioned by name in the year 755 A.D.—Probably known in the sixth century.—Described by Ammianus Marcellinus in the fourth century.—The road over the Little Mont Cenis laid down in the Peutingerian table.—The Mont Cenis crossed by Julius Cæsar.—Probably mentioned by Strabo as '*the pass through the country of the Taurini, which Hannibal crossed.*'—Conclusion.

IT is proposed in this Chapter to consider the antiquity of the route of the Mont Cenis, a pass of which it has been generally asserted that the Romans were ignorant. Yet this way across the Alps seems always to have been well known. For the last thousand years and upwards, it has, beyond all dispute, been in constant use. It is mentioned by name for the first time in the Continuation of the Chronicle of Fredegar, where it is said to have been crossed by Pepin in the year 755: 'Rex Pippinus cum exercitu suo Monte Cinisio transacto, &c.' Before these times it has been supposed that the pass was unknown: indeed it might be imagined, from the terms in which it has been spoken of, that the difficulties which it opposed to any attempt at a passage were of such a formidable nature as would have baffled all the efforts of the Romans; and that they only yielded, at length, for the first time, before the superior engineering skill of the dark ages[1].

A passage certainly existed in the sixth century between the Maurienne and Susa; for, when the bishopric of Maurienne was re-erected by king Gontran of Burgundy,

---

[1] Il nous reste à parler du Mont Cenis. Ce passage ne se trouve point dans les itinéraires romains, et il ne paroît pas qu'il ait été jamais une voie romaine, ou qu'il ait été même connu des Romains. *Il offroit de trop grandes difficultés,* car les rochers du côté de l'Italie sont presque à pic, et il a fallu tailler en zigzags dans le roc vif, le chemin par lequel on descend de la Grande Croix au village de La Ferrière.—Deluc, *Histoire du Passage des Alpes par Annibal,* p. 23.

(561—593), the recently acquired city of Susa and its territory were included in the new diocese[1]. The Maurienne had previously been comprised in the diocese of Turin[2], and not in that of Embrun, Grenoble, or Tarentaise, a fact which seems also to shew that there was a communication between the Maurienne and Italy. The pass which served as this line of communication would, in all probability, have been that of the Mont Cenis.

Yet it was not only in these times, but also in those of the Romans, that the pass of the Mont Cenis was known. To make this fact appear, it will be attempted to prove three things:

(1) The pass of the Mont Cenis is alluded to by Ammianus Marcellinus, a writer of the fourth century.

(2) The road over the Little Mont Cenis is laid down in the Peutingerian Table[3], and was therefore a Roman way.

(3) The Mont Cenis was crossed by Julius Cæsar, when on his way to intercept the Helvetii in Transalpine Gaul.

The passage in Ammianus Marcellinus, where the Mont Cenis appears to be referred to, is contained in the

---

[1] See the document relating to the foundation of this bishopric, quoted below, p. 172.

[2] Gregory of Tours 'de gloriâ martyrum.' Lib. i. cap. 14.

[3] The Peutingerian Table is an ancient Roman map, found in a library at Speyer in the fifteenth century. It is supposed to have been made originally about the middle or end of the third century of the Christian era, but to have been slightly altered by interpolations in later times. Its object was to lay down the Roman roads, and to give the names of the several stations, and the distances between them. All geographical accuracy is disregarded. The seas are represented as long straits or inlets, and no account is taken of the proper figure of the land, which generally runs in stripes or bands from west to east. Indeed, in the proper sense, the Table can hardly be called a map. Its whole extent, twenty-one feet in length, and one foot in width, is divided into eight sheets. A ninth sheet, which would have completed it on the west, is supposed to have been lost. These divisions are very abrupt, and many words are cut in two by them. One such division will be observed in the annexed copy of a part of the Table, which contains portions of two of the sheets. It is chiefly from the Peutingerian Table and the Antonine Itinerary that our information on the subject of the Roman roads is derived.

tenth chapter of the fifteenth book of his history.   It runs thus :

    ' In his Alpibus Cottiis, quarum initium a Segusione est oppido, *præcelsum erigitur jugum, nulli fere sine discrimine penetrabile. Est enim e Galliis venientibus prona humilitate devexum, pendentium saxorum altrinsecus visu terribile, præsertim verno tempore : cum liquente gelu, nivibusque solutis flatu calidiore ventorum,* per diruptas utrinque angustias, et lacunas pruinarum congerie latebrosas, descendentes cunctantibus plantis homines et jumenta procidunt *et carpenta ;* idque remedium ad arcendum exitium repertum est solum, quod pleraque vehicula vastis funibus illigata, pone cohibente virorum vel boum nisu valido, vix gressu reptante paullo tutius devolvuntur.   Et hæc, ut diximus, anni verno contingunt.   Hieme vero humus crustata frigoribus, et tanquam levigata, ideoque labilis, incessum præcipitantem impellit, et patulæ valles per spatia plana glacie perfidæ vorant nonnunquam transeuntes.   Ob quæ locorum callidi, eminentes ligneos stilos per cautiora loca defigunt, ut eorum series viatorem ducat innoxium : qui si nivibus operti latuerint, montanis defluentibus rivis eversi, agrestibus præviis difficile pervaduntur.   *A summitate autem hujus Italici clivi, planities adusque stationem nomine Martis per septem extenditur millia : et hinc alia celsitudo erectior, ægreque superabilis, ad Matronæ porrigitur verticem,* cujus vocabulum casus fœminæ nobilis dedit.   Unde declive quidem iter, sed expeditius adusque castellum Virgantiam patet.'

    The ' Mons Matrona' is the Mont Genèvre[1] : the ' præcelsum jugum,' in the first sentence, is distinguished from the Mons Matrona, as being situated between Ad Martis and Susa, and thus lying below, and not above, the former station.   Its *base,* that is to say, lay between Susa and Ad Martis ; for no mountain is *crossed,* but only *skirted,* on the road between these two places.   Ammianus Marcellinus, however, is not so clear here as might be wished. He seems not to have fully comprehended the accounts from which he compiled his description : the phenomena of this ' præcelsum jugum,' the avalanches, snow-drifts, &c.,

---

[1] See the Itinerary from Bordeaux to Jerusalem.

are rather confusedly put together; although the circumstantial manner in which they are related, and the truth and accuracy of the details given, shew that the authorities which he consulted were perfectly trustworthy. It is the expression, 'a summitate hujus Italici clivi' which introduces some difficulty. Yet the point indicated by this word 'summitas' is easily found. For about ten Roman miles from Susa, in the direction of the Genèvre, the Dora flows through a continuous defile, which never opens out into a proper valley till about two miles above Exilles. Here the mountains fall back, and a level plain is entered, which extends, for about six Roman miles, as far as Oulx, the ancient 'Ad Martis.' This level tract is clearly the 'planities' which 'adusque stationem nomine Martis per septem extenditur millia[1].' The 'summitas hujus Italici clivi' is therefore the end of the defile, about two miles above Exilles, and one below Salbertrand.

Yet this 'summitas' is clearly not the summit of the 'præcelsum jugum,' even if Ammianus supposed it to be so. For it is merely a point in the valley of the Dora, and not the crest of a pass at all. Neither would the road from this point to Susa at all answer to the description of the descent from the 'jugum.' Some other meaning must evidently be found for the 'summitas hujus Italici clivi.'

The employment of the words 'Italicus' and 'clivus' leads us readily to the meaning to be affixed to this expression. For all the main chain of the Alps separating Gaul from Italy, and every one of the different mountain-masses into which that chain may be divided, has necessarily an Italian and a Gallic slope, an 'Italicus' and a 'Gallicus clivus.' Now, between the point indicated by Ammianus as the 'summitas,' and the city of Susa, there is a continuous defile, extending from the end of the 'planities' to the beginning of the open valley called the Combe of Susa. This defile is formed on the north by a mountain-mass, which may be considered to begin at Susa, and to end at the 'summitas.' The lower extremity of the Italian declivity of this mountain-mass, or mountain, is

---

[1] Compare Cæsar, *Bell. Gall.* Lib. III. (beginning) where the 'planities' of Octodurus, or Martigny, is mentioned.

thus at Susa; the 'summitas hujus Italici clivi,' (i. e.) the upper extremity of the Italian declivity of this mountain, is at the beginning of the 'planities,' two miles above Ex-illes.   These were the limits of the Italian base of the 'præcelsum jugum,' across which lay the passage from Gaul of which we are now in search.

But over this mountain-mass only three passes exist, regarding the Great and Little Mont Cenis as one.   These passes are: the Mont Cenis, the Col de Clairée, and the Col d'Ambin or Col de Galumbre.   Yet these two last, of which the names are scarcely known, are merely difficult mountain-tracks: no 'carpentum,' however small and rude a vehicle be supposed to be designated by that term, could ever have crossed either of these cols.   Besides, the path from Savoy to the Col de Clairée passes on its way within a few yards of the Col of the Little Mont Cenis, so that the subsequent ascent would be needless.   Indeed, the Mont Cenis is the only one of these three ways that can properly be called a pass.   The others could never have been used as lines of communication between the valleys of the Arc and the Dora.

Yet it is not in position only that this 'præcelsum jugum' is found to coincide with the Mont Cenis.   The characters of the two passes, as far as the descent into Italy is concerned, are also identical.   For the descent from Gaul by the 'præcelsum jugum' was excessively steep, 'prona humilitate devexum,' flanked on both sides by frightful precipices, 'pendentium saxorum altrinsecus visu terribile,' and also liable in spring, the time of avalanches, 'nivibus solutis flatu calidiore ventorum,' to be swept by these falling masses of snow.   The first part of the descent from La Grande Croix on the Mont Cenis, by the plain of St Nicholas to La Ferrière, answers precisely to this description.   Of its extreme steepness enough has already been said: the danger from avalanches, and the precipices on both sides of the way, are also noticed in several descriptions of the pass.

In a small work, entitled *Guide du voyageur à Suse et au passage du Grand Mont-Cenis*, (Susa, 1830), the latter part of the ascent from Susa is thus described:

'Au dessous de la route actuelle[1] et à sa droite, un peu avant que d'arriver à la plaine de Saint Nicolas, se trouve une ancienne galerie en maçonnerie[2], que l'on appelait la route couverte ; elle avait été construite pour garantir les voyageurs de l'impétuosité des vents et *de la coulée des neiges ;* elle a 140 mètres de longueur et 4 mètres 80 centimètres de largeur.   Cet ouvrage est aujourd'hui presqu'entièrement enseveli sous les déblais que l'on a dû faire pour former la nouvelle route qui rejoint l'ancienne à l'entrée de la plaine de St Nicolas, dont l'horrible beauté pénétre le voyageur d'admiration et d'effroi.   Ce petit bassin est dominé *du côté droit* par des rochers très-escarpés qui semblent menacer les airs.   *A sa gauche* se trouve la nouvelle route qu'on avait premièrement essayé d'ouvrir à travers d'un rocher taillé à pic et d'une hauteur prodigieuse[3], mais que, malgré les grands travaux qu'on avait déjà faits, l'on a été forcé d'abandonner, à cause de la chûte continuelle des masses énormes de rocher qui se détachaient de la montagne, et *des dangers imminents des avalanches* auxquels on était fréquemment exposé.'

M. Albanis de Beaumont, (*Les Alpes Grecques et Cottiennes*, Vol. II. p. 652) speaking of the descent from the Mont Cenis, says of the plain of St Nicholas :

'Elle est couverte d'une belle verdure *et entourée de rochers abruptes,* dont les sommets se perdent dans les nues : c'est du haut de ces mêmes rochers que se précipitent en cascades les eaux limpides de la Cenise.   Après avoir traversé cette plaine, l'on passe sous une longue voûte[4] que l'ancien gouvernement Sarde avait fait construire *afin de prévenir les accidents autrefois si communs sur ce passage, occasionés par les avalanges toujours si dangereuses et si fatales lors de la fonte des neiges ;* ici ces avalanges sont si considérables, qu'en plusieurs occasions elles

---

[1] The present carriage-road is here spoken of.
[2] This was on the old road from La Ferrière.
[3] The 'promontorium' from which Italy is seen.   The cliff in which it terminates is pierced by a tunnel, through which the carriage-road at first ran.
[4] The new road was at this time (1802) not yet made.   The 'voûte' is the 'route couverte' previously mentioned.

ont enlevé dans leur mouvement de rotation sept à huit mulets à la fois ainsi que leurs conducteurs, qu'elles ont ensuite ensevelis dans le précipice affreux où coulent les eaux de la Cenise, et d'où leurs cadavres n'ont été retirés qu'après l'entière fonte des neiges,' &c.

The descent from the Mont Cenis into Italy is thus perfectly identical in character with the descent from the ' præcelsum jugum' of Ammianus Marcellinus, with which it has also been concluded to coincide, in respect of position. It may, therefore, be fairly supposed, that the Mont Cenis was, in fact, the pass between Gaul and Italy, of which Ammianus speaks in this place.

Before proceeding with the question of the Roman road laid down in the Peutingerian table, it will be necessary to determine the name of the tribe which dwelt in the Upper Maurienne.   This tribe will be found to be the Cottian, as distinguished from the Vocontian, Caturiges.

It is generally considered that there was in the Alps but one tribe bearing the name of Caturiges, and that they dwelt about the town of Caturigæ or Caturiges, now Chorges, between Gap and Embrun.   There is, however, no reason why there should not have been two tribes, or two branches of the same tribe, identical in name.   Instances of such a separation occur elsewhere.   In the valley of Susa dwelt the tribe of the Segusini or Segusiani; and in the modern Lyonnais there was also a tribe called Segusiani.   The Nantuates are mentioned by Cæsar[1] as dwelling on the Upper Rhine; but there was also a tribe called Nantuates to the S.E. of the lake of Geneva, and perhaps another people of the same name near the modern Nantua in the department of the Ain.   Pliny, also, expressly speaks of people descended from the Caturiges, though of different name ; a fact which seems to intimate that they were not confined to one spot in the Alps, but might have been scattered in several places[2].

---

[1] *Bell. Gall.* Lib. IV.

[2] Ligurum celeberrimi ultra Alpes Sallyi, Deceates, Oxubii: citra Veneni, et *Catarigibus orti Vagienni*, Statyelli, Vibelli, Magelli, Euburiates, Casmonates, Veliates, et quorum oppida in ora proxima dicemus.—

That there was a people in the Alps called Caturiges, who dwelt in some other district than the neighbourhood of Chorges, seems certain. Strabo, in his fourth book, speaks of the Centrones, the Catoriges, the Veragri, and the Nantuates, as dwelling on the mountains above the Salassi. Now the limit of the Salassi on the south seems to have been the Stura, or the Dora Susina[1]: they probably inhabited all the valleys on the Italian side of the main chain of the Alps, from the Roche Melon to Monte Rosa. Yet no part of their territory could be near Chorges, or its district. The whole breadth of the Cottian land intervenes between Embrun, the frontier town of the people of Chorges, and the Roche Melon, the nearest point of the country of the Salassi. The people of Chorges, also, could not possibly be associated, in respect of situation, with any one of the tribes of the Centrones, Veragri, or Nantuates, or be spoken of as a Cottian tribe. For the boundary of the Cottian territory was at Embrun, according to Strabo. Chorges would thus, on the same authority, have belonged to the Vocontii[2].

The Caturiges, or Catoriges, who bordered on the Salassi, must have inhabited the Upper Maurienne. For the other three tribes bordering on the Salassi, the Veragri, the Nantuates, and the Centrones, occupied the Lower Vallais, and Eastern Savoy as far (inclusive) as the Tarentaise. The Caturiges would therefore be sought, either in the Upper Vallais, or else in the Upper Maurienne or the valley of Susa. But they could not have dwelt in the Upper Vallais, for they are never mentioned among the people inhabiting that district, and were, besides, one of the Cottian tribes[3]: and the only parts of the

---

Nat. Hist. Lib. III. Cap. 5. And again: Sunt præterea Latio donati incolæ, ut Octodurenses, et finitimi Centrones, Cottianæ civitates; Caturiges, et *ex Caturigibus orti* Vagienni, Ligures, et qui Montani vocantur. —Lib. III. Cap. 20.

[1] The existence of a village called 'Salassa,' or 'Salazza,' on the right bank of the Orca, seems to intimate that the Salassi extended to the south beyond that river.

[2] Lib. IV. Cap. 1.

[3] The names of the Cottian tribes are found on the Arch of Susa. The following is the inscription: Imp. Cæsari . Augusto . Divi . F. Pontifici .

Cottian territory which touched the country of the Salassi were the Upper Maurienne and the valley of Susa. But the valley of Susa was inhabited by the Segusini: the Caturiges, therefore, should be sought in the Upper Maurienne.

Again, the Upper Maurienne borders on the Tarentaise. It is, accordingly, with the Centrones, the inhabitants of the Tarentaise, that we find the Caturiges leagued, when Cæsar (*Bell. Gall.* Lib. i.) crossed the Alps to intercept the Helvetii, and had to encounter the opposition of the mountaineers.

In the enumeration of the Cottian tribes on the Arch of Susa, the Caturiges are preceded by the Segusini and the Belaci, and followed by the Medulli. Now the Segusini inhabited the valley of Susa; and the Belaci are placed in the valley of Bardonèche, where the village of Beaulard is supposed to preserve their name. The Medulli dwelt in the Lower Maurienne. We thus find the Caturiges either certainly, or probably, connected in point of position with five tribes; the Salassi, the Centrones, the Medulli, the Belaci, and the Segusini. But the districts occupied by these five tribes completely encircle the Upper Maurienne. It is consequently, on the whole, highly probable, not to say certain, that the Cottian Caturiges inhabited the Upper Maurienne.

The question of the former existence of a Roman road over the Little Mont Cenis may now be considered. In the part of the Peutingerian table accompanying this book, four Roman roads across the Alps will be found, three proceeding from Turin and one from Ivrea; the first three being coincident for a certain distance. The first of these roads may be called the Turin and Arles road. It leads

---

maxumo . tribunic . potestate . xv . imp . xiii. M. Julius . Regis . Donni . F. Cottius . Præfectus . ceivitatium . quæ . subscriptæ . sunt . Segoviorum. Segusinorum . Belacorum . Caturigum . Medullorum . Tebaviorum . Adanatium . Savincatium . Egidiniorum . Veaminiorum . Venicamorum . Imeriorum . Vesubianorum . Quadiatium . et ceivitates quæ sub eo præfecto fuerunt.

from Turin to Arles, by Susa, the Mont Genèvre, (marked
Alpis Cottia on the Table) Briançon, Embrun, Gap, Sis-
teron, and Apt.   This road is, as appears by comparison
with the Itineraries, correctly laid down.   The second road
may be called the Turin and Valence road.   It is represented, (erroneously, as will be shewn) as branching off
from the first road on the Mont Genèvre.   The third road
may be called the Turin and Vienne road.   It is laid down,
(erroneously also) as striking off from the second road close
to the summit of the Mont Genèvre (no station intervening).
The fourth road may be called the Ivrea and Vienne road.
It leads by the valley of Aosta, the Little St Bernard, the
valley of the Isère, Lemincum (near Chambéry), the Chartreuse mountains, and Bourgoin, to Vienne.   It was the
third of these roads, the Turin and Vienne road, which
passed over the Little Mont Cenis.   It has, however,
hitherto been considered to have passed over the Col du
Lautaret, between Briançon and Grenoble.

The second of these roads, the Turin and Valence
road, is manifestly laid down incorrectly.   The station of
Lucus (Luc en Diois) is represented as being only 46 miles
from the summit of the Mont Genèvre.   Yet Luc, even in
a straight line, is 70 Roman miles from that mountain :
the road to Luc must, then, clearly branch off from the
Turin and Arles road at some nearer point than the Mont
Genèvre.   Besides, there is only one natural way of
reaching Luc from the Mont Genèvre ; and that is by the
valley of the Durance, down which ran the road to Arles.
The road to Luc is not likely to have branched off before
reaching Gap.   Now a very important line of way, that
given in the Itinerary from Bordeaux to Jerusalem, did
pass through Luc, and fell into the Turin and Arles road
at Gap : so that either this road must be the one erroneously laid down in the Peutingerian table, or else must
be totally omitted there, which is not very probable in the
case of so important a highway.   According to the Itinerary of Antoninus (Wesseling's *Itineraria Romanorum*) the
distance between Luc and Gap (Vapincum) was 50 miles,
a number differing but little from the 46 miles of the
Peutingerian table.   It thus appears that the Turin and

Valence road of that Table left the Turin and Arles road at Gap, and not on the summit of the Mont Genèvre[1].

The error which has vitiated the Peutingerian table in this place may now be readily perceived. The author has confounded the 'Alpis Cottia' with the 'Alpes Cottiæ.' For, though the Cottian territory terminated at Embrun, the name of the Cottian Alps, when applied to mountains, might have been extended to Gap, and even beyond. The Turin and Valence road did not separate from the Turin and Arles road 'in Alpe Cottia,' but 'in Alpibus Cottiis;' not on the Mont Genèvre, but somewhere in the Cottian Alps. The case would be similar with respect to the Turin and Vienne road.

Having now rectified the course of the Turin and Valence road, the Turin and Arles road may be left out of consideration: for it was from the Turin and Valence road that the Turin and Vienne road struck off. But at what point did it strike off? This is as yet uncertain: all that we can conclude is, that this point was somewhere in the Cottian Alps. There are consequently four roads, each of which may have a claim to be considered as the Turin and Vienne road: (1) the road of the Croix Haute, which strikes off northward from the present road to Luc, at Aspres; (the Roman road from Gap to Luc seems to have passed a little to the south of Aspres): (2) the road from Gap to Grenoble by the valley of the Drac: (3) the road from Briançon to Grenoble by the Col du Lautaret: and (4) the road over the Mont Cenis.

Now the Peutingerian table gives 85 Roman miles as the distance from Vienne to the point where the Turin and Vienne road falls into the Turin and Valence road. But, by the nearest of the four roads mentioned, the route of the Croix Haute, the distance from Vienne to Aspres

---

[1] The Peutingerian stations between Gap and Luc should probably both be read 'Geminæ.' The only station mentioned between these two places in the Itinerary of Antoninus is 'Mons Seleucus,' now 'La Bâtie Mont Saléon.' The Itinerary from Bordeaux to Jerusalem gives, from Luc: Mutatio Vologatis, (inde ascenditur Gaura Mons), Mutatio Cambono, Mansio Monte Seleuci, Mutatio Daviano, Mutatio ad fine, Mansio Vapinco.

is more than 120 Roman miles. The Peutingerian table is, therefore, doubly erroneous with respect to the Turin and Vienne road: that road does not branch off from the Turin and Valence road at the place assigned, nor does it reach Vienne at a distance of 85 miles from the point where it strikes off.

We have, therefore, a second error to remove. The principle to be applied is suggested by the detection of the error on the Turin and Valence road. For the road from Luc did not reach the summit of the Cottian Alp at a distance of 46 miles from Luc, but it fell, at about that distance, (*i. e.* at Gap) into the road leading to the Cottian Alp. The Turin and Vienne road, as it cannot reach Vienne after a course of 85 miles from the point where it leaves the Turin and Valence road, should thus, it may be expected, fall, at the termination of that length of way, into a road on the Table leading to Vienne. But this road, into which it falls, must be the Ivrea and Vienne road, for there is no other. The Turin and Vienne road must either fall into this, or return into the road from which it diverged; a supposition which is hardly possible.

The question, therefore, which has now to be determined, is this: which of the four roads, the route of the Croix Haute, the route of the valley of the Drac, the route of the Lautaret, or the route of the Mont Cenis, (the *Little* Mont Cenis will be selected) falls, at a distance of about 85 Roman miles from the point where it leaves the Turin and Valence road, into the Ivrea and Vienne road.

85 Roman miles are equivalent, neglecting fractions, to 125 French kilomètres, or 78 English miles.

For the three roads, by the Croix Haute, by the valley of the Drac, and by the Lautaret, the nearest station on the Ivrea and Vienne road is that of Augustum, now Aoste de St Genix. From Aspres to Voirons, by the Croix Haute and Grenoble, the distance is given as 124 kilomètres. From Gap to Voirons, by the valley of the Drac, the distance is 126 kilomètres. From Briançon to Voreppe, by the Lautaret, the distance is 135 kilomètres. Voirons is about 20 Roman miles from Aoste de St Genix, and 9 kilomètres from Voreppe.

By either of the two routes, that of the Croix Haute, or that by the valley of the Drac, the distance to the Ivrea and Vienne road is thus about 20 Roman miles longer that it should be. By the Lautaret, the distance is more than 30 Roman miles in excess.

The distance from Susa to Aiguebelle by the Little Mont Cenis (see page 91) is $82\frac{1}{6}$ Roman miles. The distance from Aiguebelle to Maltaverne is $4\frac{1}{4}$ Piedmontese, or 7 Roman miles. The 85 Roman miles, given in the Table, will therefore bring the road to a point about 3 Roman miles below Aiguebelle, and 4 from Maltaverne; in fact, exactly to the point where the valley of the Arc joins that of the Isère, down which ran the road from Ivrea to Vienne.

The route of the Little Mont Cenis seems thus to be the road of which we are in search. The station, at or near which the two roads to Vienne would join, must have been that of Mantala, which lay at an equal distance (16 Roman miles) from Lemincum, (Lemenc near Chambéry[1]) and Ad Publicanos, (Le Fay probably[2]), which was not very far from the modern Albertville. The station of Mantala has been fixed at Freterive, or St Pierre d'Albigny, or Bourg l'Evescal, all on the right bank of the Isère, nearly opposite Maltaverne. There seems, however, not much doubt, from the resemblance of names, that it should rather be placed at Maltaverne, otherwise Malataverne, a word probably compounded of *Mantala* and *Taberna;* and that the Roman road down this part of the valley of the Isère ran on the left, and not on the right bank of the river[3].

The comparison of the names of the stations on the Roman road from Turin to Vienne, with the names of the places with which they are identified on the supposition of that road having crossed the Little Mont Cenis, will, it is

---

[1] Maltaverne is 11 Piedmontese, or 18 Roman miles, from Chambéry.

[2] See Note A. at the end of the book.

[3] Roman remains have been found at Ayton, on the left bank of the Isère, as well as at places on the right bank. See *Les Alpes Grecques et Cottiennes*, Vol. II. p. 601.

conceived, remove all doubt as to the fact of the Roman
road having passed this way.

The following table will shew the modern places which
correspond to the old Roman stations, with the actual
distances between the various points in Roman miles, and
the same distances as given in the Peutingerian Table.

Ancient Stations.	Modern places.	Actual distances in Roman Miles.	Peutingerian distances in Roman Miles.
Segusio	Susa........................		
Stabatio	La Ferrière	$8\frac{3}{4}$	8
Durotincum	Granges de Dervieux...	$7\frac{2}{3}$	7
Mellosedum	Bramans	$10\frac{1}{3}$	10
Catorissium	Villarodin	5	5
Culabo	Orelle	$12\frac{1}{2}$	12
Morginnum	St Jean de Maurienne...	$14\frac{1}{6}$	14
Turecionicum ...	La Chapelle[1]	$14\frac{1}{3}$	14
Mantala............	Maltaverne	$16\frac{1}{4}$	15
	Total	$89\frac{1}{6}$	85

Stabatio, the first station on the way from Susa, is here
identified with *La Ferrière.* This village lies half way up
the great ascent of the Mont Cenis, beginning at La Novalèse, and ending at La Grande Croix, and is the only
village or hamlet between those two places. Its site would
thus naturally be chosen for a halting place on the ascent.

The station of *Durotincum* falls at the *Granges de Dervieux,* a place on the plateau of the Little Mont Cenis.
In the word *Dervieux,* some vestige of the Roman name
probably remains. The termination *vieux* seems, in addition, to indicate the antiquity of the place.

The word *Durotincum* is, as it stands, almost pure
Celtic. It resolves itself readily into *Dur-tin-cum,* all which
syllables are Celtic words. *Dur*[2] signifies ' water,' and
may mean here ' the river' or possibly 'the Dora.' *Tin*[3]
signifies ' a beginning,' the 'source' or 'origin' of the
river. *Cum* will be the same as the Welch *Cwm,* ' a valley,'
or ' a hollow in the mountains.' In the ' Combe of Susa'

---

[1] If XVI. were read instead of XIV., the hamlet of *Tardy* would
correspond to *Turecionicum.*

[2] O'Reilly's *Irish. Dict.*   [3] Ibid.

and the ' Combe of Malval,' the word is still used in this sense among the Alps.

Durotincum will thus mean, 'the hollow in the mountains where the river (or Dora) rises.' Now it is on the Mont Cenis that the Cenise, one of the affluents of the Dora, takes its rise. The longest of the little rills, which fall into the lake, and give origin to the Cenise, has its source on the Little Mont Cenis. The plateau of the Little Mont Cenis, enclosed by mountains, may therefore properly be called *Durotincum*.

The next station bears the name of *Mellosedum*. This word also is Celtic in origin. The first syllable exists in Melrose[1], Meldrum, &c. It is a variation of the word *Maol*, signifying ' bare,' ' barren,' ' bleak[2].' The word *Mellosedum* seems thus to be *Maol-lon-sead*, *Lon* signifying ' a meadow[3],' and *Sead* ' a way,' ' a road,' or ' a seat[4].' The signification of *Mellosedum* would therefore be, ' the station on the bare (or open) meadow.'

These ' open meadows ' are common in the Alps. Most travellers in those mountains must remember having frequently emerged from some ravine or narrow valley into a small open plain or basin, surrounded by a circuit of mountains, and sometimes almost entirely bare of everything but grass. These open spaces are called ' Matt ' in the German, and ' Pra ' or ' Praz ' in the French or Piedmontese Alps, words of continual recurrence, and all signifying ' a meadow[5].' Names nearly equivalent in

---

[1] ' *Melros* or *Maol Ross*, (i. e.) the bare promontory.'—Carlisle, *Topographical Dictionary of Scotland*.

[2] Armstrong's *Gaelic Dict.*

[3] Armstrong's *Gaelic Dict.* In Anderson's *Guide to the Highlands*, a ' Lonn' is defined as a ' meadow-strath.'

[4] Armstrong's *Gaelic Dict.* O'Reilly's *Irish Dict.*

[5] In the *Diccionario Geografico-estadistico-historico de España* by Madoz, five places bearing the name of ' Melon' are enumerated; all in the province of Orense in Galicia, a mountainous country whose original inhabitants were of Celtic origin. One of these places is described as being situated in a hollow surrounded by mountains, ' en una hondonada circuida por los montes denominados Faro y Carbela,' a locality of the same kind as a ' Matt' or ' Pra ' of the Alps. The word Melon is also found in the name of the mountain of the Roche Melon, an appella-

meaning to *Mellosedum* are still found. *Andermatt* (i.e.) (*Der Ort*) *an der Matt* is one of these. *Zermatt*, probably the same as *Zurmatt*, (i. e.) *zu der Matt,* is another.

The position of Bramans is accurately defined by the word *Mellosedum,* for it lies on a small open plain, 4000 feet above the sea, and is reached by the traveller from Modane after passing through the long defile guarded by the fort of L'Esseillon. It lies also, relatively to the Little Mont Cenis, in the same situation as Andermatt and Zermatt lie, relatively to the passes of the St Gothard and the Cervin; the valley of the Arc being entered from the Little Mont Cenis at Bramans, and the valleys of the Reuss and the Visp in the immediate neighbourhood of Andermatt and Zermatt, both these latter places lying on the open ground at the feet of their respective passes.

The name *Bramans* seems, also, nearly identical in meaning with *Mellosedum. Bramans* is *Bra-mans.* But *Bra* appears the same word as *Pra,* the term by which an open tract or *Maol-lon* is now designated. *Mans* also is easily corrupted from *Mansio,* the name which would be given to one of the more important stations on a Roman road[1]. *Bramans* might thus be *Prati Mansio.* Probably, when the Celtic language was dying out in the Alps, and a Latin or Romance dialect was taking its place, the old name *Mellosedum* fell into disuse, and was replaced by an equivalent term of Latin origin.

In the next station, *Catorissium,* (Villarodin), the name of the Caturiges or Catoriges, the people of the Upper Maurienne, appears. All the names of the other stations are in the ablative. *Catorissium* is clearly the genitive of *Catorisses,* and *vico* or some similar word, must be understood[2].

---

tion which may be taken as nearly identical in meaning with Matterhorn (Cervin). The Roche Melon rises above the fields of La Novalèse in the same manner as the Matterhorn above those of Zermatt.

[1] See the Itinerary from Bordeaux to Jerusalem, *passim.*

[2] In the Peutingerian table, *Addeam* occurs under the word *Catoris-sium.* This belongs properly to the word *Bocontiorum,* which is found below on the road from Gap to Valence; the station *Dea Vocontiorum* or *Ad deam Vocontiorum* being indicated. The name of the station *Catorissium* may possibly, however, have been, in full, *Dea Catorissium.*

In *Culabo* we have again a Celtic term. It is preserved most nearly in the Gaelic *Culaobh*[1], and appears in the Piedmontese *Culaton*[2]. The name of the Col *de la Cula*, a pass at the *extremity* of the valley of Barcelonnette, seems to derive its designation from this old word, which defines its position.

The word *Culabo* will signify 'extremity' or 'end:' it corresponds to the *Ad fines* of the Romans. *Orelle*, which is identified with *Culabo*, would be probably the last village of the Caturiges; for it is to the Upper or Caturigan valley, and not to the Lower, that it would naturally be attached[3]. The word *Orelle* seems also to signify 'extremity,' being apparently a diminutive of *ora*. It is most likely connected with the heraldic *orle* 'a border,' and with the Italian *orlo* and the Spanish *orilla*, both signifying 'extremity.' In Ponza's *Piedmontese-Italian Dictionary*, it will be seen that *cula-ton* is rendered in Italian *orl-iccio*, clearly indicating the identity of idea in the two cases.

Culabo, like *Mellosedum*, probably lost its original name with the decay of the Celtic language, and became known by the equivalent Romance appellation of *Orelle*.

The station of *Morginnum* falls at *St Jean de Maurienne*. Here the similarity of name is at once apparent; but it is in reality still closer than it seems. For the former name of St Jean was simply *Maurienne*[4], and not

---

The word *Dea* is probably the Celtic *Teagh*, 'a house.' See *Recherches sur les langues Celtiques*, par W. F. Edwards, pp. 466, 467.

[1] ' *Culaobh*, the back part of anything.'—Armstrong's *Gaelic Dictionary*.

[2] ' *Culaton*, estremità, parte deretana: *culaton d'l pan*, orliccio, estremità del pane.'—Ponza, *Vocabolario Piemontese-Italiano*. ' *Cularum* signifie proprement *lieu reculé, extremité*.'—Pilot, *Histoire de Grenoble*, p. 2.

[3] If the frontier of the Caturiges was, in the time of Hannibal, near Orelle, he would, after passing the Rock of Baune, soon enter into the territory of a different tribe from the one which had attacked him there. That such was the case, has been previously conjectured. See p. 112.

[4] Questa piccola città, di cui s' ignora la fondazione, sino dall' anno 340 avea il nome di Moriana ed un proprio vescovo: nè prese il nome di S. Giovanni che dopo la metà del secolo VI, in cui il re Gontranno di Borgogna, scacciatine i Langobardi, vi fece fabbricare la cattedrale dedicata al Santo precursore.—*Itinerario degli Stati Sardi*.

St Jean de Maurienne. In mediæval Latin it is called *Maurienna* or *Morienna*[1], while the more complete, and probably
more ancient, form of the word is *Maurigenna* or *Morigenna*[2].
Little doubt can be entertained of the identity of the Roman *Morginnum* and the *Morigenna* of the dark ages[3].

The station of *Turecionicum* falls at *La Chapelle*, an
important village in the Lower Maurienne. It has been
already spoken of in the description of the route of the
Mont Cenis. (Chap. VI. p. 82.)

From *Mantala*, (Maltaverne) the Roman roads to
Vienne from the Little Mont Cenis and the Little St

---

[1] See Hadriani Valesii *Notitia Galliarum*, where several passages are
quoted from mediæval writers, in which St Jean de Maurienne is called
'urbs Maurienna' and 'civitas Maurienna,' or, in either case, 'Morienna.'
In Baronius it is mentioned by the name 'Geneva Maurienna,' as one of
the six sees subject to Vienne. 'Porro illa sex oppida vel civitates, Gra-
tianopolis videlicet, Valentia, Dia, Alba, Vivarium, Geneva Maurienna,
in ejus tanquam in proprii Metropolitani obedientia et subjectione per-
maneant.'—Baronii *Annales,* Vol. XVIII. An. 1120. It seems to have
been ceded by the Franks, under the name of Geneva, to Theodoric the
Ostrogoth. See Lebeau, *Histoire du Bas-Empire*, Vol. VII. p. 196.

[2] *Auctoritas quod ex antiquo Morinensis ecclesia Viennensi metropoli
subdita fuit.*

. . . . Audiens autem gloriosus Guntramnus rex de
reliquiis beati Johannis et de miraculis quæ ibi Dominus ostenderat,
legatos suos *Moriennam* direxit, qui ecclesiam inibi fabricarent, cum
circumjacentibus episcopis et comitibus, ubi reliquias beati Johannis
Baptistæ reponeret, eamque perfectam episcopo Viennensi, ad cujus
diœcesim pertinebat locus, sancto Isychio sacrare præcepit. Synodum
vero postmodum in civitate Cabillonis congregare sanctorum episcoporum
fecit, et ibidem sanctum Felmasium episcopum *Morigennæ* ab episcopo
Viennensi ordinatum primum constituit, et civitati Viennensi ipsam
Mauriennam ecclesiam cum consensu episcoporum subjectam fecit.
Ad quam ecclesiam *Morigennensem*, ubi beati Johannis Baptistæ reliquias
posuerat, Secusiam civitatem jamdudum ab Italis acceptam cum omnibus
pagensibus ipsius loci subjectam fecit, et consensu etiam Romani Ponti-
ficis Viennensi ecclesiæ jure perenni episcopus civitatis et vici *Mauri-
gennæ* subditum esse decrevit.—Appendix to the *Works of Gregory of
Tours.*

[3] The '*Morginno*' of the Peutingerian Table should, perhaps, be
'*Morginna.*' Vienna, in this Table, is written 'Vigenna;' a further argument, if one were required, for the identity of 'Morienna' and 'Morigenna.'

Bernard were coincident. They went, by *Lemincum* (Lemenc), across the Chartreuse mountains (probably by the Mont du Chat), to *Augustum* (Aoste de St Genix); and thence by way of *Bergusium* (Bourgoin), to *Vienna Allobrogum*, now Vienne.

It seems, then, from the agreement of two entirely different lines of argument, that a Roman road must have crossed the Little Mont Cenis. For that conclusion has been drawn, in the first instance, from considerations quite independent of the names of the stations; the result having been arrived at by applying to the Peutingerian table an indispensable correction upon a system naturally suggested by a previously discovered and corrected error in the Table. The remarkable coincidences with respect to the names of the Roman stations seem to render it highly improbable, that the conclusion previously drawn should have been erroneous.

The grounds, on which it may be presumed that the Mont Cenis was crossed by Julius Cæsar, are derived from the following passage in the first book *de Bello Gallico*:

'Ipse (Cæsar) in Italiam magnis itineribus contendit : duasque ibi legiones conscribit; et tres, quæ circa Aquileiam hiemabant, ex hibernis educit; et, qua proximum iter in ulteriorem Galliam per Alpes erat, cum his quinque legionibus ire contendit. Ibi Centrones, et Garoceli, et Caturiges, locis superioribus occupatis, itinere exercitum prohibere conantur. Compluribus his præliis pulsis, ab Ocelo, quod est citerioris provinciæ extremum, in fines Vocontiorum ulterioris provinciæ die septimo pervenit : inde in Allobrogum fines, ab Allobrogibus in Segusianos exercitum ducit. Hi sunt extra provinciam trans Rhodanum primi.'

Cæsar's passage of the Alps was opposed by three tribes; the Centrones, the Garoceli, and the Caturiges. The Centrones lived in the Tarentaise : the Caturiges bordering on the Centrones, (who must be the Caturiges here spoken of) in the Upper Maurienne. The third tribe, the

Garoceli, is mentioned by Cæsar only. Their name does not occur in Strabo, Pliny, or Ptolemy. The natural conclusion from these omissions is, that the Garoceli are mentioned by those authors under some other name. They appear, in fact, to be identical with the Medulli, the city of St Jean de Maurienne being mentioned in old documents as Sanctus Joannes Garocellius, a fact which seems to fix the Garoceli in the Lower Maurienne, the country of the Medulli[1].

Of the three tribes, then, who opposed Cæsar's passage, two lived in the Maurienne, and one in the Tarentaise. Cæsar must thus have crossed the Alps either by the Mont Cenis or the Little St Bernard.

The Vocontian frontier, which Cæsar would arrive at by either of these passes, would be situated near the river Drac, which seems to have formed the eastern boundary of the Vocontii. He would, then, reach the banks of the Drac, or the neighbourhood of Grenoble, on the seventh day after leaving Ocelum. Now Ocelum lay, according to Strabo, at a distance of 27 Roman miles below Scingomagus or Susa[2]; a measurement which would place it

---

[1] Incolas (Mauriennæ) quamvis nonnulli putent eos esse, quos Plinius ac Strabo Medullos appellaverunt, seu qui Brannovices Cæsari memorantur, nos tamen in ea sententia sumus, ut esse credamus ejusdem Cæsaris Lib. I. Belli Gallici Garocellos, medios inter Vocontios ac Centrones, id est, inter Montanos, Delphinates, et Tarentasios: eoque magis huic sententiæ adhæremus, quo in antiquis tabulis ac monumentis, *S. Joannis Garocellii* vocabulo appellatur legimus civitatis primariæ, qua de agimus, Ecclesiam Cathedralem.—Blaev. *Theatrum Sabaudiæ.*

The root of the name *Garoceli* is probably to be found in the Welsh *Goruçel,* 'Supreme, very high, lofty.' (Owen's *Welsh Dict.*)   The Garoceli were the inhabitants of some very lofty mountains. This circumstance is perfectly in accordance with what Strabo says of the Medulli (Lib. IV. cap. 6.)   Μετὰ δὲ Οὐοκοντίους Σικόνιοι, καὶ Τρικόριοι, καὶ μετ᾽ αὐτοὺς Μέδουλοι, οἵπερ τὰς ὑψηλοτάτας ἔχουσι κορυφάς.   *Gor-uçel* (an intensive of *uçel,* 'high') and ὑψηλ-ότατος have accurately the same meaning, and, it is possible, a common root.   The lofty mountains of the Medulli present themselves under an exceedingly imposing aspect when seen across the Arc from the old road by Le Thyl and La Traverse.

[2] See Note B, at the end of the book, on the position of *Ocelum,* and of *Scingomagus.*

3 Roman miles below Avigliana, or near where Buttigliera
now stands. But for Cæsar to perform, in seven days, the
journey from Buttigliera to Grenoble by the Little St
Bernard, would have been impossible: the distance is
evidently far too great. It must have been by the Mont
Cenis that he crossed the Alps; for in this case the distance is found, as will be readily seen, to be about what
would have been previously expected.

From Ocelum to Susa the distance is 27 Roman miles.
From Susa to St Jean de Maurienne, the distance is
58 Roman miles[1]. From St Jean de Maurienne to the road
leading up the Graisivaudan on the left bank of the Isère,
the distance by the mountain-road across the Col du
Glandon and the Col de la Coche may be roughly estimated at 35 English, or 38 Roman miles. From thence to
Grenoble, the distance is about 12 English, or 13 Roman
miles. From Ocelum to Grenoble by this route the distance would thus be about 136 Roman miles[2]. This
distance might have been performed by Cæsar in seven
days; for he could have marched, when in haste, at the
rate of twenty Roman miles a day. That he was in haste,
is certain: and the mention of the seven days seems to
have been made with the view of proving the celerity
with which he marched.

When Cæsar says that he took the shortest road across
the Alps, he may probably mean, that instead of following,
from St Jean de Maurienne, the longer and easier route
by Aiguebelle, La Rochette, and Allevard, he took the
shorter way by the Col du Glandon and the Col de la
Coche, and was thus enabled to reach Grenoble in seven
days after leaving Ocelum. It is also not improbable,
that when on his way from Geneva into Italy to collect his

---

[1] By the Peutingerian measurement, 56 Roman miles.

[2] Perhaps Cæsar did not cross the Drac. Near the modern Grenoble,
he might perhaps be said to be 'in finibus Vocontiorum.' Crossing the
Isère at Grenoble, he would arrive at the suburb of Grenoble lying on
the north of the river, and corresponding to the ancient Cularo, and thus
be 'in finibus Allobrogum.' From thence, traversing the country of the
Allobroges to Vienne or Lyons, and crossing the Rhone, he would arrive
'in Segusianos.'

forces, he had given some cause of offence to the Centrones, whose country he would have skirted, or just
entered, if he followed, as is most likely, the road from
Geneva, by Annecy and Césarches, to Aiguebelle and the
Mont Cenis.   This may account for the Centrones joining
in the attack upon him on his return.   At all events, they
had probably become aware that he intended to recross
the Alps into Ulterior Gaul, and were induced to join
their neighbours, the Caturiges and Garoceli, in an
attempt to resist his passage[1].

If the Mont Cenis was known to Julius Cæsar, the road
over that mountain must necessarily have existed before
the time of Strabo.   It may now therefore be concluded
with safety, that the pass of which Strabo speaks (Lib. IV.
cap. 6) between the country of the Medulli and that of the
Taurini[2], was that of the Little Mont Cenis.   (For this, and
not the Great Mont Cenis, is the line of road traced in the
Peutingerian table.)   The distance, also, from Bramans to
Susa is, according to that Table, 25 Roman miles, or

---

[1] The earliest route over the Mont Cenis would be that followed by
Hannibal, along the left bank of the Isère, and by the towns of Allevard,
Aiguebelle, and St Jean de Maurienne. Cæsar, by taking the more difficult way from St Jean de Maurienne, across the Col du Glandon and the
Col de la Coche, would avoid the long circuit by the valley of La Rochette.
Up to this time, the Mont Cenis, the valley of the Arc, and the vale of
Graisivaudan, seem to have been used as the line of passage, both to the
neighbourhood of Valence, and also to Vienne and Lyons; for it would
probably be to one of these last two cities that Cæsar directed his
course, when he was on his way to the country of Segusiani.   When the
route over the Chartreuse mountains was opened, the road of the Mont
Cenis was, as appears from the Peutingerian table, connected with that
road, and the way by Grenoble and the Graisivaudan no longer formed the
line of approach to Vienne.   In the times of the empire, also, the road
from Gap to Die and Valence came into use, and, as would appear from
the Itineraries, displaced the Mont Cenis from being the line of passage
between Valence and Turin.   No route up the Graisivaudan is given in
the Itineraries, or traced in the Peutingerian table.   None of the great
highways of the empire seem to have passed through it, though the
older roads in that valley may still have been more or less frequented.
[2] See above, p. 132, note 2.

200 stadia. The most accurate half-way point would be where the road passed by the south-western corner óf the lake on the plateau of the Mont Cenis. From this point, reckoning to Susa on the one side, and to Bramans on the other, we should have the two lengths of one hundred stadia each, which are mentioned by Strabo[1]. The concluding question connected with this enquiry now arises.

Which of the two passes, the Little Mont Cenis and the Mont Genèvre, (a pass also known to Strabo) was described by him, on the authority of Polybius, as the pass through the country of the Taurini, which Hannibal crossed[2]? For one only of these two passes was known to Polybius, though both existed in the time of Strabo, who seems to have introduced the words ἣν Ἀννίβας διῆλθεν for the purpose of definition, (and not as a mere casual observation,) the pass which Hannibal crossed being necessarily the most ancient of the two, and therefore the one known to Polybius, of which Strabo wishes to speak.

Now the Alpine mountaineers were completely subdued for the first time by Augustus. Cottius and the tribes under his rule made their submission to the Romans, and so escaped conquest; and the Cottian territory seems to have been increased, under Augustus, by the addition of some of the conquered tribes, such as the Medulli, Caturiges, and Vesubiani. Great alterations were effected by Augustus in relation to the roads through the Alps. He seems to have repaired the old roads and opened new ones. It is in the reign of Augustus that the number of the roads across the Alps would, in all probability, have been increased.

The testimony of Cæsar's *Commentaries* is particularly valuable in indicating the roads which traversed the Alps before the time of Augustus. For Cæsar crossed the Alps

---

[1] That Strabo mentions neither the Caturiges, nor the Segusini, in connexion with this pass, seem omissions of no importance.

[2] Τέτταρας δ' ὑπερβάσεις ὀνομάζει μόνον· διὰ Λυγίων μὲν τὴν ἔγγιστα τῷ Τυρρηνικῷ πελάγει· εἶτα τὴν διὰ Ταυρίνων, ἣν Ἀννίβας διῆλθεν· εἶτα τὴν διὰ Σαλασσῶν· τετάρτην δὲ, τὴν διὰ Ῥαιτῶν· ἀπάσας κρημνώδεις.—Strabo, Lib. IV. Cap. 6.

several times, and is himself his own historian, so that the character of his evidence is perfect.   Yet he only alludes to two passes, the Mont Cenis, and the pass through the country of the Veragri, (i. e.) the Great St Bernard[1].   He does not appear ever to have crossed the Mont Genèvre. The Little Mont Cenis was thus, it is probable, the most ancient pass of the two which led through the country of the Taurini.

The route of the Mont Genèvre, as given by Strabo, led, by way of Embrun and the Durance, to Arles and Nîmes.   The cross road from Gap, to Die and Valence, is not mentioned by him.   The route of the Mont Genèvre, as far as can be gathered from Strabo, was only known by him as a road to Arles and Nîmes, and as leading to the Rhone by way of the Durance.   The route of the Little Mont Cenis passed through the country of the Medulli, and would thus lead into the Graisivaudan, and reach the Rhone by way of the Isère.

It was however, in the neighbourhood of the embou-chure of the Isère, and not of the Durance, that Hannibal struck off from the banks of the Rhone to cross the Alps. It would therefore, on this account alone, be more pro-bable, from what Strabo says, that Hannibal crossed the Alps by the Little Mont Cenis, and not by the Mont Genèvre.

It appears then, on the whole, that the Little Mont Cenis has the best claim to be considered as 'the pass through the country of the Taurini, which Hannibal crossed,' it being probably of more ancient date than the Mont Genèvre, and more consistent with what is known of Hannibal's march along the Rhone.   It is not contended, that it is certain, from this passage in Strabo, and from the fact of the antiquity of the road over the Little Mont Cenis, that it was by this way that Hannibal crossed the

---

[1] *De Bello Gallico*, Lib. III.   These two passes appear to have been known from the most remote historic times.   The passes by which the Gauls effected their earliest emigrations into Italy, according to Livy, (v. 34, 35,) were two in number; one through the country of the Tau-rini, and one by the Pennine Alps.

Alps. The evidence, however, derived from the knowledge of the Roman roads, is, as far as it goes, in favour of the Little Mont Cenis; and the amount of probability, whatever it be, which can be drawn from such testimony, rests with that pass, and weakens a theory in support of any other; and thus the very grounds, on the supposed strength of which, the claims of the Mont Cenis to be considered as the pass which Hannibal crossed have been rejected, are found, upon examination, to give additional force to those claims. In fact, on whatever authority the enquiry into Hannibal's route be based; whether it be grounded upon the narrative of Polybius or of Livy, or upon the knowledge of the ancient roads across the Alps; the conclusion reached is always the same, and the Little Mont Cenis is pointed out, in every case, as the pass by which Hannibal effected his descent into the plains of Italy.

APPENDIX.

NOTE A.

THE following routes are taken from Wesseling's *Itineraria Romanorum*. The first route is directly transcribed from the text. In the second route, three of the various readings given in the notes have been adopted. The reading *Cesuaria* has been preferred to *Casuaria*. The distance between Cesuaria and Bautas is, also, taken at xxx. instead of xviii. Roman miles. Instead of *Cenava*, the reading *Geneva* has been adopted. The modern places supposed to coincide with the ancient stations, have also been set down in the following tables: the reasons for such identification, in addition to those derived from the approximate coincidence of distances, will be afterwards given.

ROUTE FROM IVREA TO VIENNE.

Ancient Stations.	Modern Places.	Distances given in Roman miles.
Eporedia	Ivrea	
Vitricium	Verres	21
Augusta Prætoria	Aosta	25
Arebrigium	Arpi	25
Bergintrum	Bourg St Maurice	24
Darantasia	Salins (near Moutiers)	19
Oblimum	Ablêne	13
Ad Publicanos	Le Fay	3
Mantala	Maltaverne	16
Lemincum	Lemenc (near Chambéry)	16
Labiscone	doubtful	14
Augustum	Aoste de St Genix	14
Bergusium	Bourgoin	16
Vienna	Vienne	20

ROUTE FROM DARANTASIA TO GENEVA.

Darantasia	Salins	
Cesuaria	Césarches	24
Bautas	Annecy-le-vieux	30
Geneva	Geneva	25

13

It will be convenient to consider the second of these routes first. Darantasia must be either at Moutiers or at Salins. In addition to the argument drawn from the agreement of distances, the name of the station indicates that it was situated on the Doron, the river which joins the Isère by Moutiers[1]. Besides, in the Peutingerian table, Darantasia is placed 10 miles below the station of *Axima*, clearly the modern *Aime*. M. Roche, of Moutiers, identifies Darantasia rather with Salins than with Moutiers. The signification of the name of the Roman station makes Salins also preferable.

The name of *Césarches*, and its distance from Salins, point it out as the Roman *Cesuaria*. *Césarches* is a village lying on the left bank of the Arly, a short distance above Albertville. The modern road from Albertville, to Annecy and Geneva, lies on the right bank of the Arly.

Bautas is generally placed at Annecy-le-vieux, which appears to be situated at about the right distance from Césarches, and also from Geneva. The name of *Bautas* is perhaps identical with that of *Pautas* (in Italian *Pautasso*) a place one or two miles to the west of Carignano in Piedmont. *Pautass* in Piedmontese signifies 'a marsh,' so that the name *Pautas* seems identical with the French *La Palud*, which occurs in several places. The plain where the modern Annecy is built may anciently have been a marshy tract: or if the word *Bautas* be supposed entirely identical with the Latin *Palus*, the lake of Annecy itself may be pointed out under this designation[2].

It has been already conjectured, that Arebrigium, on the first route, should be placed at Arpi rather than at Pré St Didier. Nothing else, with respect to this route, calls for notice before arriving at Darantasia. *Oblimum*, (otherwise *Obilonna*), the first station after *Darantasia*, seems fixed, both by name and distance, at *Ablène*.

Ad Publicanos lay three miles below Oblimum. Le Fay, on the left bank of the Isère, is about that distance from Ablène. It would also be at about the right distance from Cesuaria or Césarches. The river was probably crossed at this place, and the Roman Provincia entered. Toll would be taken in passing by the 'Publicani[3].'

---

[1] The first part of the word *Daran-tasia* seems plainly to be the name of the river *Doron*. The second part probably remains in the name of the village of *Theys*, not far from Allevard, in Dauphiné. The Irish *Teaghais*, 'dwelling-places,' will be another variation of the old Celtic word. *Darantasia* thus means, ' the dwellings on the Doron.' See also Edwards' *Recherches sur les langues Celtiques*, pp. 466, 467.

[2] See Diefenbach's *Celtica*, i. 183, Art. 278.

[3] The Welsh word 'Fai' means ' an extreme ;' ' Faig,' ' an extremity' or 'furthest

The road, having crossed the Isère at Le Fay, would pass, by way of Ayton, and over the Arc, to Mantala or Maltaverne. Recrossing the Isère at Montmélian, it would arrive at Lemincum (Lemenc). The Chartreuse mountains were, in all probability, traversed by the route of the Mont du Chat, from whence the road descended to Yenne, and went by way of Aoste and Bourgoin to Vienne.

NOTE B.

On the position of Ocelum, and of Scingomagus.

Ocelum is mentioned by Strabo (Lib. IV. Cap. I.) as being situated at the extremity of the Cottian territory, at a distance of 99 miles from Embrun, and 27 from Scingomagus, where Italy began.

Ocelum is again mentioned by Strabo (Lib. V. Cap. I.) as being reached from Placentia by a road along the Po and the Dora, the Dora Susina being here plainly meant. This road is said to be about 60 miles long. If reckoned from Placentia, this must be a mistake for 160: if reckoned from the point, where the road would begin to follow up the Po, (i. e. from near the modern Casale) the distance would be nearly correct, if Ocelum lay not far from Avigliana. As the road from Placentia would skirt the river Po first, Ocelum must have lain by the Dora Susina. At Ocelum, Strabo says, the Alps and Gaul begin. He had previously placed the beginning of Italy at Scingomagus. It was consequently the Alps which began from Ocelum, and then, after the mountains had been entered for some time, Gaul began at Scingomagus. But perhaps Strabo here speaks of the Cottian territory as part of Gaul, in which case it would be correct to say, that Gaul began from Ocelum.

Cæsar speaks of Ocelum as the last place in the Roman province of Cisalpine Gaul.

It appears then, that Ocelum stood in the province of Cisalpine Gaul, on the frontier of the Cottian land, at the foot of the Alps, on the banks of the Dora Susina, and a distance of 99 miles from Embrun.

Ocelum is generally considered to be identical with Usseau in the Val Pragelas. The similarity of the name is the only reason for this supposition[1]. Usseau is about 70 miles from

---

point.' Owen's *Welsh Dict.* The name of Le Fay might thus point to the fact of its being the limit of the Provincia.

[1] *Ocelum* was a common name for a Celtic town. Besides the *Usseau* mentioned in the text, the towns and villages of *Ossola* and *Usseglio* in Italy, *Ussel* and *Issou-*

Embrun, by the road over the Mont Genèvre and the Col de Sestrières, is not on the banks of the Dora Susina, is not at the foot of the Alps, but far within them, and could hardly have stood on the frontier of the Cottian land, but a long way within its borders.

Avigliana (Ad Fines), according to the Itineraries, was 94 miles from Embrun, and lay on the banks of the Dora, at the foot of the Alps, and on the frontier between the Cottian land and Cisalpine Gaul. Ocelum must thus have been near Avigliana, if not actually upon that spot. The modern Buttigliera perhaps corresponds most nearly in position to the ancient Ocelum.

Scingomagus lay 27 miles from Ocelum, and therefore 72 from Embrun. By the Itineraries, Susa was 70 miles from Embrun, and, by the Peutingerian table, 72. According to Strabo, Italy began at Scingomagus; according to the Jerusalem Itinerary, Italy began at Susa. It seems thus quite evident, that Scingomagus, and Secusio or Susa, were the same place[1].

---

dun in France, and *Ochiltree* (i. e. *Uchel-tre*, ' the high-town,' Chalmers' *Caledonia*) in Scotland, all shew their connexion with the old name. The root of the word is found in the Breton *uc'hel* and the Welsh *uçel*, both signifying *high*, towns being commonly built upon heights, as defensible positions. The proper meaning of *Ocelum* seems to be a *fort* or *strong place*. The *Usseau* of the Val Pragelas would probably have been one of those *ocela :* but the mere identity of name, when the appellation was so common, is not sufficient to compensate the complete discrepancy, in point of situation, between Usseau and the Ocelum of Cæsar and Strabo.

[1] The termination *magus* is not uncommon. *Caturiges* (now *Chorges*) is called *Catorigomagus* in the Peutingerian table. In *Rotomagus* (Rouen), *Noviomagus* (Speyer), and *Borbetomagus* (Worms), it also appears. This termination seems to be the Latin form of the Celtic *magh*, ' a field,' a word apparently preserved in the names of the Irish towns of *Omagh* and *Armagh*. (See Diefenbach's *Celtica*, I. 77, Art. 105.) In the first part of the word *Scingo-magus*, (Σκιγγομάγος) the name of the tribe *Segusini* or *Secusini* is probably involved.

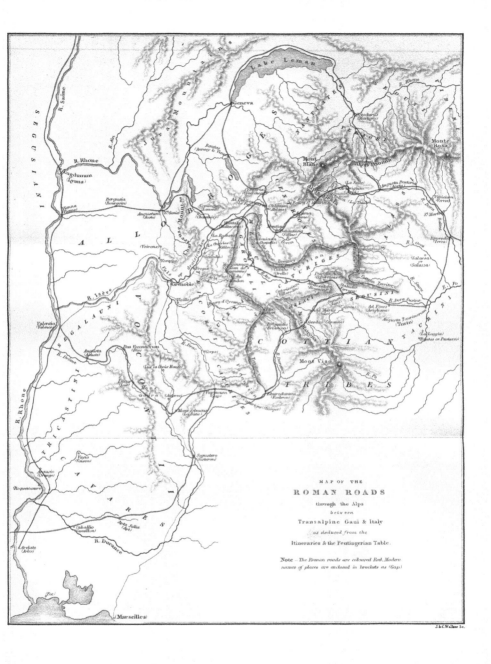

MAP OF THE
ROMAN ROADS
through the Alps
between
Transalpine Gaul & Italy
as deduced from the
Itineraries & the Peutingerian Table.

Note.—The Roman roads are coloured Red. Modern
names of places are enclosed in brackets as (Gap.)

J.&C.Walker Sc.

The material originally positioned here is too large for reproduction in this reissue. A PDF can be downloaded from the web address given on page iv of this book, by clicking on 'Resources Available'.

For EU product safety concerns, contact us at Calle de José Abascal, 56–1°,
28003 Madrid, Spain or eugpsr@cambridge.org.